KEY ACCOUNTING PRINCIPLES WORKBOOK

Volume One, V5.0

Lead Authors
Penny L. Parker, MBA, CPA, CGA
Fanshawe College

Denise Cook, CPA, CA
Durham College

Contributing Writer
Michael Van Roestel, PhD, CPA
Fanshawe College

Reviewers

Cam Beck, BBA
Holland College

Sheryl Boisvert, BEd, CGA/CPA
NorQuest College

Kolleen Brunton
Durham College

Dave Hummel, CPA, CA
Conestoga College

Kim Kennedy, CMrg, MBA, CPA, CGA, DBA
Olds College

Sai-Chung Ngan, PhD, FCMA, CPA, ACS
Fanshawe College

Leighton Reimer, MBA, CPA, CMA
Briercrest College and Seminary

Brenda Ridgeley-Ketchell, BBA, MA
Okanagan College

Jane Silver, CPA, CMA
triOS College

Lead Author of Key Accounting Principles, Volume One, Fourth Edition © 2016

Neville Joffe

Textbook ISBN: 978-1-989003-49-7
Workbook ISBN: 978-1-989003-50-3

Key Accounting Principles Workbook, Volume One, V5.0
Authors: Penny L. Parker/Denise Cook/Neville Joffe
Publisher: AME Learning Inc.
Project Manager: Lisa McManus/Suzanne Schaan
Developmental Editors: Graeme Gomes/Melody Yousefian
Production Editors: Lisa McManus/Mark John Termoso
Copy Editor: Suzanne Schaan
Typesetter: Paragon Prepress Inc.
VP Product Development and Technology: Linda Zhang
Cover Design: Soumik Dasgupta
Cover Photos: Scott Norsworthy/Shutterstock.com (front); Isabel Poulin © 123RF.com (back)
Online Course Design & Production: AME eLearning Team

1 2 3 MCRL 21 20 19

Printed in China

This book is written to provide accurate information on the covered topics.
It is not meant to take the place of professional advice.

For more information contact:

AME Learning Inc.
410-1220 Sheppard Avenue East
Toronto, ON, Canada M2K 2S5
Phone: 416.479.0200
Toll-free: 1.888.401.3881
E-mail: info@amelearning.com
Visit our website at: www.amelearning.com

Table of Contents

Chapter 1

FINANCIAL STATEMENTS: PERSONAL ACCOUNTING

LEARNING OBJECTIVES

LO 1	Describe the purpose of accounting
LO 2	Describe the balance sheet
LO 3	Describe the income statement
LO 4	Define an accounting period
LO 5	Explain how the accounting equation works
LO 6	Explain accrual-based accounting

LO 7	Explain how to account for debt
LO 8	Explain how to account for assets
LO 9	Explain how to account for prepaid expenses
LO 10	Define capital
LO 11	Demonstrate how double entries are recorded in T-accounts

AMEENGAGE™ *Access **ameengage.com** for integrated resources including tutorials, practice exercises, the digital textbook and more.*

Assessment Questions

AS-1 LO 1

Define accounting and describe the purpose of accounting.

_____

_____

_____

AS-2 LO 2

In simple terms, what are assets and liabilities?

_____

_____

AS-3 LO 3

What are revenues and expenses? Provide an example of each in your personal life.

_____

_____

_____

AS-4 LO 2

Explain the role of the balance sheet.

_____

_____

_____

AS-5 LO 3

Explain the role of the income statement.

_____

_____

_____

AS-6 LO 3

Define surplus and deficit.

_____

_____

_____

_____

AS-7 LO 4

What are some advantages of using monthly accounting periods in your personal balance sheet?

_____

_____

_____

AS-8 LO 5

What is the accounting equation in personal accounting?

_____

_____

AS-9 LO 2 5

What is net worth?

_____

_____

_____

AS-10 LO ·10

What is the equation for calculating ending net worth for a period?

_____

_____

AS-11 `LO` `6`

When does an expense need to be recorded under accrual-based accounting? What are the three possible timings the payment can be made for an expense?

_____

_____

_____

_____

_____

_____

AS-12 `LO` `6`

Explain accrual-based accounting.

_____

_____

_____

_____

_____

AS-13 `LO` `6`

Briefly describe the cash-based method of accounting.

_____

_____

_____

_____

AS-14 `LO` `7`

True or False: When you borrow money, you have more cash but your net worth decreases.

_____

_____

AS-15 `LO` `7`

True or False: When you pay off a loan, your cash decreases and your net worth increases.

_____

_____

AS-16 `LO` `8`

True or False: Buying an asset has no impact on net worth.

_____

_____

AS-17 LO 9

What is a prepaid expense?

_____

_____

AS-18 LO 9

When an expense is initially prepaid, which accounts increase or decrease?

_____

_____

AS-19 LO 10

What is capital?

_____

_____

AS-20 LO 11

Where do the opening balances of the assets and liabilities normally appear on T-accounts?

_____

_____

_____

_____

AS-21 LO 11

What is a T-account?

_____

_____

_____

Application Questions Group A

AP-1A LO 2 7 8   5

April Rose had the following financial data for the year ended December 31, 2019.

Cash	$6,000
Jewellery	10,000
Automobile	18,000
House	256,000
Bank Loan	45,000
Credit Card	5,000
Mortgage	140,000

Required

a) Calculate April's total assets.

_____

_____

_____

_____

_____

b) Calculate April's total liabilities.

_____

_____

_____

_____

AP-2A LO 2 5 7 8

Consider the following information for Julius Palanca.

Cash	$12,000
Jewellery	18,000
Automobile	22,000
House	161,000
Credit Card	5,000
Bank Loan	10,000
Mortgage	125,000

Required

a) Calculate Julius's total assets.

_____

_____

_____

_____

_____

b) Calculate Julius's total liabilities.

_____

_____

_____

_____

c) Calculate Julius's net worth.

_____

_____

_____

AP-3A LO 2 5

Darryl purchased a new laptop on January 1, 2019, worth $2,000. He paid the entire amount using cash. He also purchased a new cell phone worth $300 on account. How will these transactions affect Darryl's net worth?

_____

_____

_____

_____

_____

AP-4A LO 2 3 5 6 10 11

The following information was taken from the personal records of Juliet Lahm on April 30, 2019.

Cash	$3,000
Jewellery	2,000
House	190,000
Mortgage	80,000
Net Worth	115,000

The following transactions occurred during the month of May 2019.

1. Earned monthly salary of $5,050
2. Paid $1,200 cash for utilities
3. Purchased an automobile worth $10,000 on account
4. Paid $600 cash for food
5. Paid $400 cash for gas

Required

a) Complete the cash T-account to determine the ending balance of cash.

INCREASE		DECREASE
+	**CASH**	–
Opening Bal.		

b) Complete the personal income statement to determine the surplus or deficit for the period.

Personal Income Statement For the Month Ended May 31, 2019		

c) What is Juliet Lahm's net worth on May 31?

_____

_____

_____

_____

AP-5A LO 2 5 7 8

Peter Sims has the following personal balance sheet, but the liability section is missing.

Cash	$35,000
Automobile	58,000
House	100,000
Liabilities	?
Net Worth	55,000

Determine the total amount of liabilities.

_____

_____

_____

_____

_____

_____

AP-6A LO 2 5

Calculate the missing amounts in the table below.

	Scenario 1	Scenario 2
Total Assets	$123,000	
Total Liabilities		$34,000
Net Worth	$94,000	$114,000

AP-7A `LO` `2 5 10`

As of December 31, 2018, Maria Green had total assets of $40,000 and total liabilities of $15,000. As of December 31, 2019, Maria's total assets and liabilities increased to $50,000 and $30,000, respectively. How has Maria's net worth changed since the end of 2018?

_____

_____

_____

_____

_____

_____

AP-8A `LO` `2 3 5 7 8 11`

The following information pertains to Darius Dickson's personal finances as at January 1, 2019.

Cash	$9,000
Contents of Home	6,000
Automobile	29,000
House	156,000
Unpaid Accounts	5,500
Bank Loan	60,000
Net Worth	134,500

The following transactions occurred during the month of January 2019.

1. Deposited $4,040 from salary earned during the month of December

2. Paid maintenance expense with $120 cash

3. Purchased new furniture worth $2,500 with cash

4. Paid credit card liability of $5,500 (Unpaid Accounts) in full

5. Paid telephone, electricity and water bills for January with $1,200 cash

6. Purchased $2,000 of groceries for personal consumption with cash

Using the information provided, first record the opening balances in the T-accounts. Then, record the transactions for the month of January in the T-accounts and complete the calculations at the bottom of the table.

PERSONAL BALANCE SHEET
As at January 31, 2019

ASSETS

INCREASE	DECREASE
+	CASH	−

Opening

INCREASE	DECREASE
+	CONTENTS OF HOME	−

Opening

INCREASE	DECREASE
+	AUTOMOBILE	−

Opening

INCREASE	DECREASE
+	HOUSE	−

Opening

LIABILITIES

DECREASE	INCREASE
−	UNPAID ACCOUNTS	+

Opening

DECREASE	INCREASE
−	BANK LOAN	+

Opening

NET WORTH

DECREASE	INCREASE
−	NET WORTH	+

Opening

Total Assets   _____

Total Liabilities   _____   } _____

Net Worth   _____

PERSONAL INCOME STATEMENT
For the Month Ended Jan 31, 2019

DECREASE	INCREASE
−	REVENUE	+

LESS EXPENSES

INCREASE	DECREASE
+	ENTERTAINMENT EXPENSE	−

INCREASE	DECREASE
+	FOOD EXPENSE	−

INCREASE	DECREASE
+	INTEREST EXPENSE	−

INCREASE	DECREASE
+	MAINTENANCE EXPENSE	−

INCREASE	DECREASE
+	UTILITIES EXPENSE	−

Total Revenue   _____

Less Total Expenses   _____

Surplus (Deficit)   _____

AP-9A LO 2 3 5 7 11

Alan Marshall is preparing his balance sheet and income statement for the month ended April 30, 2019. Use the following information to help him prepare his financial statements.

Cash	$5,000
Contents of Home	1,000
Automobile	4,000
House	280,000
Unpaid Accounts	10,000
Auto Loan	30,000
Net Worth	250,000

The following transactions occurred during the month of April.

1. Deposited $4,050 from salary earned during the month
2. Purchased new home furniture worth $2,000 using a credit card
3. Paid credit card bill with $3,000 cash
4. Paid utility bills of $800 for the month of April using a credit card
5. Purchased groceries for $2,500 using cash
6. Made a principal payment of $1,250 for the automobile loan
7. Paid April's rent of $1,500 with cash

Using the information provided, first record the opening balances in the T-accounts. Then, record the transactions for the month of April in the T-accounts and complete the calculations at the bottom of the table.

PERSONAL BALANCE SHEET
As at April 30, 2019

ASSETS

INCREASE	DECREASE
+	CASH	–

Opening

INCREASE	DECREASE
+	CONTENTS OF HOME	–

Opening

INCREASE	DECREASE
+	AUTOMOBILE	–

Opening

INCREASE	DECREASE
+	HOUSE	–

Opening

LIABILITIES

DECREASE	INCREASE
–	UNPAID ACCOUNTS	+

Opening

DECREASE	INCREASE
–	AUTO LOAN	+

Opening

NET WORTH

DECREASE	INCREASE
–	NET WORTH	+

Opening

Total Assets   _____

Total Liabilities   _____ } _____

Net Worth   _____

PERSONAL INCOME STATEMENT
For the Month Ended April 30, 2019

DECREASE	INCREASE
–	REVENUE	+

LESS EXPENSES

INCREASE	DECREASE
+	ENTERTAINMENT EXPENSE	–

INCREASE	DECREASE
+	FOOD EXPENSE	–

INCREASE	DECREASE
+	INTEREST EXPENSE	–

INCREASE	DECREASE
+	MAINTENANCE EXPENSE	–

INCREASE	DECREASE
+	RENT EXPENSE	–

INCREASE	DECREASE
+	UTILITIES EXPENSE	–

Total Revenue   _____

Less Total Expenses _____

Surplus (Deficit)   _____

AP-10A LO 2 3 4 5 10

Tobias Kaufman is a senior administrator at a market research firm. In November, he received a salary increase from $3,500 per month to $4,000 per month. He would like to know how this has impacted his net worth. He has never prepared a personal balance sheet or an income statement, which would help him calculate his net worth. Tobias gathered the following information to help him understand his financial position.

	September 30, 2019	October 31, 2019	November 30, 2019
Cash	$1,000	$2,150	$4,050
House	120,000	120,000	120,000
Bank Loan	400	350	300
Salary	3,500	3,500	4,000
Entertainment Expense	200	500	400
Food Expense	1,500	1,200	1,100
Insurance Expense	150	150	150
Utilities Expense	200	400	300
Miscellaneous Expense	175	50	100

Prepare Tobias Kaufman's income statement for the three months.

Tobias Kaufman Personal Income Statement For the Month Ending				
	September 30, 2019	October 31, 2019	November 30, 2019	Total

AP-11A LO 2 3 4 5 10

Jeff Winger is working at a law firm. His salary recently increased and he would like to keep track of his net worth. Jeff has gathered the following information. Assume his net worth at the beginning of June (opening net worth) is $0.

	June 30, 2019	July 31, 2019	August 31, 2019
Cash	$2,500	$4,100	$6,300
Automobile	13,000	13,000	13,000
Credit Card Bills	1,000	800	500
Automobile Loan	12,000	11,500	11,000
Salary	4,300	4,900	4,900
Food Expense	290	500	100
Entertainment Expense	210	800	500
Rent Expense	1,300	1,300	1,300

Complete the table below.

	June 30, 2019	July 31, 2019	August 31, 2019
Opening Net Worth			
Surplus (Deficit)			
Closing Net Worth			

Analysis

Jeff notices that his cash has not increased by as much as his net worth has. Why is this the case?

_____

_____

_____

_____

_____

AP-12A LO 2 5 7 8

Using the opening balances provided in each balance sheet, enter the updated amounts for each transaction in the blank balance sheets labelled Answers.

a) Borrowed $4,000 from the bank

Opening Balances

Assets		Liabilities	
Cash	$5,000	Unpaid Accounts	$3,000
Investment	8,000	Bank Loan	0
Contents of Home	6,000	Automobile Loan	5,000
Automobile	20,000	Student Loan	6,000
House	280,000	Mortgage	250,000
		Total Liabilities	264,000
		Net Worth	55,000
Total Assets	$319,000	**Total Liabilities + Net Worth**	$319,000

Answers

b)   Purchased $3,000 of investments in cash

Opening Balances

Assets		Liabilities	
Cash	$7,000	Unpaid Accounts	$3,000
Investment	8,000	Bank Loan	0
Contents of Home	6,000	Automobile Loan	5,000
Automobile	20,000	Student Loan	6,000
House	180,000	Mortgage	150,000
		Total Liabilities	164,000
		Net Worth	57,000
Total Assets	$221,000	**Total Liabilities + Net Worth**	$221,000

Answers

c)   Paid $1,000 to reduce an outstanding automobile loan (principal portion)

Opening Balances

Assets		Liabilities	
Cash	$3,000	Unpaid Accounts	$3,000
Contents of Home	6,000	Bank Loan	0
Automobile	20,000	Automobile Loan	5,000
House	180,000	Student Loan	6,000
		Mortgage	150,000
		Total Liabilities	164,000
		Net Worth	45,000
Total Assets	$209,000	**Total Liabilities + Net Worth**	$209,000

Answers

d) Bought a motorcycle for $6,000, paid a $1,000 deposit with cash and borrowed $5,000 from the bank

Opening Balances

Assets		Liabilities	
Cash	$2,000	Unpaid Accounts	$3,000
Contents of Home	4,000	Bank Loan	1,000
Motorcycle	0	Student Loan	11,000
Automobile	20,000	Mortgage	150,000
House	180,000	**Total Liabilities**	165,000
		Net Worth	41,000
Total Assets	$206,000	**Total Liabilities + Net Worth**	$206,000

Answers

AP-13A LO 3 10

Timothy Hollister collected the following amounts in cash for the month of February 2019.

Salary paid by employer	$2,400
Winnings at the casino	$270
Gifts	$295
Performance bonus paid by employer	$450

Calculate Timothy's total revenue and total capital items for February 2019.

AP-14A LO 5

Indicate whether the parts of the accounting equation will increase or decrease for each transaction by placing a "+" or "−" in the appropriate space. If a part is not changed by the transaction, leave the space blank. The first transaction has been completed for you.

Transaction	Assets	= Liabilities	+ Net Worth
1. Deposited salary earned	+		+
2. Purchased a new TV on credit			
3. Received a cash gift			
4. Purchased gas for car on credit			
5. Made a loan payment including interest			
6. Received cash from a student loan			
7. Received a paycheque			

AP-15A LO 2 3 5 7 8 10 11

The following information is available from Drew Bernard's financial records as at September 1, 2019.

Cash	$1,500
Automobile	9,400
Boat	18,000
Instruments	7,600
House	415,000
Student Loans	67,000
Unpaid Accounts	8,500
Mortgage	250,000
Net Worth	126,000

The following transactions took place during the month of September.

1.   Purchased a piano worth $900 using cash
2.   Put $720 worth of food on a credit card
3.   Purchased an $800 guitar on credit
4.   Received a cash inheritance of $45,000
5.   Paid off unpaid accounts with $9,570 cash
6.   Received $50 interest on the bank account

Using the information provided, first record the opening balances in the T-accounts. Then, record the transactions in the T-accounts and complete the calculations at the bottom of the table.

PERSONAL BALANCE SHEET		INCOME STATEMENT
As at September 30, 2019		For the Month Ended September 30, 2019

PERSONAL BALANCE SHEET
As at September 30, 2019

ASSETS		LIABILITIES	
INCREASE	DECREASE	DECREASE	INCREASE
+ CASH –		– STUDENT LOANS +	
Opening			Opening

INCREASE	DECREASE	DECREASE	INCREASE
+ AUTOMOBILE –		– UNPAID ACCOUNTS +	
Opening			Opening

INCREASE	DECREASE	DECREASE	INCREASE
+ BOAT –		– MORTGAGE +	
Opening			Opening

INCREASE	DECREASE
+ INSTRUMENTS –	
Opening	

NET WORTH

DECREASE	INCREASE
– NET WORTH +	
	Opening

INCREASE	DECREASE
+ HOUSE –	
Opening	

Total Assets   _____
Total Liabilities   _____   } _____
Net Worth   _____

INCOME STATEMENT
For the Month Ended September 30, 2019

REVENUE	
DECREASE	INCREASE
–	+

LESS EXPENSES

INCREASE	DECREASE
+ ENTERTAINMENT EXPENSE –	

INCREASE	DECREASE
+ FOOD EXPENSE –	

INCREASE	DECREASE
+ INTEREST EXPENSE –	

INCREASE	DECREASE
+ MAINTENANCE EXPENSE –	

Total Revenue   _____
Less Total Expenses _____
Surplus (Deficit)   _____

AP-16A LO 5 7 8 9 10 11

Indicate whether assets, liabilities or net worth will increase or decrease and by how much, based on each transaction. The first one has been done for you. Always ensure the accounting equation is balanced.

Provide an explanation only if net worth is affected.

Transaction	Assets	= Liabilities	+ Net Worth	Explanation
1. Purchased a new television for $700 on credit	+ 700	+ 700		
2. Received $2,000 in salary				
3. Paid $1,200 cash for one year of insurance				
4. Purchased a new $500 gaming console with cash				
5. Paid for groceries with $80 cash				
6. Paid $400 toward the car loan				
7. Paid $30 interest on the car loan				
8. Paid $600 toward unpaid bills				
9. Used one month of insurance (from #3)				

AP-17A LO 5 7 8 10

The following information is available from Lily's financial records as at November 1, 2019.

Cash	$18,000
Furniture	3,100
Valuables & Electronics	3,200
House	255,000
Student Loans	39,000
Mortgage	100,000
Family Loan	2,000
Net Worth	138,300

Indicate whether the account balances will increase or decrease and by how much, based on each transaction. Always ensure the accounting equation is balanced.

Provide an explanation only if net worth is affected.

	Assets	= Liabilities	+ Net Worth	Explanation
1. Purchased $1,600 worth of new bedroom furniture with cash				
2. Won a tablet worth $800 as a raffle prize				
3. $350 was taken from the bank account for a car rental payment				
4. A family member accepted $2,000 worth of jewellery as repayment for the family loan				
5. Made a $2,000 mortgage payment with cash, including $400 of interest				
6. Paid $1,000 toward the student loans with cash, including $140 of interest				
7. Salary earned of $4,800 was directly deposited to the bank account				

Analysis

The net worth account is updated only at the end of an accounting period. Revenue and expense accounts, and the net worth account, track changes in net worth during the period. For each transaction that affects net worth, determine whether revenue, expense, or net worth (directly) is used to track the change.

_____

_____

_____

_____

_____

AP-18A `LO 2 5 6 7 8 9 10`

On December 1, 2019, Shervin decided to track his finances. On this date, his assets and liabilities were as follows.

Cash	$14,000
Prepaid Rent	3,000
Prepaid Insurance	300
House	160,000
Contents of Home	19,000
Automobile	30,000
Student Loan	10,000
Unpaid Accounts	17,000
Bank Loan	25,000
Mortgage	120,000

Required

a) What is the value of his total assets?

_____

_____

_____

_____

_____

_____

b) What is the value of his total liabilities?

_____

_____

_____

_____

_____

c) What is Shervin's net worth on December 1, 2019?

_____

_____

_____

d) During the month of December, $150 of Shervin's prepaid expenses were incurred and recorded on the income statement. Determine the change in his cash account and net worth.

Transaction	Change in Cash	Change in Net Worth
Recognized $150 of prepaid expenses as actual expense		

AP-19A LO 5 7 8

Nick Miller gathered the following personal accounting information but some of it was destroyed.

Bicycle	$700
Automobile	3,000
Cash	800
Furniture	?
Net Worth	3,350
Overdue Rent	?
Television	500
Total Assets	6,100
Unpaid Bills	2,300

Required

a) How much is Nick's furniture worth?

_____

_____

_____

_____

b) How much rent does Nick owe?

_____

_____

_____

_____

Analysis

Nick has worked 80 hours at his job as a bartender and earned $1,900 but will not get paid for another two weeks. According to accrual-based accounting, has Nick's net worth increased? Why or why not?

_____

_____

_____

_____

AP-20A LO 5 10

State how the following transactions would affect net worth (increase, decrease, no change).

Transaction	Effect on Net Worth
Borrow cash	
Pay for entertainment costs with cash	
Pay for food with cash	
Buy assets with cash	
Charge home repairs expense on credit card	
Pay insurance expense with cash	
Pay loan principal with cash	
Purchase assets on account	
Receive salary	
Pay rent expense with cash	

AP-21A LO 2 3 6 8 10

Using the following chart, indicate whether there would be an increase, decrease or no change to cash and net worth for the transactions provided. The first transaction has been completed for you.

Transaction	Cash			Net Worth		
	Increase	Decrease	No Change	Increase	Decrease	No Change
Deposit salary earned	X			X		
Pay cash for food						
Purchase a new car using cash						
Pay rent in advance						
Pay student loan principal						
Buy a new computer with cash						
Obtain a bank loan						
Pay entertainment expenses						
Record cash earned from a part-time job						

Application Questions Group B

AP-1B LO 2 7 8

Dana Garrison had the following personal financial information on December 31, 2019.

Cash	$7,900
Computer	700
Automobile	19,100
House	255,000
Mortgage	150,000
Credit Card	4,600
Bank Loan	37,700

Required

a) Calculate Dana's total assets.

b) Calculate Dana's total liabilities.

AP-2B LO 2 5 7 8

John Bonham was performing a year-end review of his finances and came up with this list.

Cash	$13,200
Furniture	1,900
Automobile	21,900
House	210,000
Credit Card	4,600
Student Loan	11,400
Mortgage	100,000

Required

a) Calculate John's total assets.

b) Calculate John's total liabilities.

c) Calculate John's net worth.

AP-3B LO 2 5

Consider the following information.

Cash	$6,000
Automobile	50,000
Prepaid Insurance	3,000
Bank Loan	10,000
Unpaid Credit Card Bills	2,000
Net Worth	?

How much is the net worth?

_____

_____

_____

_____

_____

AP-4B LO 2 3 5 6 10 11

Christine Sutherland compiled the following information on May 31, 2019.

Cash	$2,100
Jewellery	3,000
House	186,200
Mortgage	171,800
Net Worth	19,500

The following transactions occurred during the month of June 2019.

1. Received $4,100 cash for her monthly salary
2. Paid $590 cash for maintenance on her car
3. Paid $540 cash for telephone, water and electricity charges
4. Purchased an automobile worth $10,600 on credit
5. Received $30 interest earned on bank deposits
6. Paid $320 for food with cash

Required

a) Use the T-account to calculate the ending balance of cash.

INCREASE		DECREASE
+	**CASH**	−

b)   What is the surplus or deficit for the accounting period?

_____

_____

c)   What is Christine Sutherland's net worth on June 30?

_____

_____

AP-5B LO 2 5 7 8

Toshiro's financial records show that his assets and net worth as of May 1, 2019 are as follows.

Cash	$6,000
Computer	4,000
Contents of Home	17,500
Automobile	20,000
House	137,500
Student Loan	?
Net Worth	113,000

Required

a)   Toshiro wants to find out how much he owes for his student loan. Determine his total liabilities.

_____

_____

_____

_____

_____

_____

_____

_____

_____

b)   During the month of May, Toshiro paid $2,000 for two months of rent in advance ($1,000 per month). Calculate the change in Toshiro's cash account and personal net worth.

Transaction	Change in Cash	Change in Net Worth
Prepaid two months' rent		

AP-6B LO 2 5

Calculate the missing amounts in the following table.

	Scenario 1	Scenario 2
Total Assets	$125,900	
Total Liabilities		$33,200
Net Worth	$92,700	$117,100

AP-7B LO 2 5 10

Lucia has total assets of $35,000 and total liabilities of $20,000. She owns a few pieces of gold jewellery that were originally purchased for $1,000 total. She recently purchased some additional jewellery for $3,000 cash. Which account balances will change from this transaction and by how much? Use the accounting equation to check your answer.

_____

_____

_____

_____

_____

_____

Analysis

Lucia wants to increase her net worth, so she decides to purchase a new automobile by getting a bank loan. Has her net worth changed as expected? Explain.

_____

_____

AP-8B LO 2 3 5 7 8 11

Alan Marshall is preparing his balance sheet and income statement for the month ended July 31, 2019. The following information was available for the accounts as at July 1, 2019:

Cash	$4,400
Contents of Home	2,800
Automobile	4,800
House	287,900
Unpaid Accounts	8,500
Mortgage	239,300
Net Worth	52,100

The following transactions occurred during the month of July.

1. Deposited $4,700 of salary earned during June
2. Purchased a $1,600 high-definition television using a credit card
3. Paid a telephone bill of $640 for the month of July using a credit card
4. Paid a credit card bill with cash for $3,300
5. Purchased $1,010 of groceries using cash
6. Paid July's utilities of $1,100 with cash
7. Made a principal payment of $1,100 for the mortgage
8. Earned $60 interest on a savings account

Using the information provided, first record the opening balances in the T-accounts. Then, record the transactions for the month of July in the T-accounts and complete the calculations at the bottom of the table.

PERSONAL BALANCE SHEET
As at July 31, 2019

ASSETS

INCREASE	DECREASE
+	CASH	–

Opening

LIABILITIES

DECREASE	INCREASE
–	UNPAID ACCOUNTS	+

Opening

INCREASE	DECREASE
+	CONTENTS OF HOME	–

Opening

DECREASE	INCREASE
–	MORTGAGE	+

Opening

INCREASE	DECREASE
+	AUTOMOBILE	–

Opening

NET WORTH

DECREASE	INCREASE
–	NET WORTH	+

Opening

INCREASE	DECREASE
+	HOUSE	–

Opening

Total Assets

Total Liabilities

Net Worth

PERSONAL INCOME STATEMENT
For the Month Ended July 31, 2019

REVENUE

DECREASE	INCREASE
–	+

LESS EXPENSES

INCREASE	DECREASE
+	CLOTHING EXPENSE	–

INCREASE	DECREASE
+	FOOD EXPENSE	–

INCREASE	DECREASE
+	TELEPHONE EXPENSE	–

INCREASE	DECREASE
+	UTILITIES EXPENSE	–

Total Revenue

Less Total Expenses

Surplus (Deficit)

AP-9B LO 2 3 5 6 7 11

The following information is available from Elaine Georgiu's financial records as at February 1, 2019.

Cash	$34,000
Prepaid Insurance	3,500
Automobile	45,000
Boat	81,000
Unpaid Accounts	21,000
Automobile Loan	25,000
Net Worth	117,500

The following transactions took place during the month of February.

1. Purchased gas for the boat with $85 cash
2. Earned $1,250 in wages and deposited it in a bank account
3. Purchased $420 of groceries on a credit card
4. Won $200 cash from a lottery
5. Paid $3,600 cash for credit card bills due
6. Paid $360 interest on credit card bill with cash
7. Booked a flight on credit for $900
8. Recognized one month of car insurance used up for $350

Using the information provided, first record the opening balances in the T-accounts. Then, record the transactions in the T-accounts and complete the calculations at the bottom of the table.

PERSONAL BALANCE SHEET
As at February 28, 2019

ASSETS		LIABILITIES	
INCREASE	DECREASE	DECREASE	INCREASE
+ CASH –		– UNPAID ACCOUNTS +	
Opening			Opening

INCREASE	DECREASE	DECREASE	INCREASE
+ PREPAID INSURANCE –		– AUTOMOBILE LOAN +	
Opening			Opening

INCREASE	DECREASE
+ AUTOMOBILE –	
Opening	

NET WORTH

INCREASE	DECREASE	DECREASE	INCREASE
+ BOAT –		– NET WORTH +	
Opening			Opening

Total Assets _____
Total Liabilities _____ } _____
Net Worth _____

INCOME STATEMENT
For the Month Ended February 28, 2019

REVENUE	
DECREASE	INCREASE
–	+

LESS EXPENSES

INCREASE	DECREASE
+ ENTERTAINMENT EXPENSE –	

INCREASE	DECREASE
+ FOOD EXPENSE –	

INCREASE	DECREASE
+ FUEL EXPENSE –	

INCREASE	DECREASE
+ INSURANCE EXPENSE –	

INCREASE	DECREASE
+ INTEREST EXPENSE –	

INCREASE	DECREASE
+ TRAVEL EXPENSE –	

Total Revenue _____
Less Total Expenses _____
Surplus (Deficit) _____

Analysis

Elaine will be cancelling her auto insurance with no cancellation fee incurred. Which accounts will be affected by the insurance cancellation? How will the balances change?

_____

_____

AP-10B LO 2 3 4 5 10

Ethan is a songwriter and composer. His income is based solely on royalties that he receives regularly. Ethan opted to use three months as his accounting period.

The following information pertains to income earned and expenses incurred from January 1, 2019 to March 31, 2019.

	January	February	March
Royalty Income	$12,000	$13,000	$10,000
Interest Expense	60	60	60
Food Expense	2,000	2,100	1,900
Maintenance Expense	350	500	180
Clothing Expense	900	1,500	0
Utilities Expense	300	500	0
Rent Expense	1,500	1,500	1,500
Miscellaneous Expense	15	50	5

Required

a) Prepare a personal income statement for each of the three months.

Ethan Personal Income Statement For the Period Ended March 31, 2019				
	January	February	March	Total

b) What amount should be added to Ethan's net worth on March 31, 2019?

_____

_____

_____

_____

AP-11B LO 2 3 4·5 10

Archie always prepares an income statement and balance sheet each month, but he has fallen behind. Assume the opening net worth for October 31, 2019, is $6,770. Luckily, he has kept track of his account balances as shown below.

	October 31, 2019	November 30, 2019
Cash	$2,500	$6,900
Entertainment Expense	500	250
Food Expense	280	270
Gasoline Expense	140	130
Prepaid Rent	4,200	2,800
Rent Expense	1,400	1,400
Salary	5,050	5,050
Unpaid Accounts	700	700
Automobile	3,500	3,500

Complete the table below.

	October 31, 2019	November 30, 2019
Opening Net Worth		
Surplus (Deficit)		
Closing Net Worth		

Analysis

Archie noticed that his net worth did not increase as much as his cash did during November. Why is this the case?

_____

_____

_____

AP-12B LO 2 5 7 8

Using the opening balances provided in each balance sheet, enter the updated amounts for each transaction in the blank balance sheets labelled Answers.

a) Applied for and received a student loan of $5,700

Opening Balances

Assets		Liabilities	
Cash	$5,600	Unpaid Accounts	$2,500
Investment	8,400	Bank Loan	900
Contents of Home	6,200	Automobile Loan	4,800
Automobile	22,300	Student Loan	5,500
House	287,900	Mortgage	241,500
		Total Liabilities	255,200
		Net Worth	75,200
Total Assets	$330,400	**Total Liabilities + Net Worth**	$330,400

Answers

b) Purchased some furniture and jewellery for $5,000 cash

Opening Balances

Assets		Liabilities	
Cash	$8,200	Unpaid Accounts	$2,400
Investment	7,200	Bank Loan	200
Contents of Home	6,100	Automobile Loan	4,400
Automobile	22,900	Student Loan	6,200
House	272,300	Mortgage	242,200
		Total Liabilities	255,400
		Net Worth	61,300
Total Assets	$316,700	**Total Liabilities + Net Worth**	$316,700

Answers

c) Paid a portion of the principal of the automobile loan for $1,200

Opening Balances

Assets		Liabilities	
Cash	$4,500	Unpaid Accounts	$2,200
Contents of Home	5,500	Bank Loan	600
Automobile	19,000	Automobile Loan	4,200
House	290,000	Student Loan	6,800
		Mortgage	242,800
		Total Liabilities	256,600
		Net Worth	62,400
Total Assets	$319,000	**Total Liabilities + Net Worth**	$319,000

Answers

d) Bought a motorcycle for $7,100—paid a $1,400 deposit with cash and borrowed $5,700 from the bank

Opening Balances

Assets		Liabilities	
Cash	$5,000	Unpaid Accounts	$2,000
Contents of Home	6,700	Bank Loan	1,000
Motorcycle	0	Student Loan	11,000
Automobile	17,000	Mortgage	242,000
House	283,300	**Total Liabilities**	256,000
		Net Worth	56,000
Total Assets	$312,000	**Total Liabilities + Net Worth**	$312,000

Answers

AP-13B LO 3 10

Prisha Afsahani received the following amounts in cash for the month of November 2019.

Salary	$2,100
Gifts	$240
Winnings at the casino	$170
Performance bonus paid by employer	$460

Calculate Prisha's total revenue and total capital items for November 2019.

_____

_____

_____

_____

_____

AP-14B LO 5

Indicate whether the parts of the accounting equation will increase or decrease for each transaction by placing a "+" or "−" in the appropriate space. If a part is not changed by the transaction, leave the space blank. The first transaction has been completed for you.

Transaction	Assets	= Liabilities	+ Net Worth
1. Deposited salary earned	+		+
2. Purchased a new bicycle on credit			
3. Purchased groceries on credit			
4. Borrowed money from the bank			
5. Purchased a ring for $200 cash			
6. Received a cash gift			
7. Made a loan payment with interest			

AP-15B LO 2 3 5 7 8 10 11

The following information is available from Anna Edison's financial records as at June 1, 2019.

Cash	$18,000
Furniture	3,100
Jewellery & Electronics	3,200
House	255,000
Student Loans	39,000
Family Loan	2,000
Mortgage	100,000
Net Worth	138,300

The following transactions took place during the month of June.

1. $350 was taken from the bank account for a car lease payment
2. Paid $1,000 cash against the student loans, which includes $140 of interest
3. Won a tablet worth $800 as a raffle prize
4. Made a mortgage payment of $2,000 with cash, which includes $400 of interest
5. Salary earned of $4,800 was directly deposited to the bank account
6. A family member accepted $2,000 worth of jewellery as repayment of the family loan

Required

a) Using the information provided, first record the opening balances in the T-accounts. Then, record the transactions for the month of June in the T-accounts and complete the calculations at the bottom of the table.

PERSONAL BALANCE SHEET
As at June 30, 2019

ASSETS		LIABILITIES	

ASSETS

INCREASE	DECREASE
+	**CASH**	–

Opening

LIABILITIES

DECREASE	INCREASE
–	**STUDENT LOANS**	+

Opening

INCREASE	DECREASE
+	**FURNITURE**	–

Opening

DECREASE	INCREASE
–	**FAMILY LOAN**	+

Opening

INCREASE	DECREASE
+	**JEWELLERY & ELECTRONICS**	–

Opening

DECREASE	INCREASE
–	**MORTGAGE**	+

Opening

INCREASE	DECREASE
+	**HOUSE**	–

Opening

NET WORTH

DECREASE	INCREASE
–	**NET WORTH**	+

Opening

Total Assets _____

Total Liabilities _____ } _____

Net Worth _____

INCOME STATEMENT
For the Month Ended June 30, 2019

REVENUE

DECREASE	INCREASE
–	+

LESS EXPENSES

INCREASE	DECREASE
+	**AUTOMOBILE EXPENSE**	–

INCREASE	DECREASE
+	**ENTERTAINMENT EXPENSE**	–

INCREASE	DECREASE
+	**FOOD EXPENSE**	–

INCREASE	DECREASE
+	**INTEREST EXPENSE**	–

INCREASE	DECREASE
+	**TRAVEL EXPENSE**	–

Total Revenue _____

Less Total Expenses _____

Surplus (Deficit) _____

b)   Complete the income statement for the month of June.

Income Statement For the Month Ended June 30, 2019		

c)   Complete the personal balance sheet as at June 30, 2019.

Personal Balance Sheet As at June 30, 2019			

AP-16B LO 5 7 8 9 10 11

Indicate whether assets, liabilities or net worth will increase or decrease and by how much, based on each transaction. The first one has been done for you. Always ensure the accounting equation is balanced.

Provide an explanation only if net worth is affected.

	Assets	= Liabilities	+ Net Worth	Explanation
1. Purchased a new television for $700 on credit	+ 700	+ 700		
2. Won $700 in a lottery				
3. Deposited $2,800 in salary				
4. Purchased furniture for $400 in cash				
5. Transferred $500 from a chequing account to a savings account				
6. Paid $150 for concert tickets with a credit card				
7. Paid $200 cash for utilities				
8. Paid $1,500 toward the mortgage				
9. Paid $1,100 toward unpaid bills				

AP-17B LO 5 7 8 9 10

Indicate whether the account balances will increase or decrease and by how much, based on each transaction. The first one has been done for you. Always ensure the accounting equation is balanced.

Provide an explanation only if net worth is affected.

Transaction	Assets	= Liabilities	+ Net Worth	Explanation
1. Purchased a new television for $700 on credit	+ 700	+ 700		
2. Purchased $100 worth of gas on credit				
3. Made an $850 car loan payment				
4. Purchased a chandelier for $200 cash				
5. Prepaid three months of rent with $3,300 cash				
6. Received a cash gift of $500				
7. Used up one of three months of prepaid rent				
8. Paid interest of $50, in cash, on the car loan				
9. Received a phone bill for $110 to be paid next month				

Analysis

The net worth account is updated only at the end of an accounting period. Revenue and expense accounts, and the net worth account, track changes in net worth during the period. For each transaction affecting net worth, determine whether revenue, expense, or net worth (directly) is used to track the change.

_____

_____

_____

_____

_____

AP-18B LO 2 5 6 7 8 9 10

Consider the following financial information of Pete Griphin.

Automobile	$66,000
Boat	55,000
Automobile Loan	50,000
Cash	14,500
Coin Collection	1,200
Cottage	84,000
House and Property	510,000
Prepaid House Insurance	8,500
Mortgage Principal	450,000
Trailer	4,000

Required

a) Calculate Pete's total assets.

_____

_____

_____

_____

_____

_____

_____

_____

_____

b) Calculate Pete's total liabilities.

_____

_____

_____

_____

c) Calculate Pete's net worth.

_____

_____

_____

Analysis

Pete makes payments against his liabilities and updates all of his account balances at the end of each month. Which account balances will change at the end of the month? Which will increase and which will decrease?

_____

_____

_____

_____

AP-19B LO 5 7 8

Jess Day stored her personal accounting information in the computer but some of it was deleted by accident.

Appliances	$1,100
Cell Phone	500
Family Loan	?
Jewellery	800
Net Worth	4,500
Unpaid Bills	350
Automobile	5,000

Required

a)   What are Jess's total assets?

_____

_____

b)   What is the amount of Jess's family loan?

_____

_____

_____

Analysis

Jess works as a teacher. She has agreed to work as a substitute during one day next week for extra wages. According to accrual-based accounting, has Jess's net worth increased? Why or why not?

_____

_____

_____

_____

_____

_____

AP-20B LO 5 6 9 10

Dex had the following transactions during the month of May.

1.   Purchased a new laptop for $1,200 cash
2.   Put $1,600 of car repairs on his credit card
3.   Spent $80 on a steak dinner with his sister and paid with his credit card
4.   Prepaid his son's nanny $850 cash for future services
5.   Received a salary of $5,500

How have these transactions affected Dex's net worth?

_____

_____

_____

_____

_____

Analysis

Has Dex's cash changed the same amount as his net worth? Why or why not?

_____

_____

_____

_____

AP-21B LO 2 3 6 8 10

On June 1, 2019, Joey had $3,100 in cash (including his bank account).

Required

a) Using the following chart, indicate whether there would be an increase, decrease or no change to cash and net worth for the transactions provided. The first transaction has been completed for you.

Transaction	Cash			Net Worth		
	Increase	Decrease	No Change	Increase	Decrease	No Change
Returned groceries to the store for $50 cash	X			X		
Purchased a new laptop for $1,200 cash						
Bought a concert ticket for $90 cash						
Received wages of $3,200 for the month						
Spent $300 cash on food for the month						
Received monthly utility bills of $310, due July 21						
Received interest on a savings account of $35						

b) Based on the transactions listed in part a), what is the balance of cash on June 30? The opening cash balance is $3,100.

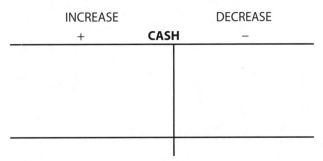

c) Prepare a personal income statement for Joey for June.

Personal Income Statement For the Month Ended June 30, 2019		
Revenue		
Expenses		
Surplus (Deficit)		

Analysis

Joey purchased his car using 0% financing. This means there is no interest on the loan. What is the effect on net worth after each car payment? Would the effect be any different if the loan had interest? Explain.

_____

_____

_____

_____

Case Study

CS–1 LO 2 3 5 6 7 8 9 10 11

After taking the first part of this financial accounting course, you excitedly tell a friend what you have learned. You tell him about assets, liabilities and net worth and how they increase and decrease in value with every financial transaction. Your friend decides to start getting organized and apply accounting principles to his personal finances. He compiles everything that he thinks is important and calculates his net worth. He then asks you to look over what he has done to make sure it is correct. His important financial items are listed below, along with his version of the T-account records.

1. He had $950 in his bank account at the beginning of the month.
2. He had a $1,200 balance on his credit card at the beginning of the month.
3. He estimates that he had about $3,000 worth of "stuff" in his apartment at the beginning of the month (TV, sound system, computer and furniture).
4. He deposited his salary of $1,500.
5. He paid in advance for three months of rent with $1,350 cash.
6. He paid $600 to pay off a portion of the credit card bill.
7. He purchased a new video game system for $350 with his credit card.
8. He bought $120 worth of food with cash.
9. He got hired at a second job. He will start next month and will earn $800 per month.
10. He spent $250 cash on movies, stage plays and Dave and Buster's Sports Bar.
11. He lived in his apartment for one of the three months he already paid for (see #5).

+	CASH		–	
1.	950	5.	1,350
4.	1,500	6.	600
		8.	120
		10.	250
Total	**$130**		

–	UNPAID ACCOUNTS		+	
6.	600	2.	1,200
		7.	350
	Total		**$950**

–	NET WORTH		+	
5.	1,350	3.	3,000
8.	120	4.	1,500
10.	250	7.	350
		9.	800
	Total		**$3,930**

Required

a) What are some immediate problems that you see with what your friend has prepared?

_____

_____

_____

_____

_____

b) With all the problems you see, your friend asks you to show him what the correct records should look like. Use the templates at the end of this problem to record the transactions.

_____

_____

After showing your friend the corrected version, he asks a number of questions.

c) Why did you use all of these accounts when I only used three (Cash, Unpaid Accounts and Net Worth)?

_____

_____

_____

_____

_____

d) Why is the $3,000 worth of "stuff" not considered net worth?

_____

_____

_____

_____

e) I was having trouble figuring out how to record my second job which I start next month. They are going to be paying me $800 a month! I figured it will increase my net worth, but I didn't know where else to put it. I knew it couldn't be cash, because they haven't paid me yet. What did you do with it and why?

_____

_____

_____

f) What did you do with my rent? Shouldn't the entire $1,350 decrease my net worth? And what would happen if I did it my way?

_____

_____

_____

_____

_____

_____

_____

g) I forgot to tell you that the $600 credit card payment included $30 of interest. I didn't think it mattered since the total payment amount is the same. This won't change anything, right?

_____

_____

h) You may have noticed that I am running low on cash. Any suggestions on how I can raise more cash?

_____

_____

_____

_____

_____

_____

_____

_____

i) This is very useful and I would like to do this more often. I can do it this weekend, then two weeks from now once I finish my exams, then probably not for another month after that. I'm going on a well-deserved vacation after my exams, so I won't be around to look after it. Do you think this will work out well?

_____

_____

_____

_____

_____

_____

_____

_____

_____

_____

_____

_____

_____

_____

_____

_____

_____

_____

j)   Using the information provided, record the transactions in the T-accounts and complete calculations at
     the bottom of the personal balance sheet and income statement (on the next page).

PERSONAL BALANCE SHEET

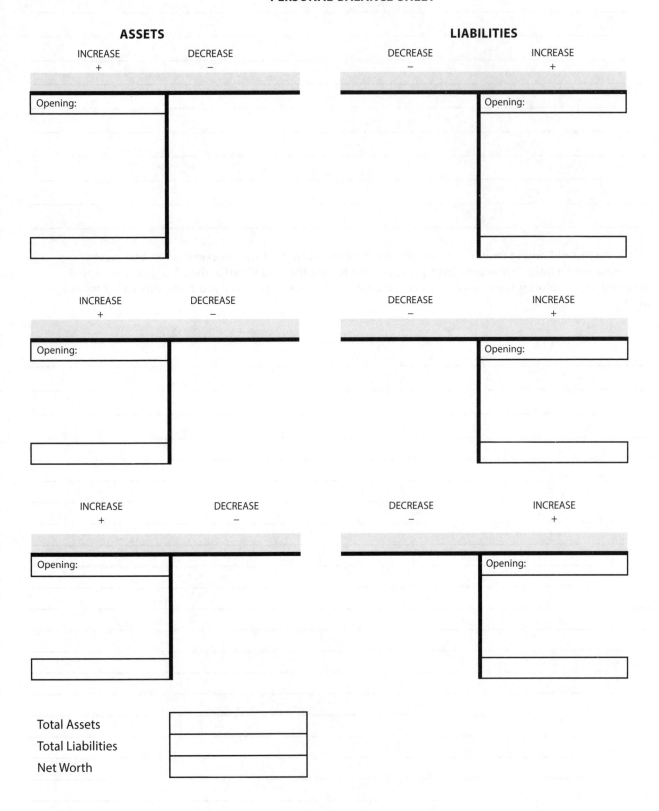

Total Assets	
Total Liabilities	
Net Worth	

PERSONAL INCOME STATEMENT

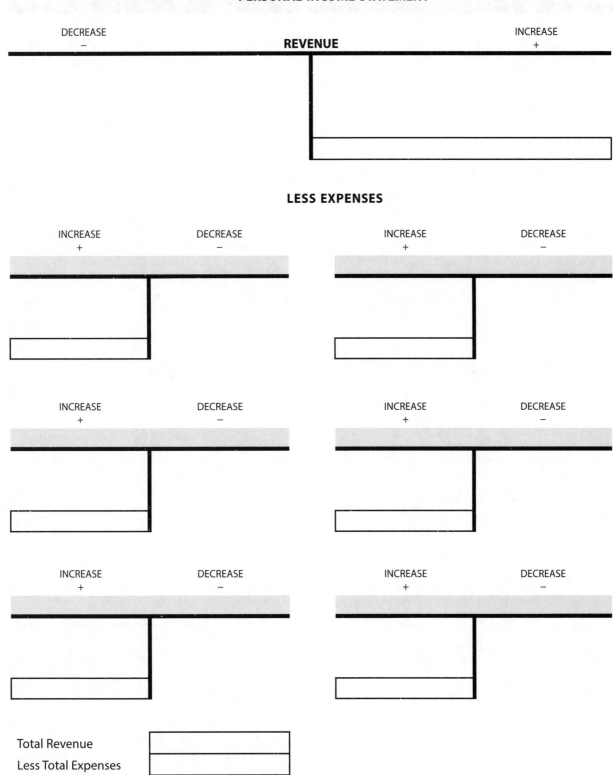

LESS EXPENSES

Total Revenue	
Less Total Expenses	
Surplus (Deficit)	

Notes

Chapter 2

LINKING PERSONAL ACCOUNTING TO BUSINESS ACCOUNTING

LEARNING OBJECTIVES

LO 1　List the differences between personal accounts and business accounts

LO 2　Describe the three main types of businesses

LO 3　Record revenue based on the concept of accruals

LO 4　Record expenses based on the concept of accruals

LO 5　Record business transactions in T-accounts

LO 6　Identify the four required financial statements and prepare three financial statements

LO 7　Describe ethics relating to financial statement reporting

AMEENGAGE™　*Access ameengage.com for integrated resources including tutorials, practice exercises, the digital textbook and more.*

Assessment Questions

AS-1　LO 1

Net worth in personal accounting is similar to which item in accounting for businesses?

AS-2　LO 1

What is equity?

AS-3　LO 1

What is the formula for calculating the ending owner's equity balance?

AS-4　LO 1

Describe owner's contributions and owner's withdrawals and explain how they affect the balance sheet.

AS-5　LO 2

List the three main types of businesses.

AS-6 LO 2

Describe what a service business does. Provide two examples of service businesses.

_____

_____

_____

AS-7 LO 2

Describe what a merchandising business does. Provide an example of a merchandising business.

_____

_____

_____

AS-8 LO 2

Describe what a manufacturing business does. Provide two examples of a manufacturing business.

_____

_____

AS-9 LO 3

What does it mean to *recognize* revenue?

_____

_____

AS-10 LO 3

Describe the three different times cash can be received from a customer related to earning revenue.

_____

_____

_____

AS-11 LO 3

What is the entry to record revenue if a customer pays *when* the service is delivered?

_____

_____

AS-12 LO 3

What is the entry to record revenue if a customer pays *after* the service is delivered?

_____

_____

AS-13 LO 3

What is the entry if a customer pays *before* the service is delivered?

_____

_____

AS-14 `LO 3`

What type of account is unearned revenue?

_____

_____

AS-15 `LO 4`

Give three examples of expenses that businesses commonly prepay.

_____

_____

_____

_____

AS-16 `LO 4`

Describe the three different times cash can be paid to a supplier related to an expense.

_____

_____

_____

_____

_____

AS-17 `LO 4`

What does it mean to _incur_ an expense?

_____

_____

AS-18 `LO 4`

What is the entry to record an expense if a company pays _when_ the expense is incurred?

_____

_____

AS-19 `LO 4`

What is the entry to record an expense if a company pays _after_ the expense is incurred?

_____

_____

_____

AS-20 `LO 4`

What is the entry to record an expense if a company pays _before_ the expense is incurred?

_____

_____

AS-21 `LO 6`

In what order are the assets of a business listed? Explain.

_____

_____

_____

AS-22 `LO 6`

In what order are the liabilities of a business listed? Explain.

_____

_____

_____

AS-23 `LO 6`

What are the three categories on the statement of cash flows?

_____

_____

_____

AS-24 `LO 6`

On the statement of cash flows, where would cash received from customers be reported, and is it an inflow or outflow of cash?

_____

_____

_____

AS-25 `LO 7`

What factors can lead a person to commit fraud?

_____

_____

Application Questions Group A

AP-1A LO 1 3 4

For each transaction, indicate whether the total assets, liabilities or owner's equity increased (+), decreased (−) or did not change (o) by placing the symbol in the appropriate column.

	Assets	Liabilities	Owner's Equity
1. Paid salaries for current month	−		−
2. Purchased equipment on credit	+	+	
3. Purchased furniture using cash	+/−		
4. Made an additional investment into the business	+		+
5. Received payment for services to be provided next month			
6. Made partial payment for equipment purchased on credit	−	−	
7. Billed customers for services performed	+		+
8. Withdrew cash for personal use	−		−
9. Received payment from customers already billed		−	
10. Received bills for utilities to be paid next month			

AP-2A LO 1 3 4

The given transactions were completed by Juliet's Delivery Services during May 2019. Indicate the effects of each transaction by placing the appropriate letter in the space provided.

- A   Increase in asset, decrease in another asset
- B   Increase in asset, increase in liability
- C   Increase in asset, increase in owner's equity
- D   Decrease in asset, decrease in liability
- E   Decrease in asset, decrease in owner's equity

_____   Received cash for providing delivery services
_____   Paid amount owing that was outstanding to a creditor
_____   Owner invested additional cash in the business
_____   Paid advertising expense with cash
_____   Billed customers for delivery services on account
_____   Purchased office furniture on account
_____   Paid rent for the month
_____   Received cash from customers on account
_____   Received cash in advance for services to be provided in the next month
_____   Owner withdrew cash for personal use

AP-3A LO 6

Organize the following asset and liability accounts in the order they are likely to appear in a balance sheet.

Assets	Liabilities
Accounts Receivable	Bank Loan
Cash	Accounts Payable
Equipment	Unearned Revenue
Prepaid Expenses	

AP-4A LO 3 4

Simpson Moving had the following transactions during the month. Indicate whether assets, liabilities or owner's equity will increase or decrease and by how much, based on each transaction. Provide an explanation only if equity is affected. The first entry has been done for you. Always ensure the accounting equation is balanced.

	Assets =	Liabilities +	Owner's Equity	Explanation
1. Paid $200 cash for maintenance expense	−200		−200	Paid for maintenance expense
2. The owner invested $4,000 cash in the business	+ 4000		4000	owner investment
3. Paid $2,400 cash for one year of insurance	+ 2400 −2400			
4. Received a telephone bill for $150, which will be paid later		+150	−150	
5. Purchased equipment worth $1,000 on account	+1000	+1000		
6. Provided services and collected $4,200 cash	4200		4200	
7. Paid $500 toward the bank loan	−500		−500	
8. Paid $50 interest related to the bank loan	−50			
9. Paid $700 of accounts payable	−700	−700		

AP-5A LO 3 4 5

Dry Cleanest offers extensive dry cleaning services. Riya Kapoor started this company one year ago. The opening balances of the accounts on August 1, 2019, are shown below.

Cash	$980
Accounts Receivable	620
Prepaid Expenses	300
Machinery	3,800
Accounts Payable	1,020
Bank Loan	0
Kapoor, Capital	4,680

Required

a) Indicate whether assets, liabilities or owner's equity will increase or decrease and by how much, based on each transaction during August. Provide an explanation only if equity is affected. The first one has been done for you. Always ensure the accounting equation is balanced.

	Assets =	Liabilities +	Owner's Equity	Explanation
1. Borrowed $10,000 from the bank	+10,000	+10,000		
2. Purchased machinery for $7,300 cash				
3. Billed clients $2,950 for completed services, which is due in 30 days				
4. Paid $130 cash for regular maintenance on the machine				
5. Collected $1,300 from clients who owed money				
6. Paid $3,000 in advance for four months of rent				
7. Recorded $1,600 of cash sales for the month				
8. Paid $700 owed to a supplier				

b) Based on the information provided, first record the opening balances in the T-accounts. Then, record the transactions for the month of August in the T-accounts, and complete the calculations at the bottom of the table.

Dry Cleanest
Balance Sheet
As at August 31, 2019

ASSETS

INCREASE	DECREASE
+ CASH	−
Opening 980	7300
40000	130
1300	3000
1600	700
2480	

INCREASE	DECREASE
+ ACCOUNTS RECEIVABLE −	
Opening 620	1300
2950	
2270	

INCREASE	DECREASE
+ PREPAID EXPENSES −	
Opening 300	
3000	
3300	

INCREASE	DECREASE
+ MACHINERY −	
Opening 3800	
7300	
11100	

LIABILITIES

DECREASE	INCREASE
− ACCOUNTS PAYABLE +	
1300	1020 Opening
700	
	320

DECREASE	INCREASE
− BANK LOAN +	
	0
	Opening 10000
	10000

OWNER'S EQUITY

DECREASE	INCREASE
− KAPOOR, CAPITAL +	
	4680 Opening
	4680

INCREASE	DECREASE
+ KAPOOR, WITHDRAWALS −	
	0

Total Assets	19410
Total Liabilities	10320
Owner's Equity	9100

4680 − 0 + 4420 − 0

Dry Cleanest
Income Statement
For the Month Ended August 31, 2019

REVENUE

DECREASE	INCREASE
− SERVICE REVENUE +	
	2950
	1600
	4550

LESS EXPENSES

INCREASE	DECREASE
+ INSURANCE EXPENSE −	
	0

INCREASE	DECREASE
+ MAINTENANCE EXPENSE −	
130	
130	

INCREASE	DECREASE
+ SALARIES EXPENSE −	
	0

INCREASE	DECREASE
+ UTILITIES EXPENSE −	
	0

Total Revenue	4550
Less Total Expenses	1130
Net Income (Loss)	4420

Analysis

The owner of Dry Cleanest wants to withdraw cash from the business, but she does not want the net income to fall below $4,000. What is the maximum amount of cash she can withdraw in order to keep net income above $4,000? Explain.

_____

_____

_____

_____

AP-6A LO 1 6

Alex Limbo is the owner of Double Duplicator. The following is a list of Double Duplicator's accounts and balances as at March 31, 2019.

Cash	$4,700
Limbo, Capital	2,000
Accounts Payable	5,000
Unearned Revenue	2,000
Prepaid Insurance	2,300
Bank Loan	10,000
Automobile Loan	18,000
Prepaid Rent	5,000
Automobile	25,000

Prepare a balance sheet as at March 31, 2019, using the above information.

AP-7A LO 6

Alex Papanov operates a construction company as a sole proprietorship called Papanov Construction. Alex is creating some financial records for the company for the end of April 2019 and has come up with the following account balances.

Accounts Payable	$750
Accounts Receivable	350
Bank Loan	5,000
Cash	11,250
Storage Warehouse	36,200
Tools and Equipment	7,900
Vehicle	13,800

Prepare the balance sheet as at April 30, 2019, for Papanov Construction.

AP-8A LO 5

Paul Stiles runs a small landscaping business. During the month of July 2019, he had the following transactions. For each transaction, provide the appropriate T-account names and fill in the amounts.

1. Earned service revenue from a client and received $600 cash

2. Paid $150 cash for gas for the lawn cutting equipment

3. Purchased a new lawn mower for $700 and will pay for it next month

4. Went to the bank and took out a $3,000 loan

AP-9A LO 5

Brad Picton operates a consulting business. During the month of December 2019, he had the following transactions. For each transaction, provide the appropriate T-account names and fill in the amounts.

1. Invested $4,000 cash into the business

2. Paid $1,400 cash for a one-year insurance policy

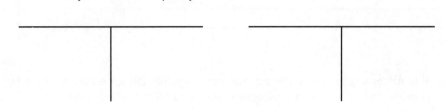

3. Received a $300 bill for utilities, which will be paid next month

4. A customer paid $500 cash for work that was completed last month

AP-10A LO 6

Isabela Paloma owns a painting business called Paloma Painters. She has recorded all the transactions for the month of July 2019. The balances of the accounts are shown below.

Account	Balance
Accounts Payable	$1,000
Accounts Receivable	500
Cash	1,500
Equipment	10,000
Maintenance Expense	100
Bank Loan	5,000
Paloma, Capital	3,750
Paloma, Withdrawals	1,400
Prepaid Insurance	1,200
Rent Expense	200
Service Revenue	5,200
Telephone Expense	150
Travel Expense	300
Unearned Revenue	400

Required

a) Using the information provided, prepare the income statement for Paloma Painters for the month of July.

b) Prepare the statement of owner's equity for Paloma Painters for the month of July. Isabela did not make any investments in the business during the month.

c) Prepare the balance sheet for Paloma Painters as at July 31, 2019.

AP-11A LO 1 3 4 5

Jessica Holmes recently started her own shoe repair business. Transactions for the first month of operations (June 2019) are as follows.

1. Jessica invested $10,000 cash in the business
2. Paid two months of rent in advance, in the amount of $1,000
3. Purchased store equipment worth $3,000 with cash
4. Incurred business registration expenses, paid with $600 cash
5. Paid travel expenses with $1,100 cash
6. Received $2,300 cash from customers for shoe repair services performed during the month
7. Provided shoe repair services worth $1,200 on account
8. Paid $1,300 salary to an assistant
9. Borrowed $3,000 cash from the bank
10. Received $800 in bills for electricity, water and telephone, to be paid next month
11. Jessica withdrew $500 cash for personal purposes
12. Received $200 owing from a customer for service provided earlier this month

Record the above transactions on the T-account worksheet, and complete the calculations at the bottom of the table.

Holmes Shoe Repair
Balance Sheet
As at June 30, 2019

ASSETS

INCREASE	DECREASE
+ CASH	−
Opening	

INCREASE	DECREASE
+ ACCOUNTS RECEIVABLE −	
Opening	

INCREASE	DECREASE
+ PREPAID RENT −	
Opening	

INCREASE	DECREASE
+ EQUIPMENT −	
Opening	

LIABILITIES

DECREASE	INCREASE
− ACCOUNTS PAYABLE +	
	Opening

DECREASE	INCREASE
− BANK LOAN +	
	Opening

OWNER'S EQUITY

DECREASE	INCREASE
− HOLMES, CAPITAL +	
	Opening

INCREASE	DECREASE
+ HOLMES, WITHDRAWALS −	
Opening	

Total Assets _____

Total Liabilities _____ ⎫
Owner's Equity _____ ⎭ _____

_____

Holmes Shoe Repair
Income Statement
For the Month Ended June 30, 2019

REVENUE

DECREASE	INCREASE
− SERVICE REVENUE +	

LESS EXPENSES

INCREASE	DECREASE
+ REGISTRATION & LICENSES EXPENSE −	

INCREASE	DECREASE
+ RENT EXPENSE −	

INCREASE	DECREASE
+ SALARIES EXPENSE −	

INCREASE	DECREASE
+ TELEPHONE & UTILITIES EXPENSE −	

INCREASE	DECREASE
+ TRAVEL EXPENSE −	

Total Revenue _____

Less Total Expenses _____

Net Income (Loss) _____

AP-12A LO 1 3 4 5

Sheila Abney opened a dormitory locator business called Room Finders near a college campus. During the first month of operations, June 2019, Sheila had the following transactions.

1. Sheila invested $10,000 of personal funds to start the business
2. Incurred travel expenses for $650, which will be paid later
3. Paid $700 cash for maintenance expense
4. Received $5,000 cash for services provided to clients
5. Paid $650 related to the purchase in transaction #2
6. Paid three months of office rent in advance, in the amount of $1,500
7. Incurred $300 of utilities expense, which will be paid next month
8. Received $1,000 cash from a customer for services to be provided in two months
9. Provided $1,200 in services for a customer who will pay later
10. Recognized one month of office rent that was prepaid
11. Sheila withdrew $1,000 cash for personal use
12. Purchased a second-hand car worth $10,000 for business use, with cash
13. Received $700 from the customer in transaction #9

Prepare a T-account worksheet.

Room Finders
Balance Sheet
As at June 30, 2019

ASSETS

INCREASE	DECREASE
+	−

Opening

INCREASE	DECREASE
+	−

Opening

INCREASE	DECREASE
+	−

Opening

INCREASE	DECREASE
+	−

Opening

LIABILITIES

DECREASE	INCREASE
−	+

Opening

DECREASE	INCREASE
−	+

Opening

DECREASE	INCREASE
−	+

OWNER'S EQUITY

DECREASE	INCREASE
−	+

Opening

INCREASE	DECREASE
+	−

Total Assets _____

Total Liabilities _____ }

Owner's Equity _____ _____

Room Finders
Income Statement
For the Month Ended June 30, 2019

REVENUE

DECREASE	INCREASE
−	+

LESS EXPENSES

INCREASE	DECREASE
+	−

INCREASE	DECREASE
+	−

INCREASE	DECREASE
+	−

INCREASE	DECREASE
+	−

INCREASE	DECREASE
+	−

Total Revenue _____

Less Total Expenses _____

Net Income (Loss) _____

AP-13A LO 1 3 4 5

John Cheng Communications is a public relations firm. On April 30, 2019, the firm had the following ending balances.

Cash	$20,000
Prepaid Rent	10,000
Equipment	25,000
Accounts Payable	8,000
Capital	47,000

During the month of May, the company completed the following transactions.

1. Purchased $800 of office equipment on account
2. Paid $6,000 to reduce the amount owing to a supplier
3. Received $5,000 cash from customers for services rendered
4. Paid May's utility bill with $700 cash
5. Purchased a computer worth $1,500 on account
6. Received a bill for $1,000 for advertisements during the month of May; the amount will be paid in July
7. Paid May's salaries with $1,900 cash
8. Owner withdrew $3,000 cash for personal use
9. Recognized $2,000 rent for May (which was prepaid)
10. Received $4,000 cash in advance for a contract to be completed in three months

Prepare the T-account worksheet.

Note: The ending balances for the month of April are the opening balances for the month of May.

Cheng Communications
Balance Sheet
As at May 31, 2019

ASSETS	
INCREASE	DECREASE
+	–

Opening

INCREASE	DECREASE
+	–

Opening

INCREASE	DECREASE
+	–

Opening

LIABILITIES	
DECREASE	INCREASE
–	+

Opening

DECREASE	INCREASE
–	+

Opening

DECREASE	INCREASE
–	+

Opening

OWNER'S EQUITY	
DECREASE	INCREASE
–	+

Opening

INCREASE	DECREASE
+	–

Total Assets _____

Total Liabilities _____ } _____

Owner's Equity _____

_____

Cheng Communications
Income Statement
For the Month Ended May 31, 2019

REVENUE	
DECREASE	INCREASE
–	+

LESS EXPENSES

INCREASE	DECREASE
+	–

INCREASE	DECREASE
+	–

INCREASE	DECREASE
+	–

INCREASE	DECREASE
+	–

INCREASE	DECREASE
+	–

Total Revenue _____

Less Total Expenses _____

Net Income (Loss) _____

AP-14A LO 1 3 4 5

On December 1, 2019, Laila Ann established City Laundry. During the first month, the following transactions occurred.

1. Laila deposited $15,000 into City Laundry's bank account
2. Bought tables and chairs worth $1,000 with cash
3. Received and paid a utilities bill for $1,200 in cash
4. Purchased washers and dryers worth $4,000; paid $2,000 cash with the remainder due in 30 days
5. Purchased two additional dryers worth $1,100 from Marky Distributors, on account
6. Received $4,000 cash for laundry services provided for the first half of the month
7. Paid $900 cash for a one-year insurance policy
8. Paid $1,000 cash for this month's rent
9. Paid the amount owing to Marky Distributors
10. Provided $3,500 of laundry services during the second half of the month for customers who will pay at a later date
11. Paid employee salaries of $1,400
12. Laila withdrew $2,000 cash for personal use
13. Recorded first month's insurance expense of $75
14. Collected $3,000 cash from customers as payment on their accounts
15. Received $2,000 cash in advance for services to be provided next year

Prepare the T-account worksheet.

City Laundry
Balance Sheet
As at December 31, 2019

ASSETS	
INCREASE	DECREASE
+	−
Opening	

INCREASE	DECREASE
+	−
Opening	

INCREASE	DECREASE
+	−
Opening	

INCREASE	DECREASE
+	−
Opening	

LIABILITIES	
DECREASE	INCREASE
−	+
	Opening

DECREASE	INCREASE
−	+
	Opening

OWNER'S EQUITY	
DECREASE	INCREASE
−	+
	Opening

INCREASE	DECREASE
+	−

Total Assets _____

Total Liabilities _____ }

Owner's Equity _____ _____

_____

City Laundry
Income Statement
For the Month Ended December 31, 2019

REVENUE	
DECREASE	INCREASE
−	+

LESS EXPENSES

INCREASE	DECREASE
+	−

INCREASE	DECREASE
+	−

INCREASE	DECREASE
+	−

INCREASE	DECREASE
+	−

INCREASE	DECREASE
+	−

INCREASE	DECREASE
+	−

Total Revenue _____

Less Total Expenses _____

Net Income (Loss) _____

AP-15A LO 1 3 4 5

On April 1, 2019, Aaron Ragan established a business to manage rental properties. He had the following transactions during the business's first month of operations.

1. Aaron invested $20,000 cash into the business from his personal savings; amount was deposited into the business's bank account
2. Purchased $1,000 worth of office equipment on account
3. Received $5,000 cash for managing rental properties for a client
4. Purchased furniture worth $350 on account
5. Paid a utilities bill of $400 for the month in cash
6. Used a bank loan to purchase office furniture for $5,000
7. Paid $500 cash to reduce the amount of the bank loan principal
8. Paid rent for the month with $1,800 cash
9. Paid office staff salaries with $1,500 cash
10. Aaron withdrew $1,000 cash for personal use
11. Provided $2,000 worth of services for a customer on account

Prepare the T-account worksheet.

Ragan Properties
Balance Sheet
As at April 30, 2019

ASSETS

INCREASE	DECREASE
+	−

Opening

INCREASE	DECREASE
+	−

Opening

INCREASE	DECREASE
+	−

Opening

LIABILITIES

DECREASE	INCREASE
−	+

Opening

DECREASE	INCREASE
−	+

Opening

OWNER'S EQUITY

DECREASE	INCREASE
−	+

Opening

INCREASE	DECREASE
+	−

Total Assets _____

Total Liabilities _____ } _____

Owner's Equity _____

_____

Ragan Properties
Income Statement
For the Month Ended April 30, 2019

REVENUE

DECREASE	INCREASE
−	+

LESS EXPENSES

INCREASE	DECREASE
+	−

INCREASE	DECREASE
+	−

INCREASE	DECREASE
+	−

INCREASE	DECREASE
+	−

INCREASE	DECREASE
+	−

Total Revenue _____

Less Total Expenses _____

Net Income (Loss) _____

AP-16A LO 1 3 4 5 6

Edward James decided to start his own car rental business after graduation, called James Rent-A-Car. He recorded these transactions during the first month of operations (January 2019).

1. Edward invested $20,000 cash in the business
2. Borrowed $20,000 from the bank
3. Paid $35,000 cash for a new car to be used in the business
4. Paid the principal of the bank loan with $2,000 cash
5. Paid for $800 of maintenance expense with cash
6. Paid monthly salaries for personnel with $1,000 cash
7. Paid miscellaneous expenses with $300 cash
8. Received $8,000 in cash for service revenue for the month
9. Received a utilities bill for the month for $600, payable next month
10. Paid monthly interest on the bank loan with $200 cash
11. Paid $1,500 of insurance for the next five months in advance
12. Edward withdrew $1,000 cash for personal use
13. Received $3,000 cash from customers for services to be provided next month

Required

a) Prepare the T-account worksheet.

James Rent-A-Car
Balance Sheet
As at January 31, 2019

ASSETS

INCREASE	DECREASE
+	CASH	–

Opening

INCREASE	DECREASE
+	PREPAID INSURANCE	–

Opening

INCREASE	DECREASE
+	AUTOMOBILE	–

Opening

LIABILITIES

DECREASE	INCREASE
–	ACCOUNTS PAYABLE	+

Opening

DECREASE	INCREASE
–	UNEARNED REVENUE	+

Opening

DECREASE	INCREASE
–	BANK LOAN	+

Opening

OWNER'S EQUITY

DECREASE	INCREASE
–	JAMES, CAPITAL	+

Opening

INCREASE	DECREASE
+	JAMES, WITHDRAWALS	–

Total Assets _____

Total Liabilities _____

Owner's Equity _____ } _____

James Rent-A-Car
Income Statement
For the Month Ended January 31, 2019

REVENUE

DECREASE	INCREASE
–	SERVICE REVENUE	+

LESS EXPENSES

INCREASE	DECREASE
+	INTEREST EXPENSE	–

INCREASE	DECREASE
+	MAINTENANCE EXPENSE	–

INCREASE	DECREASE
+	MISCELLANEOUS EXPENSE	–

INCREASE	DECREASE
+	RENT EXPENSE	–

INCREASE	DECREASE
+	SALARIES EXPENSE	–

INCREASE	DECREASE
+	UTILITIES EXPENSE	–

Total Revenue _____

Less Total Expenses _____

Net Income (Loss) _____

b)   Prepare the income statement for the month of January.

c)   Prepare the statement of owner's equity for the month of January.

d)   Prepare the balance sheet as at January 31, 2019.

AP-17A LO 1 3 4 5 6

Lina D'Amico is the owner of Lina's Computer Services. The balance sheet of Lina's Computer Services on February 28, 2019, is shown below.

Lina's Computer Services Balance Sheet As at February 28, 2019			
Assets		**Liabilities**	
Cash	$4,000	Accounts Payable	$3,000
Prepaid Insurance	3,000	Bank Loan	0
Furniture and Equipment	25,000	**Total Liabilities**	3,000
		Owner's Equity	
		D'Amico, Capital	29,000
Total Assets	$32,000	**Total Liabilities + Owner's Equity**	$32,000

During March, the business engaged in the following transactions.

1. Borrowed $20,000 from bank
2. Purchased computer equipment for $5,000 cash
3. Performed services for a customer and received $4,000 cash
4. Purchased furniture for $1,000 on credit
5. Paid $1,500 to a supplier for the amount owed
6. Paid the following expenses in cash: salaries, $1,000; rent, $1,500; and interest, $200
7. Received a $900 utilities bill, due next month
8. Lina withdrew $3,500 cash for personal use
9. Received $1,000 cash in advance for services to be completed next month

Required

a) Prepare the T-account worksheet.

Note: The ending balance for the month of February is the opening balance for the month of March.

Lina's Computer Services
Balance Sheet
As at March 31, 2019

ASSETS		
INCREASE	DECREASE	
+	–	
Opening		

LIABILITIES		
DECREASE	INCREASE	
–	+	
	Opening	

INCREASE	DECREASE
+	–
Opening	

DECREASE	INCREASE
–	+
	Opening

INCREASE	DECREASE
+	–
Opening	

DECREASE	INCREASE
–	+
	Opening

OWNER'S EQUITY		
DECREASE	INCREASE	
–	+	
	Opening	

INCREASE	DECREASE
+	–

Total Assets _____

Total Liabilities _____ }

Owner's Equity _____ _____

Lina's Computer Services
Income Statement
For the Month Ended March 31, 2019

REVENUE	
DECREASE	INCREASE
–	+

LESS EXPENSES

INCREASE	DECREASE
+	–

INCREASE	DECREASE
+	–

INCREASE	DECREASE
+	–

INCREASE	DECREASE
+	–

INCREASE	DECREASE
+	–

INCREASE	DECREASE
+	–

Total Revenue _____

Less Total Expenses _____

Net Income (Loss) _____

b) Prepare the income statement for the month of March.

c) Prepare the statement of owner's equity for the month of March.

d) Prepare the balance sheet as at March 31, 2019.

AP-18A LO 7

Over the summer, you were hired by your uncle as an accounting intern for his landscaping company, which operates as a sole proprietorship. While working as an intern, you discovered that Sandra, the company's only accountant, has been using the company's money to pay for some of her personal expenses. Sandra recorded these personal expenses in the company's books as business expenses. Sandra told you that she needed the money to pay the hospital bills of her sick child. She also requested that you not tell your uncle about her actions, because she is simply borrowing this money and will try to pay the company back in about a year. Because you were hired for only three months, there is no way for you to know whether Sandra will in fact return the money. While your uncle is a great landscaper, he has very limited accounting knowledge and therefore does not know how to check Sandra's accounting work. He generally trusts Sandra because of her college degree in accounting.

Analyze Sandra's actions using the fraud triangle as the framework. Discuss whether you should reveal Sandra's actions to your uncle and why or why not.

Application Questions Group B

AP-1B LO 1 3 4

For each of the given transactions, determine the effect on owner's equity by placing an "X" in the space provided.

	Increase	Decrease	No Effect
1. Invested money in the business			
2. Purchased equipment on account			
3. Paid one third of the amount owing for the purchase of equipment			
4. Received cash for the services rendered			
5. Paid salaries for the month			
6. Withdrew cash for personal use			
7. Paid monthly rent			
8. Additional investment by the owner			
9. Provided services for a customer who will pay in two months			
10. Acquired land using cash			

Effect on Owner's Equity

AP-2B LO 1 3 4

For the following transactions, indicate the two accounts related to each transaction.

	Account 1	Account 2
1. Invested cash in the business		
2. Purchased service vehicle for business use		
3. Collected cash for services provided today		
4. Provided services this week on credit		
5. Paid operating expenses in cash		
6. Received a bill for operating expenses incurred this week to be paid later		
7. Received a loan from the bank		
8. Collected cash from a customer for services provided previously		
9. Paid monthly salaries to employees with cash		
10. Incurred operating expenses this week, to be paid next month		
11. Paid cash for expenses incurred previously		
12. Received cash in advance for the service to be performed next month		

AP-3B LO 2

Match each term with the appropriate description.

    A   Merchandising
    B   Service
    C   Manufacturing
    D   Accounts Receivable
    E   Cash

_____ A law firm is an example of this type of business.
_____ This account represents the amount owed to the business by its customers for services preformed earlier.
_____ This type of business buys goods to resell to customers.
_____ An automaker is an example of this type of business.
_____ This is the most liquid asset.

AP-4B `LO` `3` `4`

Focus In had the following transactions during the month. Indicate whether assets, liabilities or owner's equity will increase or decrease and by how much, based on each transaction. Provide an explanation only if equity is affected. Always ensure the accounting equation is balanced.

	Assets =	Liabilities +	Owner's Equity	Explanation
1. The owner invested $10,000 into the business	+10,000		+10,000	Owner investment
2. Paid $3,300 cash for three months of rent				
3. Borrowed $5,000 from the bank				
4. Purchased furniture for $2,500 on account				
5. Paid $700 cash for advertising				
6. Provided services and received $2,300 cash				
7. Paid $400 for the furniture purchased earlier				
8. The owner withdrew $2,500 for personal use				
9. Used up one month of rent				

AP-5B `LO` `3` `4` `5` `6`

Vu's Auto Repair is a new business owned by Sam Vu, that started operations on April 1, 2019.

Required

a)   Indicate whether assets, liabilities or owner's equity will increase or decrease and by how much, based on each transaction during April. Provide an explanation only if equity is affected. The first one has been done for you. Always ensure the accounting equation is balanced.

	Assets =	Liabilities +	Owner's Equity	Explanation
1. Sam invested $8,000 cash into the business	+8,000		+8,000	Owner invested cash
2. Sam invested $2,500 worth of equipment into the business				
3. Purchased tools and supplies for $6,030 on credit				
4. Paid 12 months of insurance in advance at $250/month				
5. Made cash sales of $4,420 during the month				
6. Received a utility bill for $370 for the month, which will be paid later				
7. Paid wages to employees of $5,800				
8. Sam withdrew $2,000 cash from the business				
9. Recorded one month of insurance used up				
10. Received $2,000 cash for services to be provided in two months				

b) Record the transactions in the T-accounts, and complete the calculations at the bottom of the table.

Vu's Auto Repair
Balance Sheet
As at April 30, 2019

ASSETS

INCREASE	DECREASE
+ CASH	−
Opening	

INCREASE	DECREASE
+ PREPAID INSURANCE	−
Opening	

INCREASE	DECREASE
+ TOOLS AND SUPPLIES	−
Opening	

INCREASE	DECREASE
+ EQUIPMENT	−
Opening	

LIABILITIES

DECREASE	INCREASE
− ACCOUNTS PAYABLE	+
	Opening

DECREASE	INCREASE
− UNEARNED REVENUE	+
	Opening

DECREASE	INCREASE
− BANK LOAN	+
	Opening

OWNER'S EQUITY

DECREASE	INCREASE
− VU, CAPITAL	+
	Opening

INCREASE	DECREASE
− VU, WITHDRAWALS	+

Total Assets _____

Total Liabilities _____ } _____

Owner's Equity _____

Vu's Auto Repair
Income Statement
For the Month Ended April 30, 2019

REVENUE

DECREASE	INCREASE
− SERVICE REVENUE	+

LESS EXPENSES

INCREASE	DECREASE
+ INSURANCE EXPENSE	−

INCREASE	DECREASE
+ SALARIES EXPENSE	−

INCREASE	DECREASE
+ UTILITIES EXPENSE	−

Total Revenue _____

Less Total Expenses _____

Net Income (Loss) _____

c) Complete the income statement for the month of April.

d) Complete the statement of owner's equity for the month of April.

e) Complete the balance sheet as at April 30, 2019.

AP-6B LO 6

Maya's Music offers music lessons to the public for all age groups. Maya Matlin is trying to assess her business by analyzing her balance sheet. Here are the accounts and balances of Maya's Music on October 31, 2019.

Accounts Payable	$1,250
Bank Loan	55,000
Building	120,000
Cash	8,150
Instruments	21,650
Prepaid Insurance	3,600
Supplies	280
Unearned Revenue	1,000

Prepare the balance sheet as at October 31, 2019 for Maya's Music.

Analysis

Maya thinks her business is doing well because her capital is so high. Is the balance sheet a useful tool to analyze performance? What other information is needed to assess whether Maya's Music has been performing well or not? Explain.

_____

_____

_____

_____

_____

_____

AP-7B LO 6

Some numbers are missing from the following balance sheet and statement of cash flows of Caldwell Enterprises.

Caldwell Enterprises			
Balance Sheet			
As at August 31, 2019			
Assets		**Liabilities**	
Cash	a)	Accounts Payable	$18,000
Accounts Receivable	15,000	Bank Loan	5,000
Office Supplies	3,000	**Total Liabilities**	b)
Furniture	10,000	**Owner's Equity**	
		Caldwell, Capital	c)
Total Assets	$35,100	**Total Liabilities + Owner's Equity**	d)

Caldwell Enterprises		
Statement of Cash Flows		
For the Month Ended August 31, 2019		
Cash Flow from Operating Activities		
Cash Received from Customers	$13,450	
Cash Paid to Employees	(6,000)	
Cash Paid for Interest	(50)	
Net Cash Provided by Operating Activities		e)
Cash Flow from Investing Activities		
Cash Payments for Furniture Purchase	(10,000)	
Net Cash Used by Investing Activities		f)
Cash Flow from Financing Activities		
Cash Received from Bank Loan	5,000	
Cash Withdrawal by Owner	(1,000)	
Net Cash Provided by Financing Activities		g)
Net Increase in Cash		h)
Cash Balance, August 1, 2019		i)
Cash Balance, August 31, 2019		j)

Required

Calculate the missing numbers for the following balances.

a) Cash balance in the balance sheet: _____

b) Total liabilities: _____

c) Caldwell, capital: _____

d) Total liabilities + owner's equity: _____

e) Net cash provided by operating activities: _____

f) Net cash used by investing activities: _____

g) Net cash provided by financing activities: _____

h) Net increase in cash: _____

i) Cash balance, August 1, 2019: _____

j) Cash balance, August 31, 2019: _____

AP-8B LO 5

Macy Stewart operates a nail and spa business. For the month of May 2019, she had the following transactions. For each transaction, provide the appropriate T-account names and fill in the amounts.

1. Received a deposit of $400 from a wedding party for a spa treatment to be done next month

2. Took $800 from the business for personal use

3. Performed a manicure/pedicure for a client and charged her $100; the client will pay next month

4. Received and paid the telephone bill for $150

AP-9B LO 5

Stacy Dixon operates a small accounting business. During the month of October 2019, she had the following transactions. For each transaction, provide the appropriate T-account names and fill in the amounts.

1. Provided services to a client and billed him $1,200; the client paid immediately with cash

2. Paid $80 for the telephone bill that was received and recorded last month

3. Paid $800 of the bank loan principal.

4. Provided services to a client and billed her $900; the client will pay next month

AP-10B LO 6

Faiyaz Dhawan Architects has recorded all the transactions for the month of March 2019. The balances of all the accounts are shown below. During the month, Faiyaz invested an extra $2,000 into the business.

Account	Balance
Accounts Payable	$3,500
Accounts Receivable	6,700
Cash	8,500
Equipment	18,000
Insurance Expense	700
Maintenance Expense	400
Bank Loan	7,500
Prepaid Rent	3,600
Dhawan, Capital	17,650
Dhawan, Withdrawals	2,600
Salaries Expense	5,200
Service Revenue	16,400
Travel Expense	1,400
Unearned Revenue	800
Utilities Expense	750

Required

a) Using the accounts and balances, prepare the income statement for Faiyaz Dhawan Architects for the month of March.

b) Prepare the statement of owner's equity for the month of March.

c) Prepare the balance sheet as at March 31, 2019.

AP-11B LO .1 3 4 5

Brenda Darby recently started her own consulting business, and completed these transactions during the first month of operations (May 2019).

1. Brenda invested $10,700 cash in the business
2. Purchased store furniture for $4,000 cash
3. Paid $1,100 cash for two months of insurance in advance
4. Incurred business registration expenses, paid with $640 cash
5. Paid travel expenses with $1,200 cash
6. Received $2,300 cash from clients for consulting services provided during the month
7. Borrowed $3,800 cash from the bank
8. Paid salary to an assistant with $790 cash
9. Received bills of $900 for May's electricity, water and telephone, to be paid next month
10. Brenda withdrew $700 cash for personal purposes
11. Received $1,000 cash for a consulting service to be completed next month

Record the above transactions in the T-account worksheet, and complete the calculations at the bottom of the table.

Darby Consulting
Balance Sheet
As at May 31, 2019

ASSETS		LIABILITIES	

CASH

INCREASE	DECREASE
+	−
Opening	

PREPAID INSURANCE

INCREASE	DECREASE
+	−
Opening	

FURNITURE

INCREASE	DECREASE
+	−
Opening	

ACCOUNTS PAYABLE

DECREASE	INCREASE
−	+
	Opening

UNEARNED REVENUE

DECREASE	INCREASE
−	+
	Opening

BANK LOAN

DECREASE	INCREASE
−	+
	Opening

OWNER'S EQUITY

DARBY, CAPITAL

DECREASE	INCREASE
−	+
	Opening

DARBY, WITHDRAWALS

INCREASE	DECREASE
+	−

Total Assets	
Total Liabilities	
Owner's Equity	

Darby Consulting
Income Statement
For the Month Ended May 31, 2019

REVENUE

SERVICE REVENUE

DECREASE	INCREASE
−	+

LESS EXPENSES

REGISTRATION EXPENSE

INCREASE	DECREASE
+	−

SALARIES EXPENSE

INCREASE	DECREASE
+	−

TRAVEL EXPENSE

INCREASE	DECREASE
+	−

UTILITIES EXPENSE

INCREASE	DECREASE
+	−

Total Revenue	
Less Total Expenses	
Net Income (Loss)	

AP-12B LO 1 3 4 5

Deep Drains is a plumbing company that started operations in February 2018. The company is fully owned by Emma Reno. Consider the following opening balances as of February 1, 2019.

Cash	$13,200
Prepaid Rent	5,700
Prepaid Insurance	4,000
Property, Plant & Equipment	38,200
Accounts Payable	3,300
Bank Loan	11,300
Reno, Capital	46,500

The following transactions were completed during the month of February.

1. Purchased plane tickets for business travel with $1,140 cash
2. Paid $3,300 cash to reduce the balance of accounts payable
3. Purchased equipment worth $3,400 with a bank loan
4. The owner invested $6,700 additional cash in the company
5. Paid $850 cash for registration expenses
6. Received a bill for $590 for utilities used during the month; the bill was immediately paid with cash
7. Earned revenue and received $10,000 cash
8. Recognized prepaid rent as an expense for $1,110
9. Paid interest for the month of February with $50 cash
10. Paid monthly salaries with $4,100 cash
11. The owner withdrew $2,500 cash from the business to pay for personal expenses
12. Received $2,000 cash in advance for services to be rendered in three months

Using the information provided, first record the opening balances in the T-accounts. Then, record the transactions for the month of February in the T-accounts, and complete the calculations at the bottom of the table.

Deep Drains
Balance Sheet
As at February 28, 2019

ASSETS

INCREASE	DECREASE
+ CASH	−

Opening

INCREASE	DECREASE
+ PREPAID RENT	−

Opening

INCREASE	DECREASE
+ PREPAID INSURANCE	−

Opening

INCREASE	DECREASE
+ EQUIPMENT	−

Opening

Total Assets _____

Total Liabilities _____ } _____

Owner's Equity _____

LIABILITIES

DECREASE	INCREASE
− ACCOUNTS PAYABLE	+

Opening

DECREASE	INCREASE
− UNEARNED REVENUE	+

Opening

DECREASE	INCREASE
− BANK LOAN	+

Opening

OWNER'S EQUITY

DECREASE	INCREASE
− RENO, CAPITAL	+

Opening

INCREASE	DECREASE
+ RENO, WITHDRAWALS	−

Deep Drains
Income Statement
For the Month Ended February 28, 2019

REVENUE

DECREASE	INCREASE
− SERVICE REVENUE	+

LESS EXPENSES

INCREASE	DECREASE
+ INTEREST EXPENSE	−

INCREASE	DECREASE
+ REGISTRATION EXPENSE	−

INCREASE	DECREASE
+ RENT EXPENSE	−

INCREASE	DECREASE
+ SALARIES EXPENSE	−

INCREASE	DECREASE
+ UTILITIES EXPENSE	−

INCREASE	DECREASE
+ TRAVEL EXPENSE	−

Total Revenue _____

Less Total Expenses _____

Net Income (Loss) _____

AP-13B LO 1 3 4 5

Candace Harris Legal is a law firm. On July 31, 2019, the firm had the following ending balances.

Cash	$18,500
Prepaid Insurance	9,200
Property, Plant & Equipment	22,300
Accounts Payable	8,100
Harris, Capital	41,900

During the month of August, the company completed the following transactions.

1. Purchased $1,000 of office equipment on account
2. Received $4,600 cash from customers for services rendered
3. Paid $4,900 owing to a supplier
4. Paid a $570 utilities bill for August with cash
5. Purchased a computer on account for $1,420
6. Paid August's salaries with $3,600 cash
7. Received a $1,150 advertising bill to be paid in September for advertisements during the month of August
8. Performed services worth $2,000 for customers on account
9. Owner withdrew $3,200 cash for personal use
10. Recognized $1,700 insurance for August (which was prepaid)
11. Received $1,500 cash for legal services to be provided next month
12. Collected all the balances owing from customers for services performed earlier

Using the information provided, first record the opening balances in the T-accounts. Then, record the transactions for the month of August in the T-accounts, and complete the calculations at the bottom of the table.

Candace Harris Legal
Balance Sheet
As at August 31, 2019

ASSETS

INCREASE	DECREASE
+	CASH –

Opening

INCREASE	DECREASE
+ ACCOUNTS RECEIVABLE –	

Opening

INCREASE	DECREASE
+ PREPAID INSURANCE –	

Opening

INCREASE	DECREASE
+ EQUIPMENT –	

Opening

LIABILITIES

DECREASE	INCREASE
– ACCOUNTS PAYABLE +	

Opening

DECREASE	INCREASE
– UNEARNED REVENUE +	

Opening

OWNER'S EQUITY

DECREASE	INCREASE
– HARRIS, CAPITAL +	

Opening

INCREASE	DECREASE
+ HARRIS, WITHDRAWALS –	

Total Assets _____

Total Liabilities _____ } _____

Owner's Equity _____

Candace Harris Legal
Income Statement
For the Month Ended August 31, 2019

REVENUE

DECREASE	INCREASE
– SERVICE REVENUE +	

LESS EXPENSES

INCREASE	DECREASE
+ ADVERTISING EXPENSE –	

INCREASE	DECREASE
+ INSURANCE EXPENSE –	

INCREASE	DECREASE
+ SALARIES EXPENSE –	

INCREASE	DECREASE
+ UTILITIES EXPENSE –	

Total Revenue _____

Less Total Expenses _____

Net Income (Loss) _____

AP-14B LO 1 3 4 5

Christine Jacob is a financial planning consultant. During the month of February 2019, she completed the following transactions.

1. Christine invested $8,000 cash in the business
2. Paid $1,400 cash for office rent for the month of February
3. Received $6,500 from a client for services rendered
4. Paid $500 cash for gas
5. Paid $700 cash to Helpful Entrepreneur for consulting services
6. Purchased office equipment worth $900 on account
7. Owner withdrew $2,500 cash for personal use
8. Donated $800 cash to the Canadian Red Cross
9. Provided $2,000 worth of services for a client for services on account
10. Made partial payment of $500 on the equipment that was purchased on account
11. Received $500 cash for services to be provided next month
12. Collected $1,000 cash from a client who owed for services provided earlier in the month

Prepare the T-account worksheet.

Christine Jacob Financial Planning
Balance Sheet
As at February 28, 2019

ASSETS		LIABILITIES	

ASSETS

INCREASE	DECREASE
+	−

Opening

INCREASE	DECREASE
+	−

Opening

INCREASE	DECREASE
+	−

Opening

LIABILITIES

DECREASE	INCREASE
−	+

Opening

DECREASE	INCREASE
−	+

Opening

OWNER'S EQUITY

DECREASE	INCREASE
−	+

Opening

INCREASE	DECREASE
+	−

Total Assets _____

Total Liabilities _____ } _____

Owner's Equity _____

Christine Jacob Financial Planning
Income Statement
For the Month Ended February 28, 2019

REVENUE

DECREASE	INCREASE
−	+

LESS EXPENSES

INCREASE	DECREASE
+	−

INCREASE	DECREASE
+	−

INCREASE	DECREASE
+	−

INCREASE	DECREASE
+	−

INCREASE	DECREASE
+	−

INCREASE	DECREASE
+	−

Total Revenue _____

Less Total Expenses _____

Net Income (Loss) _____

AP-15B LO 1 3 4 5

Troy Dale, a graphic designer, opened his own business on March 1, 2019. During the month, he completed the following transactions related to his professional practice.

1. Troy transferred $30,000 cash from his personal bank account to the business account
2. Provided services for $3,000 cash
3. Purchased office and computer equipment worth $8,000 on account, which will be paid next month
4. Paid $1,100 cash for meals and entertainment
5. Paid insurance expense with $800 cash
6. Performed services for clients for $4,000 on account
7. Paid $600 cash for miscellaneous expenses
8. Received a utilities bill of $1,000, to be paid next month
9. Paid $1,200 cash for office rent for the month of March
10. Paid $1,000 salary to his assistant
11. Collected 50% of the balance owing from clients for services performed earlier this month
12. Received $1,000 cash for services to be performed in three months

Prepare the T-account worksheet.

Dale Design
Balance Sheet
As at March 31, 2019

ASSETS

INCREASE	DECREASE
+	−

Opening

INCREASE	DECREASE
+	−

Opening

INCREASE	DECREASE
+	−

Opening

LIABILITIES

DECREASE	INCREASE
−	+

Opening

DECREASE	INCREASE
−	+

Opening

OWNER'S EQUITY

DECREASE	INCREASE
−	+

Opening

INCREASE	DECREASE
+	−

Total Assets _____

Total Liabilities _____

Owner's Equity _____ } _____

Dale Design
Income Statement
For the Month Ended March 31, 2019

REVENUE

DECREASE	INCREASE
−	+

LESS EXPENSES

INCREASE	DECREASE
+	−

INCREASE	DECREASE
+	−

INCREASE	DECREASE
+	−

INCREASE	DECREASE
+	−

INCREASE	DECREASE
+	−

INCREASE	DECREASE
+	−

Total Revenue _____

Less Total Expenses _____

Net Income (Loss) _____

AP-16B LO 1·3 4 5 6

Ella Kates founded Health-Plus Clinic as a medical clinic that started operations in January 2018. Consider the following opening balances as of January 1, 2019.

Cash	$15,000
Prepaid Rent	6,000
Prepaid Insurance	5,000
Equipment	30,000
Accounts Payable	3,000
Bank Loan	10,000
Kates, Capital	43,000

The following transactions occurred during the month of January.

1. Purchased plane tickets with $1,500 cash; the plane tickets are to attend a business conference
2. Paid $3,000 cash to reduce the balance of accounts payable
3. The owner invested $5,000 additional cash in the company
4. Purchased $4,000 worth of equipment with a bank loan
5. Paid $1,000 cash for maintenance expenses
6. Earned $15,000 revenue from patients on a cash basis
7. Received a $900 bill for utilities used during the month; a cheque was issued to pay the bill immediately
8. Recognized $2,000 of prepaid rent as an expense
9. Paid $100 interest for the month with cash
10. Paid $4,000 in monthly salaries to all medical practitioners and clinic personnel
11. Received $2,000 cash from one of its clients for services to be provided in March
12. The owner withdrew $2,000 cash from the business to pay for personal expenses

Required

a) Prepare the T-account worksheet.

Health-Plus Clinic
Balance Sheet
As at January 31, 2019

ASSETS

INCREASE +	DECREASE −
Opening	

INCREASE +	DECREASE −
Opening	

INCREASE +	DECREASE −
Opening	

INCREASE +	DECREASE −
Opening	

LIABILITIES

DECREASE −	INCREASE +
	Opening

DECREASE −	INCREASE +
	Opening

DECREASE −	INCREASE +
	Opening

OWNER'S EQUITY

DECREASE −	INCREASE +
	Opening

INCREASE +	DECREASE −

Total Assets _____

Total Liabilities _____

Owner's Equity _____ } _____

Health-Plus Clinic
Income Statement
For the Month Ended January 31, 2019

REVENUE

DECREASE −	INCREASE +

LESS EXPENSES

INCREASE +	DECREASE −

INCREASE +	DECREASE −

INCREASE +	DECREASE −

INCREASE +	DECREASE −

INCREASE +	DECREASE −

INCREASE +	DECREASE −

Total Revenue _____

Less Total Expenses _____

Net Income (Loss) _____

b)   Prepare the income statement for the month of January.

c)   Prepare the statement of owner's equity for the month of January.

d)   Prepare the balance sheet as at January 31, 2019.

AP-17B LO 1 3 4 5 6

Helga Stiles operates a hairstyling company. The opening balances from Helga's Hairstyling's financial records on March 1, 2019, are shown below.

Cash	$18,000
Equipment	4,300
Prepaid Insurance	1,200
Building	140,000
Accounts Payable	3,600
Bank Loan	100,000
Stiles, Capital	59,900

The following transactions took place during the month of March.

1. $5,000 cash was taken from the bank account for a bank loan payment
2. Paid down a portion of the accounts payable with $1,000 cash
3. Recorded cash sales of $5,500
4. Recognized $100 of insurance used for the month
5. Received a bill of $650 for maintenance on equipment, which will be paid next month
6. Paid salaries to employees with $1,500 cash
7. Helga withdrew $2,000 cash from the business
8. Provided services worth $2,000 for clients on account
9. Received $1,500 cash in advance of service to be done next month
10. Collected $1,000 of the amount owing from clients

Required

a) Prepare the T-account worksheet.

Helga's Hairstyling Balance Sheet As at March 31, 2019	Helga's Hairstyling Income Statement For the Month Ended March 31, 2019

ASSETS

INCREASE	DECREASE
+	CASH	–
Opening	

INCREASE	DECREASE
–	ACCOUNTS RECEIVABLE	+
Opening	

INCREASE	DECREASE
+	PREPAID INSURANCE	–
Opening	

INCREASE	DECREASE
+	EQUIPMENT	–
Opening	

INCREASE	DECREASE
+	BUILDING	–
Opening	

LIABILITIES

DECREASE	INCREASE
–	ACCOUNTS PAYABLE	+
	Opening

DECREASE	INCREASE
–	UNEARNED REVENUE	+
	Opening

DECREASE	INCREASE
–	BANK LOAN	+
	Opening

OWNER'S EQUITY

DECREASE	INCREASE
–	STILES, CAPITAL	+
	Opening

INCREASE	DECREASE
+	STILES, WITHDRAWALS	–

REVENUE

DECREASE	INCREASE
–	SERVICE REVENUE	+

LESS EXPENSES

INCREASE	DECREASE
+	INSURANCE EXPENSE	–

INCREASE	DECREASE
+	MAINTENANCE EXPENSE	–

INCREASE	DECREASE
+	SALARIES EXPENSE	–

INCREASE	DECREASE
+	TELEPHONE EXPENSE	–

Total Assets _____

Total Liabilities _____

Owner's Equity _____ } _____

Total Revenue _____

Less Total Expenses _____

Net Income (Loss) _____

b) Complete the income statement for the month of March.

c) Complete the statement of owner's equity for the month of March.

d) Complete the balance sheet as at March 31, 2019.

AP-18B LO 7

After facing a financial shortage, Antonio, the owner of a toy manufacturer, decided to apply for a bank loan for his business. The bank requested important reports, including the company's financial statements, to review. To maximize his chance of getting the bank loan approved, Antonio suppressed a product safety report stating that the material used to manufacture the company's new toys can be harmful if children bite on them. Additionally, he asked the accountant to reclassify some expenses as assets in order to show a higher net income figure to the bank.

Required

a) Discuss whether Antonio is behaving in an ethical manner by omitting the product safety report and re-classifying expenses as assets.

b) Discuss whether Antonio and the bank share any common interests.

Case Study

CS-1 LO `1 3 4 5 6 7`

Granyard Clockworks is a service company that repairs damaged watches and clocks. The company is owned by Maurice Granyard. Maurice is fully liable for all activities of the business. In the most recent month (May 2019), Granyard Clockworks had the following transactions.

1. Maurice deposited $40,000 of additional cash into the business
2. Borrowed $15,000 in cash from the bank
3. Paid $3,500 cash for May's rent
4. Paid $6,000 in salaries for May
5. Performed services and earned $18,000 in cash
6. Incurred telephone expenses of $500 (to be paid next month)
7. Performed services for a client for $3,000 on account
8. Prepaid insurance for one year in the amount of $11,000
9. Incurred maintenance expense of $1,000 (on account)
10. Maurice withdrew $5,000 from the business for personal use
11. Received $2,000 cash for repair services to be done in July
12. Collected 80% of the $3,000 amount owing from a client for services performed earlier this month

As at April 30, 2019, the ending account balances for Granyard Clockworks were as follows.

Cash	$50,000
Accounts Receivable	12,000
Prepaid Insurance	800
Equipment	40,000
Accounts Payable	2,000
Bank Loan	60,000
Granyard, Capital	40,800

Required

a) Complete the T-account worksheet for May 2019.

Granyard Clockworks
Balance Sheet
As at May 31, 2019

ASSETS

INCREASE	DECREASE
+	CASH	−

Opening

INCREASE	DECREASE
−	ACCOUNTS RECEIVABLE	+

Opening

INCREASE	DECREASE
+	PREPAID INSURANCE	−

Opening

INCREASE	DECREASE
+	EQUIPMENT	−

Opening

LIABILITIES

DECREASE	INCREASE
−	ACCOUNTS PAYABLE	+

Opening

DECREASE	INCREASE
−	UNEARNED REVENUE	+

Opening

DECREASE	INCREASE
−	BANK LOAN	+

Opening

OWNER'S EQUITY

DECREASE	INCREASE
−	GRANYARD, CAPITAL	+

Opening

INCREASE	DECREASE
+	GRANYARD, WITHDRAWALS	−

Total Assets   _____

Total Liabilities   _____ }

Owner's Equity   _____   _____

Granyard Clockworks
Income Statement
For the Month Ended May 31, 2019

REVENUE

DECREASE	INCREASE
−	REVENUE	+

LESS EXPENSES

INCREASE	DECREASE
+	MAINTENANCE EXPENSE	−

INCREASE	DECREASE
+	RENT EXPENSE	−

INCREASE	DECREASE
+	SALARIES EXPENSE	−

INCREASE	DECREASE
+	TELEPHONE EXPENSE	−

Total Revenue   _____

Less Total Expenses   _____

Net Income (Loss)   _____

b) Using the information above, prepare the following financial statements for Granyard Clockworks.

   i.   Income Statement for the month of May 2019.

   ii.   Statement of Owner's Equity for the month ended May 31, 2019

   iii.   Balance Sheet as at May 31, 2019

c)   Explain the impact on each of the above financial statements if Maurice recorded transaction #11 as
     revenue in May. Are you concerned with this reporting? Include in your explanation the parties who would
     be most impacted by this reporting if it is not corrected, and why Maurice may have chosen to report the
     transaction this way.

Notes

Chapter 3

THE ACCOUNTING FRAMEWORK

LEARNING OBJECTIVES

LO **1** Describe the users of accounting information

LO **2** Describe the fields of accounting

LO **3** Compare the different forms of business organization

LO **4** Identify the objective and qualitative characteristics of financial information

LO **5** Identify the key financial statement foundations

LO **6** Illustrate the similarities and differences between ASPE and IFRS

LO **7** Explain the importance of ethics in accounting

AMEENGAGE™ *Access **ameengage.com** for integrated resources including tutorials, practice exercises, the digital textbook and more.*

Assessment Questions

AS-1 LO **1**

What is an internal user? What do internal users use financial information for?

_____

_____

_____

AS-2 LO **1**

What is an external user? What do external users use financial information for?

_____

_____

_____

AS-3 LO **2**

Briefly define financial accounting.

_____

_____

_____

AS-4 LO **2**

Briefly define managerial accounting.

_____

_____

AS-5 LO 3

What is a sole proprietorship? What is the title of a sole proprietorship's equity section?

_____

_____

AS-6 LO 3

Explain the concept of unlimited liability.

_____

_____

AS-7 LO 3

What is a partnership?

_____

_____

AS-8 LO 3

What are the three types of partnerships that can be created?

_____

_____

AS-9 LO 3

What is the difference between a general partnership and a limited partnership?

_____

_____

_____

AS-10 LO 3

Describe a corporation.

_____

_____

_____

AS-11 LO 3

What is a non-profit organization?

_____

_____

_____

AS-12 `LO` `3`

Provide four examples of non-profit organizations.

_____

_____

_____

AS-13 `LO` `4 6`

Briefly define and explain GAAP. What are the two frameworks that have evolved from Canadian GAAP?

_____

_____

_____

_____

AS-14 `LO` `4`

What are the qualitative characteristics of effective and useful financial information?

_____

_____

_____

AS-15 `LO` `4`

Describe the characteristic of relevance.

_____

_____

_____

_____

AS-16 `LO` `4`

Describe the characteristic of timeliness.

_____

_____

_____

AS-17 `LO` `4`

Describe the characteristic of faithful representation.

_____

_____

_____

AS-18 LO 4

Describe the characteristic of verifiability.

_____

_____

AS-19 LO 4

Describe the characteristic of understandability.

_____

_____

AS-20 LO 4

What is neutrality? Neutrality is a component of which characteristic?

_____

_____

AS-21 LO 4

Describe the characteristic of comparability.

_____

_____

AS-22 LO 4

Describe what is meant by consistency in financial reporting.

_____

_____

_____

AS-23 LO 4

Describe what is meant by materiality in financial reporting.

_____

_____

_____

_____

AS-24 LO 5

Describe the business entity assumption.

_____

_____

_____

AS-25 `LO 5`

Explain what the basis of accounting means.

_____

_____

AS-26 `LO 5`

Describe what is meant by the term "going concern" in financial reporting.

_____

_____

AS-27 `LO 5`

Describe the monetary unit assumption.

_____

_____

AS-28 `LO 5`

Describe what is meant by measurement in financial reporting.

_____

_____

_____

AS-29 `LO 5`

Describe the revenue recognition process in financial reporting.

_____

_____

_____

AS-30 `LO 5`

Describe the expense recognition process in financial reporting.

_____

_____

_____

AS-31 `LO 5`

Describe what is meant by disclosure in financial reporting.

_____

_____

_____

AS-32 LO 6

What is ASPE and which forms of organization can adhere to it?

_____

_____

_____

AS-33 LO 6

What is IFRS and which forms of organization can adhere to it?

_____

_____

_____

_____

AS-34 LO 7

List two ethical standards for accountants.

_____

_____

_____

_____

Application Questions Group A

AP-1A `LO 3`

Match each form of an organization with the appropriate description.

A	Sole Proprietorship
B	Partnership
C	Corporation
D	Non-Profit Organization

_____ This type of organization usually does not have an identifiable owner.

_____ There are two types: one that limits the liability of the owners and one that does not.

_____ This type of business is operated by a single owner.

_____ This type of business often elects a board of directors.

AP-2A `LO 4`

Match each of the following financial statement reporting terms to the appropriate description in the table below.

- Benefit versus cost
- Prudence
- Substance over form
- Freedom from material error
- Neutrality

Term (fill in)	Description
	Concept that financial information is free from bias
	Cost of providing perfect financial information should not exceed benefit to the users
	Financial information is free from intentional omissions
	Exercising professional judgment
	Reporting an accurate economic representation of transactions or events

AP-3A `LO 4`

Identify the qualitative characteristic(s) of financial information violated in each of the following scenarios.

a) Thorn Company has reported several gains for the period but has not provided any explanation or proof of how they occurred.

_____

b) Due to recent layoffs, Monte Carlo Ltd. was not able to complete and issue its 2018 financial statements and accompanying notes. The information was instead included with the 2019 financial report in the following year.

_____

c) To value inventory, Toland and Sons uses a different accounting policy from the rest of the companies in the same industry. There is no justification for the use of this accounting policy in the notes to the financial statements.

_____

d)   Eris Laboratories used many uncommon medical terms and scientific language in the notes to the financial statements. This language was not explained anywhere else.

_____

e)   A bank decided not to grant a loan to Mida Ltd. after a customer filed a substantial lawsuit. Mida Ltd. did not include any mention of the lawsuit in the financial statements or in the notes to the financial statements.

_____

AP-4A `LO` `4 5`

Identify the financial statement qualitative characteristic or foundation that has been violated in each of the following scenarios.

a)   Bill Co. purchased a two-year insurance policy and expensed the entire amount in period of purchase.

_____

b)   Charlie Co. listed inventory at its market value of $31,000 on the balance sheet, even though it was purchased for $20,000.

_____

c)   Percy Co. did not include the details of its property, plant and equipment, even though this information is relevant to the users.

_____

d)   Fred Co. made a sale on the last day of the accounting period. The customer paid for the item in the following month, so this sale was included in the next period's financial statements.

_____

e)   George Co. has plans to restructure its operations next year and will sell off about half of the business. This information was not included in the notes to the financial statements because it does not affect the current financial information.

_____

f)   Ron Co. applied a certain accounting policy that allowed the company to report higher assets and net income. A different accounting policy was available that would have resulted in a lower balance of assets and net income.

_____

g)   Ginny Co. changed the accounting policy used to value property, plant, and equipment after using a different policy for 10 years. There was no justification for the change.

_____

AP-5A `LO` `4`

Sood Supplies is in the business of selling electronic components to computer manufacturers. Sood Supplies' financial statements are issued on an annual basis for a large number of users, such as investors and the bank. The financial reporting of the company is based on ASPE.

Prior to the issuance of the current year's financial statements, the head of engineering and the accounting manager had a discussion regarding the amount of warranty expense that should be recognized for the year. The head of engineering believes that only 2% of sales needs to be calculated as a provision for the warranty expense, while the accounting manager believes that 6% of sales should be recorded as an expense. The accounting manager argues that the 6% is estimated based on historical trends of the company and the industry; however, the engineering department claims that its new method of quality assurance will reduce the future warranty expenses. The engineering department could not submit any documents to support the claim. Eventually, the accounting manager decides to trust the engineering department and uses the 2% calculation.

Do you believe any of the qualitative characteristics of financial accounting or related considerations have been violated by Sood Supplies? Explain.

_____

_____

_____

_____

_____

_____

_____

_____

_____

_____

AP-6A LO 4 5 6

Hawkton Publishing Corporation is a publisher of math textbooks. The company is a large, well-known publicly traded corporation with thousands of shareholders. It produces financial statements on an annual basis. The most recent financial statements (for the year ended December 31, 2019) showed comparative balances for 2019 and 2018. The 2019 balances were derived using accrual-based accounting whereas the 2018 balances were derived using cash-based accounting.

Which characteristic(s) of information did Hawkton fail to represent? Explain.

_____

_____

_____

_____

_____

_____

AP-7A LO 4 6

Suppose that a company has changed its policy for depreciation from one year to the next. An employee in the accounting department addressed this change with the owner. The employee asked the owner why the accounting policy was changed and why the reasoning for the change was not disclosed in the financial statements. The owner replied, "IFRS gives you the option to use a different depreciation method from one year to the next. We also are not required to explain our choices." Is the owner correct in his reasoning? Explain.

_____

_____

_____

_____

_____

AP-8A `LO 5`

Match each of the following financial statement foundations to the appropriate description in the table below.

- Business entity assumption
- Going concern
- Monetary unit assumption
- Revenue recognition
- Measurement

Term (fill in)	Description
	Sales must be recorded when ownership of a good transfers from the seller to the buyer
	Assumes that a business will continue to operate into the foreseeable future
	Financial reports should be expressed in a single currency
	Accounting for a business must be kept separate from the personal affairs of its owner or any other business
	Purchases must be recorded at their values on the date of purchase

AP-9A `LO 5`

Alton Floral is a new company that operates in the gardening industry. The owner of the company has decided not to hire an accountant, rather maintain the financial records on his own. He has reported his employees as assets on the balance sheet in an account called "Human Resources." He has valued them at the present value of their future salaries on the balance sheet. Also, the financial statements are not supported by notes explaining some of the figures.

Which of the basic financial statement foundations has Alton Floral violated? Explain.

_____

_____

_____

_____

AP-10A `LO 5 6`

Heggy Company, a privately owned corporation, is producing cellphone accessories. It relies on ASPE to prepare its financial statements. The company is doing well and is planning to expand its product line. Assume you are a newly hired accountant reviewing Heggy's financial statements.

You realize that the company recently purchased machinery for $700,000 as part of its expansion strategy. After a long negotiation, Heggy's purchasing department was able to negotiate the price well below the market value of $740,000. The machinery has been recorded in Heggy's books at $740,000.

Also, Heggy Company has paid $15,000 for the cost of the plant's insurance for the upcoming year and expensed the whole amount. Heggy believes that this expensing would be an effective cost-saving strategy in the long run, as it will avoid the extra bookkeeping associated with updating the prepaid insurance account.

Has Heggy Company violated any of the financial statement foundations of ASPE? Explain.

_____

_____

_____

_____

_____

AP-11A LO 5 6

Tasai Corporation is a Canadian manufacturer of wings for commercial aircrafts. Tasai is a large public company that is famous for the unique design of its wings. You are appointed as its audit manager.

As you go through the financial statements you notice, on the income statement, that the company has set aside one line item under revenue that shows an amount of 800,000 in Brazilian currency (reals). In the notes related to this item, it is indicated that the company has completed a project in Brazil; due to the large amount of foreign exchange loss, the company has decided to report the figure in reals. The accounting department thinks this practice is permitted under IFRS as long as it is clearly explained in the notes.

You also note this year's travel expense is significantly larger than last year's. As part of the audit procedures, you examine travel documents and invoices and realize that one of the owners included his personal travel expenses as part of his business-related travels. In addition, Tasai Corporation has changed one of its accounting policies and disclosed the nature, impact and reason of this change in the notes.

As the audit manager, discuss if any accounting assumptions or principles have been violated.

_____

AP-12A LO 6

Assume you are running a small business as a sole proprietorship. You need to borrow money from the bank, and they have asked you for your most recent financial statements. Would you report the financial statements using IFRS or ASPE? Explain your answer.

_____

AP-13A LO 5 7

Joan is a senior accountant who recently agreed to give a professional review of the financial statements of Baker Consulting Inc. Joan is a personal friend of the president of this company and has an outstanding loan to the company. Baker Consulting Inc. is having cash flow issues that may force it to lay off some employees, but the owner has assured Joan that everything is under control and that the company is about to land several large sales contracts. He also explained that if the financial statements revealed any issues, the company would lose potential customers and suppliers. After some discussion, Joan decided to issue a positive opinion of the financial statements and not disclose any issues. Has Joan violated any ethical standards of accounting? Discuss.

_____

_____

_____

_____

_____

_____

_____

Application Questions Group B

AP-1B LO 3

Match each form of an organization with the appropriate description.

A	Sole Proprietorship
B	Partnership
C	Corporation
D	Non-Profit Organization

_____ An organization aimed to improve society in some way

_____ A business that can be set up as either public or private

_____ A business in which the owner receives all the net income and suffers from any net loss

_____ A business operated by two or more people

AP-2B LO 4

Match each of the following financial statement reporting terms with the appropriate definition.

- Completeness
- Timeliness
- Neutrality
- Verifiability
- Materiality

Term (fill in)	Description
	Financial information should be received before it is no longer able to influence decisions
	Refers to the significance of information to users' decisions
	Concept that financial information is free from bias
	Documentation that supports financial information being reported on
	Financial statements contain all information regarding transactions or events related to the reporting period

AP-3B LO 4

Identify the qualitative characteristic that describes each of the following scenarios.

a) Titus Group presented its financial information in a way that allowed informed users to comprehend the meaning of the information.

_____

b) Hunt Manufacturing included references to source documents to explain where certain financial figures originated from.

_____

c) Arloc Games Company uses the same accounting methods each year when preparing the financial statements.

_____

d) Crypt Technologies reported all financial information that could have an impact on the decisions of the users of the financial statements.

_____

AP-4B LO 4 5

Identify the qualitative characteristic or financial statement foundation that describes each of the following scenarios.

a) Pangea Construction recorded revenue for a five-year construction contract evenly over the five years.

_____

b) Athena Spa has committed to opening a second location in the next eight months. Details regarding this expansion were included in the financial information.

_____

c) Zeus Electric used the same accounting policy for depreciation as last year, even though it could have reported a higher net income by switching to a different method.

_____

d) Neptune Water Supply grouped small expenses such as pens, staplers and notepads together as office supplies expense because the cost of recording them in separate accounts outweighed the benefits.

_____

e) Hermes Athletics had its land appraised at $60,000. The land was listed on the balance sheet at $50,000, which was the price originally paid for it.

_____

f) Hera Consulting prepaid cash for its annual insurance policy. The amount was expensed on a monthly basis as it was used up.

_____

AP-5B LO 4 5 6

Imzy Company is a small private company that relies on ASPE to prepare financial statements. During the year, the company has experienced a number of tax disputes with the government. This issue was not included in the notes to the financial statements, as the bookkeeper believes this type of tax dispute is common for a small business. In addition, the bookkeeper does not keep purchase invoices because he thinks the costs of holding all those receipts would outweigh their benefits for a small company. Explain whether any accounting foundations or qualitative characteristics have been violated by the bookkeeper.

_____

_____

_____

_____

_____

_____

_____

_____

_____

_____

AP-6B LO 4 6

Reflex Sports Inc. is a manufacturer of sports equipment for children. It relies on IFRS to prepare its financial statements. The nature of its accounting transactions can be quite complex at times. However, the financial statements have no additional notes to support them. The company also does not keep all invoices on record to back up expense amounts reported on the financial statements. Which characteristic(s) of information did Reflex Sports fail to represent? Explain.

_____

_____

_____

_____

AP-7B LO 4 5

Team Toro Inc., a unionized company, is in the business of planning and hosting events for various colleges and universities. Its service includes a wide range of activities such as decor and design, accommodation for guests and catering. At the end of the year, prior to issuance of its financial statements, the head of the accounting department realized that the union was not able to negotiate a collective agreement with the board, and it is planning to go on strike legally at the beginning of next year. After discussing the matter with the board members, the accounting manager decides not to disclose this issue, since the strike will happen next year and this year's financial statements are not affected. In addition, the accounting manager thinks the disclosure may have an unnecessarily negative impact on the company's financial position and reputation in the market. Discuss whether any accounting foundations or qualitative characteristics have been violated.

_____

_____

_____

_____

_____

_____

_____

_____

AP-8B LO 4 5

Match each of the following terms to the appropriate description in the table below.

- Comparability
- Disclosure
- Expense recognition
- Faithful representation
- Relevance
- Understandability

Term (fill in)	Description
	Information is free from material error and bias
	The financial statements of a company should be prepared in a similar way year after year
	Financial information can be comprehended by users with a reasonable knowledge of the business
	All information for decision-making is present in the financial statements
	The costs of doing business must be recorded in (or matched to) the same accounting period as the revenues that they helped to generate
	Any and all information that affects the full understanding of a company's financial statements must be included with the financial statements

AP-9B LO 5

Mackenzie Attire is currently preparing its annual financial statements for the past fiscal year. The company uses cash-based accounting. The company's policy includes receiving payment for its services well before the service is performed. The owner recently purchased a fish tank for his home and the transaction included a decrease to Mackenzie Attire's equity (an expense was recorded in the income statement). The value of inventory is adjusted annually to be stated at fair value. Which of the financial statement foundations has Mackenzie Attire violated? Explain.

_____

_____

_____

_____

_____

_____

_____

_____

_____

AP-10B LO 5

IMORI is large publicly traded construction company. IMORI has entered into a three-year construction contract with Siano Company. Siano paid upfront for the full value of the contract, and IMORI has recorded the entire amount as revenue immediately. Explain the financial statement foundation that has been violated.

_____

_____

_____

_____

_____

_____

AP-11B LO 5

Blossoma Inc. is a private supplier of organic beauty products. The company prepares its financial statements in compliance with ASPE. Due to recent economic difficulties, Blossoma Inc. had to file for bankruptcy. The company's property, plant and equipment are listed on the balance sheet at what they could be sold for, which is lower than their original purchase price. Has Blossoma Inc. violated any of the financial statement foundations? Explain.

_____

_____

_____

_____

_____

_____

_____

AP-12B `LO 6`

A private corporation is planning on going public next year. Explain how this decision may impact the financial reporting requirements of the business.

_____

_____

_____

_____

AP-13B `LO 7`

Marcus is the senior accountant for a small accounting firm. He is currently performing the year-end audit of a particular client: Le Jardin Oak Inc. (LJO), a manufacturer of high-quality furniture. After Marcus met with Le Jardin's CEO in a restaurant, the CEO noticed that Le Jardin's financial records, which were provided to Marcus, were scattered on the ground. The CEO was extremely disappointed because the records were meant for internal use only. Which ethical standard did Marcus violate? Explain.

_____

_____

_____

_____

_____

Case Study

CS-1  LO 1 4 5 6

Gordon is the majority owner of Gordon House Restaurant (GHR), a publicly traded chain of family restaurants. GHR has adopted ASPE for recording accounting transactions. The company is owned by hundreds of shareholders who expect timely, reliable and accurate financial statements. GHR produces financial statements periodically.

It is now June 15, 2019. The accountant has prepared the financial statements for the eight-month period ended May 31, 2019. The previous financial statements covered a one-year period.

GHR was recently sued by another company, the details of which are not disclosed in the financial statements. The court proceedings have not yet ended. However, as of May 31, 2019, it was believed that GHR was very likely to lose the case and would eventually have to pay a significant amount in damages to the plaintiff.

Also consider the following information:

- Cash disbursements are not supported by additional source documents
- GHR has recognized revenue in a different accounting period from that in which the costs associated with producing that revenue were recognized

Required

a) Which of the qualitative characteristics of financial information has GHR failed to apply? Explain.

_____
_____
_____
_____
_____
_____
_____
_____
_____
_____
_____
_____
_____
_____
_____

b) Which of the financial statement foundations has GHR violated? Explain.

_____
_____
_____
_____
_____
_____
_____
_____

c) Based on the information provided, should GHR have adopted ASPE or IFRS? Explain.

_____

_____

d) Who would be the internal or external users of GHR's financial information?

_____

_____

Notes

Chapter 4

THE ACCOUNTING CYCLE: JOURNALS AND LEDGERS

LEARNING OBJECTIVES

LO 1   Distinguish between debits and credits

LO 2   Describe the accounting cycle

LO 3   Explain how to analyze a transaction

LO 4   Record transactions in the general journal

LO 5   Post journal entries to the general ledger

LO 6   Prepare a trial balance

LO 7   Describe ethics and internal controls relating to recording and posting transactions

AMEENGAGE *Access **ameengage.com** for integrated resources including tutorials, practice exercises, the digital textbook and more.*

Assessment Questions

AS-1 LO 1

What does the term debit refer to?

_____

_____

AS-2 LO 1

True or False: A credit will always be an increase to any account.

_____

_____

AS-3 LO 1

Which three types of accounts use the debit side of the T-account to increase their value?

_____

_____

AS-4 LO 1

Which three types of accounts use the credit side of the T-account to increase their value?

_____

_____

AS-5 LO 1

What is the normal balance of an asset?

_____

_____

AS-6 LO 1

What is the normal balance of a liability?

_____

_____

AS-7 LO 2

In the accounting cycle, what is the purpose of creating the general journal?

_____

_____

AS-8 LO 4

In the journal, what information is entered in the PR (posting reference) column?

_____

_____

_____

AS-9 LO 5

Explain the purpose of a chart of accounts.

_____

_____

_____

AS-10 LO 2 5

In the accounting cycle, what is the purpose of the general ledger?

_____

_____

AS-11 LO 5

What is the relationship between the closing balance and the opening balance for an asset?

_____

_____

_____

AS-12 LO 2 6

In the accounting cycle, what is the purpose of the trial balance?

_____

_____

AS-13 LO 6

What is meant by "balancing a trial balance"?

_____

_____

_____

AS-14 LO 6

If an error is found in a journal entry that has already been prepared and posted to the general ledger, how should the error be corrected?

_____

_____

AS-15 LO 2 3 4 5 6

List and describe the first four steps of the accounting cycle.

_____

_____

_____

_____

AS-16 LO 7

Does using a computerized accounting information system automatically mean that accounting information is reliable and accurate? Explain.

_____

_____

_____

_____

_____

_____

_____

_____

_____

_____

_____

_____

Application Questions Group A

AP-1A LO 1

For the following list of accounts, indicate which side of the T-account causes an increase or decrease. The first account has been done for you.

Account Title	Debit	Credit
Cash	Increase	Decrease
Advertising Expense		
Service Revenue		
Unearned Revenue		
Accounts Receivable		
Accounts Payable		
Owner's Capital		
Owner's Withdrawals		
Prepaid Rent		
Rent Expense		

AP-2A LO 1

For each of the following accounts, identify whether the normal balance is a debit (DR) or a credit (CR).

a) Cash	DR
b) Equipment	DR
c) Unearned Revenue	CR
d) Rent Expense	DR
e) Bank Loan	CR
f) Prepaid Expenses	DR
g) Service Revenue	CR
h) Accounts Payable	CR

AP-3A LO 1 3

Esteem Fitness provides fitness services for its customers. During June 2019, Esteem Fitness had the following transactions.

Jun 1   Sold one-month memberships to customers for $4,500 on account
Jun 3   Received a telephone bill for $250, which will be paid next month
Jun 6   Paid an employee's salary of $1,200
Jun 10   Received $3,000 cash from customers paying in advance for upcoming one-year memberships
Jun 15   Paid $6,000 cash in advance for six months of rent
Jun 20   Received a $10,000 loan from the bank
Jun 26   Purchased equipment with $8,000 cash

Complete the table to analyze each transaction.

	Account Name	Category	Increase or Decrease	Debit or Credit
Jun 1				
Jun 3				
Jun 6				
Jun 10				
Jun 15				
Jun 20				
Jun 26				

AP-4A LO 1 3

Bendari Tutoring Services had the following transactions for the month of November 2019.

Nov 1   Purchased supplies for $100 on account
Nov 4   Received $4,200 cash from clients as payment for tutoring
Nov 9   Received a telephone bill in the mail for $150
Nov 16   Paid an employee's salary of $3,500 in cash
Nov 25   Collected $500 from clients who owed money for previous services

Complete the table to analyze each transaction.

	Account Name	Category	Increase or Decrease	Debit or Credit
Nov 1				
Nov 4				
Nov 9				
Nov 16				
Nov 25				

AP-5A LO 3 4

Kick-off Sports Training helps train children in various sporting activities. During May 2019, the following transactions took place.

May 3   Received a maintenance bill for $500, which will be paid next month
May 3   Received $2,750 cash for training services provided
May 4   Borrowed $4,000 cash from the bank
May 4   Received $220 from a customer who owed money on training services already provided
May 10   Prepaid $1,200 cash for insurance for one year
May 10   Paid telephone expenses of $150 for the month with cash
May 11   Paid $700 cash to reduce the amount owed to a supplier
May 15   Paid $25 interest on the bank loan

Prepare the journal entries for the transactions.

Date	Account Title and Explanation	PR	Debit	Credit
Jun 2	Cash		3000	
	unearned revenue			3000
	Received payment for future			
Jun 3			496	
				455
Jun 8				

AP-6A LO 3 4

Rejuvenation Spa is a sole proprietorship owned by Claire Sawyer. During the month of July 2019, the following transactions took place.

Jul 3   Provided services to a customer on account worth $3,600

Jul 4   Borrowed $2,000 cash from the bank

Jul 6   Provided services to a customer and received $2,400 in cash

Jul 10   Received a telephone bill for $250, which will be paid later

Jul 11   Paid $600 cash to reduce the amount owed to a supplier

Jul 15   Collected $1,800 cash from customers owing on account

Jul 20   Paid the telephone bill from July 10

Jul 21   Paid a portion of the bank loan principal with $1,500 cash

Jul 31   Paid salaries for the month with $1,600 cash

Jul 31   Purchased equipment for $1,900, which will be paid later

Prepare the journal entries for the above transactions.

Date	Account Title and Explanation	PR	Debit	Credit

AP-7A LO 3 4

Cherry Consulting Firm is owned by Ron Cherry and offers consulting services for small businesses. During June 2019, the following transactions occurred.

Jun 2   Received a deposit of $3,000 from a customer for services to be provided in the future

Jun 3   Paid a $495 utility bill that was received and recorded last month

Jun 8   Charged $1,400 in travel costs to a credit card

Jun 17   Paid $1,000 cash to reduce the bank loan; of that amount, $75 is interest and the remainder is principal

Jun 19   Ron withdrew $2,100 cash from the business for personal use

Jun 28   Paid $4,900 for salaries for the month

Prepare the journal entries for the above transactions.

Date	Account Title and Explanation	PR	Debit	Credit

AP-8A LO 3 4

Greg Carlin is the owner of Carlin Consulting. During the month of April 2019, he had the following transactions.

Apr 1   Greg invested $5,000 cash and equipment valued at $3,000 into the business

Apr 3   Provided consulting services to a customer; the customer paid $1,000 now and will pay $1,500 later

Apr 6   Received a loan from the bank for $6,000

Apr 8   Paid $1,300 for utilities for the month

Apr 17   Purchased equipment with $4,000 cash

Apr 20   Paid employee salaries with $2,100 cash

Apr 22   Provided consulting services to a customer on account for $1,600

Apr 28   Received the balance owing from the customer on April 3

Record the transactions in the journal.

Date	Account Title and Explanation	PR	Debit	Credit

AP-9A LO 1 6

Micro Company, owned by Steven Upton, showed these accounts and their corresponding normal balances on May 31, 2019.

Account Title	Balance
Upton, Capital	$23,500
Insurance Expense	900
Accounts Payable	15,500
Service Revenue	8,900
Equipment	34,500
Supplies Expense	3,000
Cash	6,400
Salaries Expense	4,000
Rent Expense	3,000
Upton, Withdrawals	3,000
Utilities Expense	1,300
Bank Loan	10,200
Prepaid Insurance	2,000

Prepare Micro Company's trial balance at May 31, 2019.

AP-10A LO 1 6

A part-time bookkeeper for Wombat Tours has created the trial balance at the end of the year and cannot get it to balance.

Wombat Tours Trial Balance December 31, 2019		
Account Title	**DR**	**CR**
Accounts Payable	$3,150	
Accounts Receivable	2,350	
Advertising Expense		$2,100
Bank Loan		5,200
Sharpe, Capital		6,170
Cash	6,200	
Interest Expense	560	
Maintenance Expense	240	
Sharpe, Withdrawals		3,900
Prepaid Insurance	1,200	
Equipment	13,500	
Rent Expense	6,200	
Salaries Expense	5,300	
Service Revenue		25,800
Telephone Expense	450	
Unearned Revenue	1,680	
Total	**$40,830**	**$43,170**

All the entries have been journalized and posted to the general ledger properly, and all the accounts should have normal balances.

Recreate the trial balance for Wombat Tours so that the accounts are listed in the order they would typically appear in a chart of accounts, and ensure that debits equal credits.

AP-11A LO 5 6

Glam Stars' complete general ledger for March 2019 is shown below.

Account: Cash					GL No: 101	
Date	Description	PR	DR	CR	Balance	
Mar 1	Opening Balance				7,800	DR
Mar 1		J1		1,800	6,000	DR
Mar 2		J1	2,900		8,900	DR
Mar 3		J1		1,440	7,460	DR
Mar 10		J1		10	7,450	DR
Mar 10		J1		780	6,670	DR
Mar 20		J1	2,600		9,270	DR
Mar 22		J1	800		10,070	DR
Mar 24		J1		710	9,360	DR
Mar 31		J1		2,000	7,360	DR

Account: Accounts Receivable					GL No: 105	
Date	Description	PR	DR	CR	Balance	
Mar 1	Opening Balance				2,460	DR
Mar 22		J1		800	1,660	DR

Account: Prepaid Insurance					GL No: 110	
Date	Description	PR	DR	CR	Balance	
Mar 1	Opening Balance				0	DR
Mar 1		J1	1,800		1,800	DR

Account: Equipment					GL No: 120	
Date	Description	PR	DR	CR	Balance	
Mar 1	Opening Balance				11,140	DR
Mar 20		J1		2,350	8,790	DR

Account: Accounts Payable					GL No: 200	
Date	Description	PR	DR	CR	Balance	
Mar 1	Opening Balance				2,900	CR
Mar 4		J1		250	3,150	CR
Mar 24		J1	710		2,440	CR

Account: Unearned Revenue					GL No: 210	
Date	Description	PR	DR	CR	Balance	
Mar 1	Opening Balance				1,800	CR

Account: Bank Loan					GL No: 215	
Date	Description	PR	DR	CR	Balance	
Mar 1	Opening Balance				5,100	CR
Mar 10		J1	780		4,320	CR

Account: Roberts, Capital					GL No: 300	
Date	Description	PR	DR	CR	Balance	
Mar 1	Opening Balance				11,600	CR

Account: Roberts, Withdrawals					GL No: 310	
Date	Description	PR	DR	CR	Balance	
Mar 31		J1	2,000		2,000	DR

Account: Service Revenue					GL No: 400	
Date	Description	PR	DR	CR	Balance	
Mar 2		J1		2,900	2,900	CR

Account: Interest Expense					GL No: 530	
Date	Description	PR	DR	CR	Balance	
Mar 10		J1		10	10	DR

Account: Rent Expense					GL No: 540	
Date	Description	PR	DR	CR	Balance	
Mar 3		J1	1,440		1,440	DR

Prepare a trial balance. Place the accounts in the order shown in the general ledger.

AP-12A LO 3 4 5 6

Thomas Topology provides surveying services to construction companies and municipalities. The company is owned and operated by Thomas Edwards. The closing balances at the end of March 2019 and the chart of accounts are shown below.

Thomas Topology Balance Sheet As at March 31, 2019			
Assets		**Liabilities**	
Cash	$22,000	Accounts Payable	$10,500
Accounts Receivable	9,000	Unearned Revenue	4,500
Equipment	8,000	Bank Loan	6,000
		Total Liabilities	21,000
		Owner's Equity	
		Edwards, Capital	18,000
Total Assets	$39,000	**Total Liabilities and Owner's Equity**	$39,000

Account Description	Account #
ASSETS	
Cash	101
Accounts Receivable	105
Prepaid Insurance	110
Equipment	120
LIABILITIES	
Accounts Payable	200
Unearned Revenue	210
Bank Loan	215
OWNER'S EQUITY	
Edwards, Capital	300
Edwards, Withdrawals	310

Account Description	Account #
REVENUE	
Service Revenue	400
EXPENSES	
Insurance Expense	515
Interest Expense	520
Rent Expense	540
Salaries Expense	545
Telephone Expense	550
Travel Expense	555

During the month of April, Thomas Topology had the following transactions.

Apr 1   Purchased office equipment on account worth $7,000

Apr 2   Received $25,000 cash for services provided

Apr 3   Paid $1,000 cash for April's rent

Apr 4   Prepaid $1,200 for insurance for one year

Apr 10   Paid $200 cash to reduce the balance of accounts payable

Apr 14   Paid $8,000 cash for employee's salaries

Apr 22   Received a telephone bill for $250, which will be paid next month

Apr 24   Recorded travel expenses for $8,000 to be paid next month

Apr 30   Paid $4,550 to bank for the bank loan principal and interest; interest was $50 and the remainder was principal

Required

a)   Prepare the journal entries for the month of April.

Date	Account Title and Explanation	PR	Debit	Credit
Apr 1	Equipment	120	7000	
	Accounts payable	200		7000
Apr 2	cash	101	25000	
	service revenue	400		25000
Apr 3	Rent Expense	540	1000	
	cash	101		1000
Apr 4	Prepaid insurance	110	1200	
	cash			1200
Apr 10	Accounts payable		200	
	cash			200
Apr 14	salaries		8000	
	cash			8000
Apr 22	Telephone		250	
	Accounts payable			250
Apr 24	Travel		8000	
	Accounts payable			8000
Apr 30	Interest Expense		50	
	Bank loan		4500	
	Cash			4550

b) Post the journal entries to the ledger accounts.

Account: Cash					GL No: 101	
Date	Description	PR	DR	CR	Balance	
Apr 1	Opening balance				22000	DR
Apr 2			25000		47000	DR
Apr 3		J1		1000	46000	DR
Apr 4				1200	44800	DR

Account: Receivable

GL No:

Date	Description	PR	DR	CR	Balance	
Ap 1	Opening				9000	Dr

Account: Equipment

GL No: 00

Date	Description	PR	DR	CR	Balance	
April	Opening balance	J1			8000	DR
April			7000		15000	DR

Account: Prepaid insurance

GL No:

Date	Description	PR	DR	CR	Balance	
Apr 1	Opening capital					

Account: Accounts payable

GL No: 110

Date	Description	PR	DR	CR	Balance	
	Opening balance			10500		CR
april		J1		7000	14500	CR

Account: Unearned revenue

GL No: 210

Date	Description	PR	DR	CR	Balance	
	Opening balance					

Account: Bank Loan

GL No: 215

Date	Description	PR	DR	CR	Balance	
	Opening Balance				6000	Dr

Account: Edwards capital

GL No: 300

Date	Description	PR	DR	CR	Balance
	0				

Account: Insurance Expense				GL No: 51?	
Date	Description	PR	DR	CR	Balance

Account: Interest Expense				GL No: 5 ?0	
Date	Description	PR	DR	CR	Balance

Account: Rent expense				GL No: 540	
Date	Description	PR	DR	CR	Balance
Apr 3		J1	1000		1000 DR

Account: Salaries expense				GL No: 54?	
Date	Description	PR	DR	CR	Balance

Account: Telephone Expense				GL No: 550	
Date	Description	PR	DR	CR	Balance

Account: Travel expense				GL No: 555	
Date	Description	PR	DR	CR	Balance

Account: Service Revenue				GL No:	
Date	Description	PR	DR	CR	Balance
apr 1.		J1		25000	25000 CR

Account:				GL No:	
Date	Description	PR	DR	CR	Balance

c) Prepare a trial balance at the end of April.

AP-13A LO 3 4 5 6

High Flying Biplane provides sightseeing tours in vintage biplanes. The company is owned by Sky Singh. The closing balances at the end of May 2019 and the chart of accounts are shown below.

High Flying Biplane
Balance Sheet
As at May 31, 2019

Assets		Liabilities	
Cash	$8,000	Accounts Payable	$8,200
Accounts Receivable	6,000	Unearned Revenue	3,200
Prepaid Insurance	1,200	Bank Loan	20,000
Equipment	60,000	**Total Liabilities**	31,400
		Owner's Equity	
		Singh, Capital	43,800
Total Assets	$75,200	**Total Liabilities and Owner's Equity**	$75,200

Account Description	Account #
ASSETS	
Cash	101
Accounts Receivable	105
Prepaid Insurance	110
Equipment	120
LIABILITIES	
Accounts Payable	200
Interest Payable	205
Unearned Revenue	210
Bank Loan	215
OWNER'S EQUITY	
Singh, Capital	300
Singh, Withdrawals	310

Account Description	Account #
REVENUE	
Service Revenue	400
EXPENSES	
Advertising Expense	500
Insurance Expense	515
Interest Expense	520
Telephone Expense	550

During the month of June, High Flying Biplane had the following transactions.

Jun 1   The owner invested $5,000 cash into the business
Jun 2   Received $1,500 cash for tours that will be provided in August
Jun 3   Received an advertising bill for $400, which will be paid next month
Jun 4   Paid the telephone bill with $200 cash
Jun 10   Provided tours worth $2,400 to a customer who will pay next month
Jun 14   Purchased equipment with $4,000 cash
Jun 20   Received payments totaling $1,600 from customers paying their accounts
Jun 22   Paid $900 toward accounts payable
Jun 24   Paid $1,000 toward the bank loan principal
Jun 30   The owner withdrew $1,200 cash for personal use

Required

a)   Prepare the journal entries for the month of June.

Date	Account Title and Explanation	PR	Debit	Credit

Date	Account Title and Explanation	PR	Debit	Credit

b) Post the journal entries to the ledger accounts.

Account:						GL No:	
Date	Description	PR	DR	CR	Balance	

Account:						GL No:	
Date	Description	PR	DR	CR	Balance	

Account:						GL No:	
Date	Description	PR	DR	CR	Balance	

Account:						GL No:	
Date	Description	PR	DR	CR	Balance	

Account:					GL No:	
Date	Description	PR	DR	CR	Balance	

Account:					GL No:	
Date	Description	PR	DR	CR	Balance	

Account:					GL No:	
Date	Description	PR	DR	CR	Balance	

Account:					GL No:	
Date	Description	PR	DR	CR	Balance	

Account:					GL No:	
Date	Description	PR	DR	CR	Balance	

Account:					GL No:	
Date	Description	PR	DR	CR	Balance	

Account:					GL No:	
Date	Description	PR	DR	CR	Balance	

Account:					GL No:	
Date	Description	PR	DR	CR	Balance	

Account:					GL No:	
Date	Description	PR	DR	CR	Balance	

Account:					GL No:	
Date	Description	PR	DR	CR	Balance	

Account:					GL No:	
Date	Description	PR	DR	CR	Balance	

c) Prepare a trial balance at the end of June.

AP-14A LO 7

Xavier works as an accountant for O'Hara Travel Services. He prepared the trial balance at the end of the period and discovered that it did not balance. The total debit balance was significantly larger than the total credit balance. Xavier believes that Mrs. O'Hara, the company's owner, would be happy if the net income figure was higher so that she can show higher profitability to the lender. Therefore, Xavier decides to balance the debit and credit sides by increasing the service revenue account balance and therefore increasing the credit side of the trial balance. Did Xavier behave in an ethical manner? Explain.

_____

_____

_____

_____

_____

_____

AP-15A LO 3 4 7

On June 23, 2019, the bookkeeper for Henson Company discovered an error in the journal entries. On June 2, equipment was purchased on account for $9,000; however, it was recorded in the journals and ledgers for $90,000. Prepare the entries to correct this error.

Date	Account Title and Explanation	PR	Debit	Credit

AP-16A LO 3 4 7

On November 22, 2019, the bookkeeper for Fraggle Company discovered an error in the journal entries. On November 16, an entry was made for the cash purchase of small parts inventory for $550 that incorrectly debited equipment. Prepare the entries to correct this error.

Date	Account Title and Explanation	PR	Debit	Credit

Application Questions Group B

AP-1B LO 1

For the accounts listed below, determine if the normal balance is a debit or a credit. Also, indicate if a debit or a credit will decrease the account balance.

	Normal Balance	Decrease
Cash		
Accounts Receivable		
Accounts Payable		
Bank Loan		
Owner's Capital		
Service Revenue		
Insurance Expense		
Prepaid Insurance		
Equipment		
Unearned Revenue		
Owner's Withdrawals		
Salaries Expense		

AP-2B LO 1

Indicate whether increases and decreases in the following groups of accounts correspond to debits or credits.

	Increase	Decrease
Liabilities		
Owner's Equity		
Expenses		
Owner's Withdrawals		
Revenues		
Assets		

Analysis

What is a normal balance? Provide an example.

_____

_____

_____

AP-3B LO 1 3

Perfect Party is owned by Candace Rodriguez and provides party planning services. During April 2019, Perfect Party had the following transactions.

Apr 1   The owner invested $5,800 cash into the business
Apr 4   Planned a party for a customer for $740; the customer will pay later
Apr 6   Paid $600 cash for rent for the month
Apr 8   Received a $370 telephone bill, which will be paid later
Apr 15   Paid $300 toward the bank loan principal
Apr 19   Received cash from a customer who owed $840
Apr 27   Paid the telephone bill received earlier

Complete the table to analyze each transaction.

	Account Name	Category	Increase or Decrease	Debit or Credit
Apr 1				
Apr 4				
Apr 6				
Apr 8				
Apr 15				
Apr 19				
Apr 27				

AP-4B LO 1 3

Have-a-Bash, owned by Finn Tymes, provides party planning services. During October 2019, Have-a-Bash had the following transactions.

Oct 1	Finn invested $5,000 cash into the business
Oct 2	Planned a party for a customer and received $900 cash
Oct 4	Received a $500 utilities bill, which will be paid later
Oct 10	Paid $200 cash for maintenance for the month
Oct 12	Paid $400 toward the bank loan principal
Oct 18	Received cash from a customer who owed $1,100
Oct 22	Paid the utilities bill received on October 4
Oct 28	Paid $3,000 cash in advance for office rent

Complete the table to analyze each transaction.

	Account Name	Category	Increase or Decrease	Debit or Credit
Oct 1				
Oct 2				
Oct 4				
Oct 10				
Oct 12				
Oct 18				
Oct 22				
Oct 28				

AP-5B LO 3 4

HomeStyle provides interior design solutions for residential and commercial spaces. During the month of July 2019, the following transactions took place.

Jul 3   Provided services to a customer and received $3,100 cash

Jul 4   Borrowed $2,500 from the bank

Jul 6   Provided services worth $2,800 to a customer on account

Jul 10   Received the utilities bill for $240, which will be paid later

Jul 11   Paid $690 cash to reduce the balance of accounts payable

Jul 15   Collected $1,900 cash from customers owing on account

Jul 20   Paid $2,600 toward the bank loan principal

Jul 21   Paid the amount owing from July 10

Jul 27   Paid salaries of $1,700 for the month with cash

Jul 31   Purchased equipment worth $3,100, which will be paid later

Prepare the journal entries for the above transactions.

Date	Account Title and Explanation	PR	Debit	Credit

Date	Account Title and Explanation	PR	Debit	Credit

AP-6B LO 3 4

Tracts of Land provides surveying services to construction companies and municipalities. During the month of February 2019, Tracts of Land had the following transactions.

Feb 1   Purchased equipment worth $8,200, which will be paid later

Feb 2   Provided services worth $20,200 to a customer on account

Feb 3   Paid $1,900 cash for February's utilities

Feb 4   Paid $1,600 for four months of insurance coverage

Feb 10   Paid $2,000 cash to reduce the balance of accounts payable

Feb 14   Paid $6,600 cash for a monthly maintenance contract

Feb 22   Received a bill for $5,800 in travel expenses to be paid next month

Feb 24   Received an advertising bill for $400, which will be paid next month

Feb 28   Paid $2,730 to the bank to reduce the bank loan; interest was $30 and the remainder was principal

Prepare the journal entries for the transactions.

Date	Account Title and Explanation	PR	Debit	Credit

Date	Account Title and Explanation	PR	Debit	Credit

AP-7B LO 3 4

Noel Dy opened an automobile repair shop. The following transactions occurred during the month of March 2019.

Mar 1	Noel Dy invested $10,000 cash and $8,000 worth of equipment in the business
Mar 3	Paid $1,000 cash to rent the shop space
Mar 5	Purchased $1,200 worth of shop tools using cash
Mar 7	Received $2,000 cash for repair work done for MJ Gonzales
Mar 8	Purchased $1,000 worth of shop tools from Adrian Cruz on account
Mar 15	Paid half of the amount due to Adrian Cruz with cash
Mar 18	Paid $200 cash to a local publication for advertising
Mar 19	Paid salaries with $1,000 in cash
Mar 20	Noel Dy withdrew $1,500 cash for personal use
Mar 29	Bought $1,000 worth of chairs and tables for the shop on account
Mar 31	Noel Dy personally invested additional equipment worth $5,000 for business use
Mar 31	Received $3,000 cash from various customers for repairs done on their automobiles

Prepare journal entries for the above transactions.

Date	Account Title and Explanation	PR	Debit	Credit

Date	Account Title and Explanation	PR	Debit	Credit

AP-8B LO 3 4

Helen Long owns and operates Long Landscaping, which provides landscaping and gardening services. During the month of August 2019, she had the following transactions.

Aug 1   Provided services to a customer who paid $800 cash

Aug 3   Paid $1,000 to the bank to repay a bank loan; of that amount, $100 was interest

Aug 6   Received a maintenance bill for $500, which will be paid later

Aug 8   Paid $1,600 for a one-year insurance policy

Aug 17   Paid $2,200 for rent for the month

Aug 20   Provided services to a customer for $1,300 and the customer will pay later

Aug 22   Paid the maintenance bill received on August 6

Aug 28   Received payment from the customer from August 20

Record the transactions in the journal.

Date	Account Title and Explanation	PR	Debit	Credit

AP-9B LO 1 6

The following are the accounts of DRAM Company and their corresponding normal balances on October 31, 2019.

Account	Balance
David, Capital	$20,400
Accounts Payable	13,200
Insurance Expense	1,000
Service Revenue	6,800
Equipment	30,500
Supplies Expense	2,900
Cash	5,700
Salaries Expense	4,100
David, Withdrawals	3,100
Rent Expense	2,200
Telephone Expense	1,200
Bank Loan	11,700
Prepaid Rent	1,400

Prepare DRAM Company's trial balance for the month ended October 31, 2019.

AP-10B LO 1 6

A part-time bookkeeper for Bright Lights has created the trial balance at the end of the year and cannot get it to balance.

Bright Lights Trial Balance December 31, 2019		
Account Title	**DR**	**CR**
Accounts Payable		$2,500
Accounts Receivable		6,000
Advertising Expense	$1,500	
Bank Loan		5,000
Bright, Capital		20,600
Bright, Withdrawals		10,000
Cash	7,600	
Interest Expense	750	
Maintenance Expense	1,500	
Office Supplies Expense	1,200	
Rent Expense	12,000	
Salaries Expense		15,000
Service Revenue	30,000	
Telephone Expense	5,000	
Unearned Revenue		2,950
Utilities Expense	500	
Total	**$60,050**	**$62,050**

155

All the entries have been journalized and posted to the general ledger properly, and all the accounts should have normal balance. Recreate the trial balance for Bright Lights so that the accounts are listed in the order they would typically appear in a chart of accounts, and ensure that debits equal credits.

Analysis

The accountant at Bright Lights was worried that he may have recorded some entries incorrectly in the journal, but upon seeing that the trial balance is in balance, he assumed that he must have done everything correctly. Is his assumption correct? Explain.

_____

_____

_____

_____

AP-11B LO 5 6

Winter Sports is owned by Robert Blue and provides winter sport equipment and apparel. The complete general ledger for November 2019 is shown below.

Account: Cash					GL No: 101	
Date	Description	PR	DR	CR	Balance	
Nov 1	Opening Balance				15,600	DR
Nov 1		J1		3,600	12,000	DR
Nov 2		J1	5,800		17,800	DR
Nov 3		J1		2,880	14,920	DR
Nov 10		J1		20	14,900	DR
Nov 10		J1		1,560	13,340	DR
Nov 20		J1	5,200		18,540	DR
Nov 22		J1	1,600		20,140	DR
Nov 24		J1		1,420	18,720	DR
Nov 30		J1		4,000	14,720	DR

Account: Accounts Receivable					GL No: 105	
Date	Description	PR	DR	CR	Balance	
Nov 1	Opening Balance				4,920	DR
Nov 22		J1		1,600	3,320	DR

Account: Prepaid Insurance					GL No: 110	
Date	Description	PR	DR	CR	Balance	
Nov 1	Opening Balance				0	DR
Nov 1		J1	3,600		3,600	DR

Account: Equipment					GL No: 120	
Date	Description	PR	DR	CR	Balance	
Nov 1	Opening Balance				22,280	DR
Nov 20		J1		5,200	17,080	DR

Account: Accounts Payable					GL No: 200	
Date	Description	PR	DR	CR	Balance	
Nov 1	Opening Balance				5,800	CR
Nov 4		J1		500	6,300	CR
Nov 24		J1	1,420		4,880	CR

Account: Unearned Revenue					GL No: 210	
Date	Description	PR	DR	CR	Balance	
Nov 1	Opening Balance				3,600	CR

Account: Bank Loan					GL No: 215	
Date	Description	PR	DR	CR	Balance	
Nov 1	Opening Balance				10,200	CR
Nov 10		J1	1,560		8,640	CR

Account: Blue, Capital					GL No: 300	
Date	Description	PR	DR	CR	Balance	
Nov 1	Opening Balance				23,200	CR

Account: Blue, Withdrawals					GL No: 310	
Date	Description	PR	DR	CR	Balance	
Nov 30		JI	4,000		4,000	DR

Account: Service Revenue					GL No: 400	
Date	Description	PR	DR	CR	Balance	
Nov 2		J1		5,800	5,800	CR

Account: Interest Expense					GL No: 520	
Date	Description	PR	DR	CR	Balance	
Nov 10		J1	20		20	DR

Account: Maintenance Expense					GL No: 530	
Date	Description	PR	DR	CR	Balance	
Nov 4		J1	500		500	DR

Account: Rent Expense					GL No: 540	
Date	Description	PR	DR	CR	Balance	
Nov 3		J1	2,880		2,880	DR

Prepare a trial balance. Place the accounts in the order shown in the general ledger.

AP-12B LO 3 4 5 6

Lowe Consulting provides advice and resources to entrepreneurs starting their own businesses. The company is a sole proprietorship owned by Leslie Lowe. The closing balances at the end of August 2019 and the chart of accounts are shown below.

Lowe Consulting Balance Sheet As at August 31, 2019			
Assets		**Liabilities**	
Cash	$7,200	Accounts Payable	$3,400
Accounts Receivable	2,300	Unearned Revenue	1,400
Prepaid Insurance	850	Bank Loan	5,600
Equipment	11,500	**Total Liabilities**	10,400
		Owner's Equity	
		Lowe, Capital	11,450
Total Assets	$21,850	**Total Liabilities and Owner's Equity**	$21,850

Account Description	Account #
ASSETS	
Cash	101
Accounts Receivable	105
Prepaid Insurance	110
Equipment	120

Account Description	Account #
LIABILITIES	
Accounts Payable	200
Unearned Revenue	210
Bank Loan	215

Account Description	Account #
OWNER'S EQUITY	
Lowe, Capital	300
Lowe, Withdrawals	310

Account Description	Account #
REVENUE	
Service Revenue	400

Account Description	Account #
EXPENSES	
Insurance Expense	515
Interest Expense	520
Office Supplies Expense	530
Rent Expense	540

During the month of September, Lowe Consulting had the following transactions.

Sep 1	Paid $1,800 cash in advance for a one-year insurance policy
Sep 2	Received $1,900 cash for services provided
Sep 3	Paid $1,350 cash for September's rent
Sep 4	Purchased office supplies on account worth $250
Sep 10	Paid $960 toward the bank loan principal and $40 of interest on the loan
Sep 20	Received $2,200 cash from a customer booking consulting services in advance
Sep 22	Collected $850 from a customer paying their account
Sep 24	Paid $600 toward accounts payable
Sep 30	The owner withdrew $1,600 cash for personal use

Required

a) Prepare the journal entries for the month of September.

Date	Account Title and Explanation	PR	Debit	Credit

b) Post the journal entries to the ledger accounts.

Account:						GL No:	
Date	Description	PR	DR	CR	Balance	

Account:					GL No:	
Date	Description	PR	DR	CR	Balance	

Account:					GL No:	
Date	Description	PR	DR	CR	Balance	

Account:					GL No:	
Date	Description	PR	DR	CR	Balance	

Account:					GL No:	
Date	Description	PR	DR	CR	Balance	

Account:					GL No:	
Date	Description	PR	DR	CR	Balance	

Account:					GL No:	
Date	Description	PR	DR	CR	Balance	

Account:					GL No:	
Date	Description	PR	DR	CR	Balance	

Account:					GL No:	
Date	Description	PR	DR	CR	Balance	

Account:					GL No:	
Date	Description	PR	DR	CR	Balance	

Account:					GL No:	
Date	Description	PR	DR	CR	Balance	

Account:					GL No:	
Date	Description	PR	DR	CR	Balance	

Account:					GL No:	
Date	Description	PR	DR	CR	Balance	

Account:					GL No:	
Date	Description	PR	DR	CR	Balance	

c)   Prepare a trial balance at the end of September.

AP-13B LO 3 4 5 6

Sokatoa, owned by Hiromi Nakata, had the following transactions for the month of July 2019.

Jul 1   Purchased a new machine with $12,000 cash

Jul 5   Provided services worth $10,000 to clients who will pay later

Jul 12   Hiromi withdrew $5,000 cash from the business

Jul 19   Received a maintenance bill for $1,100, which will be paid later

Jul 31   Got a loan from the bank for $25,000

Required

a)   Prepare the journal entries for the month of July.

Date	Account Title and Explanation	PR	Debit	Credit

Date	Account Title and Explanation	PR	Debit	Credit

b) Post the journal entries to the ledger accounts.

Account: Cash — GL No: 101

Date	Description	PR	DR	CR	Balance	
	Opening Balance				31,800	DR

Account: Accounts Receivable — GL No: 105

Date	Description	PR	DR	CR	Balance	
	Opening Balance				5,000	DR

Account: Machine — GL No: 120

Date	Description	PR	DR	CR	Balance	
	Opening Balance				6,000	DR

Account: Accounts Payable — GL No: 200

Date	Description	PR	DR	CR	Balance	
	Opening Balance				3,500	CR

Account: Bank Loan — GL No: 215

Date	Description	PR	DR	CR	Balance	
	Opening Balance				0	CR

Account: Nakata, Capital						GL No: 300	
Date	Description	PR	DR	CR	Balance	
	Opening Balance				39,300	CR

Account: Nakata, Withdrawals						GL No: 310	
Date	Description	PR	DR	CR	Balance	

Account: Sales Revenue						GL No: 400	
Date	Description	PR	DR	CR	Balance	

Account: Maintenance Expense						GL No: 520	
Date	Description	PR	DR	CR	Balance	

Account: Salaries Expense						GL No: 540	
Date	Description	PR	DR	CR	Balance	

c) Prepare a trial balance at the end of July.

Analysis

Explain how the general ledger is similar to the T-accounts used in earlier chapters.

_____

_____

_____

_____

AP-14B LO 7

Sassy Salon is a small hair salon with only three employees—two hairdressers, and an accountant who also acts as the receptionist and cashier, and who performs other miscellaneous tasks to keep the salon operational. Sassy Salon uses a computerized accounting system, where the accountant is supposed to enter each credit card and cash receipt transaction as soon as a customer pays. Based on the accountant's input, the computerized accounting system automatically prepares journal entries, posts the entries to ledgers and prepares a trial balance at the end of the period. Sometimes, the amount of cash on hand at the end of the period is not the same as the cash balance reported by the computerized accounting system. This is mostly due to the accountant forgetting to input a transaction or making other mistakes, especially when the salon is busy and the amount of work is overwhelming. When there is a discrepancy, the accountant always has a difficult time locating the error and explaining the discrepancy to the business owner. Therefore, the accountant proposes to the owner that rather than inputting each sales transaction separately, she will wait until the end of the period to count the amount of cash on hand and enter sales transactions based on that amount. By doing so, there will never be a discrepancy. It also reduces the amount of work for the accountant, which allows her to focus on servicing customers. Should the owner approve the accountant's proposed change? Why or why not?

_____

_____

_____

_____

_____

_____

_____

AP-15B LO 3 4 7

On August 16, 2019, the bookkeeper for Reliable Administration discovered that an entry was made on August 9 to pay for a one-year insurance policy for $1,800; however, accounts payable was used instead of cash. Prepare the entries to correct this error.

Date	Account Title and Explanation	PR	Debit	Credit

AP-16B LO 3 4 7

On February 21, 2019, the bookkeeper for Balsdon Consulting discovered that an entry was made on February 6 to pay for repairs expense with $800 cash; however, rent expense was debited. Prepare the entries to correct this error.

Date	Account Title and Explanation	PR	Debit	Credit

Case Study

CS-1 LO 1 2 3 4 5 6 7

Renu Mawani has been operating her own interior design business called Mawani Interiors for a couple of years. The following transactions occurred in March 2019.

Mar 2	Paid $2,000 cash for March's office rental
Mar 3	Renu invested $7,000 cash into the business
Mar 4	Purchased equipment on account for $8,000
Mar 6	Received $2,800 cash from a client that owed the company for last month's services
Mar 8	Purchased office supplies using $370 cash
Mar 10	Paid $6,900 cash for a consulting invoice received and recorded last month
Mar 13	Completed work for a client and the client paid $2,900 cash
Mar 15	Prepaid $1,800 cash for a one-year insurance policy
Mar 16	Completed work for a client, who will pay $3,200 next month
Mar 20	Discovered that an error was made on the transaction recorded on March 4; the equipment cost $8,800, not $8,000
Mar 23	Received a $6,000 cash deposit from a client for work to be completed in the next few months
Mar 29	Received utility bills for $410 to be paid next month
Mar 29	Obtained a bank loan of $12,000
Mar 30	Renu withdrew $3,000 cash for personal use
Mar 31	Paid $18,000 cash for employee salaries

Required

a) Below is the list of account names that the company uses and their respective opening account balances as at the beginning of March. For each of the accounts, identify the account category (assets, liabilities, owner's capital, owner's withdrawals, revenue or expenses) and input the opening account balance in the debit or credit column based on the side of its normal balance. The answers have been filled in for the accounts payable account as an example. Be sure to total both the debit and credit sides. (Hint: If all your answers are correct, the total debit will be equal to the total credit.)

Account Name	Balance	Account Category	Debit	Credit
Accounts Payable	$6,900	Liabilities		$6,900
Accounts Receivable	5,400			
Cash	2,400			
Equipment	11,600			
Mawani, Capital	12,500			
Mawani, Withdrawals	0			
Bank Loan	0			
Prepaid Insurance	0			
Insurance Expense	0			
Office Supplies Expense	0			
Rent Expense	0			
Salaries Expense	0			
Service Revenue	0			
Unearned Revenue	0			
Utilities Expense	0			
Total				

b) Identify the steps in the accounting cycle that need to be done repeatedly during the accounting period before the trial balance can be prepared at the end of the accounting period.

_____

_____

_____

_____

c) Record all of March's transactions in the journal and post them to the ledger. The account number can be found on the top right corner of each account's ledger.

Date	Account Title and Explanation	PR	Debit	Credit

Date	Account Title and Explanation	PR	Debit	Credit

Account: Cash   **GL No: 110**

Date	Description	PR	DR	CR	Balance	

Account: Accounts Receivable   **GL No: 120**

Date	Description	PR	DR	CR	Balance	

Account: Prepaid Insurance					GL No: 130	
Date	Description	PR	DR	CR	Balance	

Account: Equipment					GL No: 150	
Date	Description	PR	DR	CR	Balance	

Account: Accounts Payable					GL No: 210	
Date	Description	PR	DR	CR	Balance	

Account: Unearned Revenue					GL No: 220	
Date	Description	PR	DR	CR	Balance	

Account: Bank Loan					GL No: 230	
Date	Description	PR	DR	CR	Balance	

Account: Mawani, Capital					GL No: 310	
Date	Description	PR	DR	CR	Balance	

Account: Mawani, Withdrawals					GL No: 320
Date	Description	PR	DR	CR	Balance

Account: Service Revenue					GL No: 410
Date	Description	PR	DR	CR	Balance

Account: Office Supplies Expense					GL No: 500
Date	Description	PR	DR	CR	Balance

Account: Salaries Expense					GL No: 510
Date	Description	PR	DR	CR	Balance

Account: Rent Expense					GL No: 520
Date	Description	PR	DR	CR	Balance

Account: Insurance Expense					GL No: 530
Date	Description	PR	DR	CR	Balance

Account: Utilities Expense					GL No: 540
Date	Description	PR	DR	CR	Balance

d) Prepare the trial balance.

e) In order to improve the efficiency of the accounting process, Renu is considering recording transactions directly to the ledger and eliminating the use of a journal. Would it be ethical to do so? Explain.

_____

_____

_____

_____

_____

_____

_____

_____

_____

_____

_____

_____

_____

_____

_____

_____

_____

_____

_____

Notes

Chapter 5

THE ACCOUNTING CYCLE: ADJUSTMENTS

LEARNING OBJECTIVES

LO **1** Describe the purpose of adjustments

LO **2** Prepare adjusting entries for accrued revenue

LO **3** Prepare adjusting entries for accrued expenses

LO **4** Prepare adjusting entries for unearned revenue

LO **5** Prepare adjusting entries for prepaid expenses

LO **6** Prepare adjusting entries for depreciation

LO **7** Prepare an adjusted trial balance

LO **8** Describe ethics and internal controls relating to adjusting entries

AMEENGAGE™ Access **ameengage.com** for integrated resources including tutorials, practice exercises, the digital textbook and more.

Assessment Questions

AS-1 LO **1**

What is an accounting period?

AS-2 LO **1**

Is a fiscal year always the same as a calendar year? Explain how a natural business year is related to a fiscal year.

AS-3 LO **1**

Why must adjustments be made at the end of the accounting period?

AS-4 LO **1**

What does accrual-based accounting state regarding revenue and expenses?

AS-5 LO 1

What are the five broad categories of adjusting entries?

_____

_____

AS-6 LO 2

Define accrued revenue.

_____

_____

AS-7 LO 2

When making an adjustment to record accrued revenue, which accounts are used and how are they affected?

_____

_____

AS-8 LO 3

Define accrued expenses.

_____

_____

AS-9 LO 3

When making an adjustment to record accrued interest on a bank loan, which accounts are used and how are they affected?

_____

_____

AS-10 LO 4

When making an adjustment to record unearned revenue that is now earned, which accounts are used and how are they affected?

_____

_____

AS-11 LO 5

When making an adjustment to record the used portion of prepaid insurance, which accounts are used and how are they affected?

_____

_____

AS-12 LO 6

When making an adjustment to record depreciation on equipment, which accounts are used and how are they affected?

_____

_____

AS-13 `LO 6`

What is the purpose of a contra account?

_____

_____

_____

AS-14 `LO 6`

True or False: All assets that are part of property, plant and equipment depreciate.

_____

_____

AS-15 `LO 6`

How does accumulated depreciation affect the value of property, plant and equipment?

_____

_____

_____

AS-16 `LO 7`

What is an adjusted trial balance?

_____

_____

_____

AS-17 `LO 7`

What is the purpose of a worksheet?

_____

_____

_____

AS-18 `LO 8`

Provide an example of an internal control procedure that can ensure that all necessary adjustments are accounted for.

_____

_____

_____

_____

_____

_____

Application Questions Group A

AP-1A [LO 2]

Metropolitan Tailors finished tailoring clothes for a client on December 31, 2019. The client picked up the clothes and paid the invoice of $180 on January 3, 2020. Record any necessary adjusting entries for Metropolitan Tailors in 2019 and the cash receipt transaction in 2020. Metropolitan Tailors has a December 31 year end.

Date	Account Title and Explanation	PR	Debit	Credit
2019				
Dec 31	Accounts receivable		180	
	Service Revenue			180
	To accrue service rev			
2020				
Jan 3	Cash			
	Accounts receivable			
	received payment			

AP-2A [LO 3]

Lexcon Farm employs one worker. The employee works Monday to Friday and is paid a weekly salary of $560 every Friday. As of April 30, 2019, all of April's weekly salaries have been paid except the amounts for Monday, April 29, and Tuesday, April 30. The last two days of April's salary are paid on Friday, May 3, along with the first three days of May's salary. Lexcon Farm records all adjusting entries on a monthly basis.

Required

a) Prepare an adjusting entry on April 30, 2019, to accrue the employee's salary for Monday, April 29, and Tuesday, April 30.

Date	Account Title and Explanation	PR	Debit	Credit
Apr 30	Salary payable		224	
	Salaries expense			224
	to accrue salaries			

b) Record the payment of salary on May 3, 2019.

Date	Account Title and Explanation	PR	Debit	Credit
May 3	Salaries payable		224	
	Salaries expense		336	
	Cash			560

AP-3A LO 4

On December 15, 2019, Peaceful Living Inc. received $200 cash from a customer in advance for two rounds of bug spraying services, which took place on December 31, 2019, and January 31, 2020.

Required

a) Record the cash receipt transaction on December 15, 2019.

Date	Account Title and Explanation	PR	Debit	Credit
Dec 15	Cash		200	
	Unearned revenue			200

b) Record any necessary adjusting entries on December 31, 2019.

Date	Account Title and Explanation	PR	Debit	Credit
Dec 31	Unearned Revenue		100	
	Service revenue			100
	To adjust for 1 round of service			

AP-4A LO 5

At the beginning of the fiscal year 2019, Samat Company negotiated a new one-year lease. On January 2, 2019, Samat paid a total of $1,600 representing first and last month's rent. Prepare all journal entries related to Samat Company's rental space for the month of January 2019.

Date	Account Title and Explanation	PR	Debit	Credit
Jan 2	Prepaid rent		1600	
	Cash			1600
Jan 31	Rent expense		800	
	Prepaid rent			800
	to expense january rent			

$$\frac{100000 - 0}{5} = 20000\text{\textdollar}$$

AP-5A [LO 6]

On January 1, 2019, Precision Machinery purchased a new piece of equipment for $100,000. The equipment is expected to last five years and will have no residual value. Precision Machinery has a December 31 year end. Prepare the table below showing the yearly depreciation, accumulated depreciation and net book value of the equipment.

Year	Original Cost of Equipment	Depreciation Expense	Accumulated Depreciation	Net Book Value
2019	100000	20000	20000	80000
2020	1000000	20000	40000	60000
2021	100000	20000	60000	40000
2022	100000	20000	80000	20000
2023	100000	20000	100000	0

AP-6A [LO 6]

$$\frac{Cost - residual\ value}{useful\ life}$$

On March 1, 2019, Jefferson Consulting purchased new computers for $19,000. The computers are expected to last three years and have an estimated residual value of $1,000. Jefferson has a December 31 year end. Prepare the table below showing the yearly depreciation, accumulated depreciation and net book value of the computers.

Year	Original Cost of Computers	Depreciation Expense	Accumulated Depreciation	Net Book Value
2019	19000	5000	5000	14000
2020	19000	6000	11,000	8000
2021	19000	6000	17000	2000
2022	19000	1000	18000	1000

AP-7A [LO 8]

Gwen MacDonals works as an accountant for Sky High Condos, which is owned by Sam Huang. The business currently owns two buildings with 100 units in each. Sky High is in the process of expanding by building new condo buildings in other provinces. In order to finance the expansion, Sam needs to borrow from the bank. His concern is that the bank may not approve his current financial statements. In December 2019, Sam suggests that Gwen reclassify all of the unearned revenue to the income statement. The unearned revenue includes deposits on hand from tenants: 60% are last month's rent, and 40% are security deposits. Sam's argument is that at least 40% of the balance can be recognized as he has never seen damage to any of the units and therefore believes it isn't a liability. Gwen is in an awkward position as she doesn't want to offend her boss, but she thinks that recording the reclassification would be wrong. What course of action would you suggest for Gwen? In your answer, include the impact the reclassification would have on the financial statements and how the bank might interpret them.

_____

_____

_____

_____

_____

_____

_____

_____

_____

AP-8A LO 2 3 4 5

Susan Richards opened up a consulting business in late August 2019, called North Star Inc. The following transactions took place in September 2019, her first month of operations.

Sep 1   Susan signed a one-year lease for her space and prepaid the first and last months' rent. The payment was recorded as $3,000 in the prepaid rent account on that date. Rent is $1,500/month and paid on the last day of each month.

Sep 16   Susan hired an administrative assistant. The assistant worked 20 hours per week for the last two weeks of September at an hourly rate of $15/hour. Susan intends to pay her on October 1.

Sep 24   Susan agreed to offer consulting work for a customer in early October. The customer paid $1,000 in advance to secure the contract.

Sep 27   Susan performed consulting work for a client in the amount of $2,000, which will be paid at a later date.

Record the adjusting entries Susan must record on September 30, 2019.

Date	Account Title and Explanation	PR	Debit	Credit

AP-9A LO 2·3 5 6

Allan Poe operates an advertising business called A-Plus Advertising. The company had the following adjustments for the month of December 2019.

Dec 31   Recognized $1,250 rent expense used for the month

Dec 31   A monthly magazine subscription was prepaid for one year on December 1, 2019 for $600; by December 31, one issue had been received

Dec 31   Computer depreciation for the month is $400

Dec 31   Salaries for employees accrued by $1,300 by the end of the month

Dec 31   A 30-day contract was started on December 16; the customer will pay $5,000 at the end of the contract in January; accrue the revenue earned by the end of December

Prepare the journal entries for the adjustments.

Date	Account Title and Explanation	PR	Debit	Credit
	Rent expense		1250	
	Prepaid rent			1250
	Prepaid subscription		600	
	Cash			600
	Depreciation expense		400	
	Accumulated depreciation			400
	Salaries expense		1300	
	Salaries payable			1300
	"Service" revenue			
	Accounts receivable			

AP-10A LO 2 3 4 5 6

MJ Sandblasting is in its second year of operations. At the end of April 2019, it had the following adjustments.

Apr 30   Recognized $300 of prepaid insurance expense for the month

Apr 30   Depreciation on equipment for the month was $200

Apr 30   Work worth $650 was done for a client; the client will pay in May

Apr 30   Accrued interest on a bank loan was $30

Apr 30   Outstanding work for a client worth $800 was completed during the month; the client had paid for the work in March

Prepare the journal entries for the adjustments.

Date	Account Title and Explanation	PR	Debit	Credit

AP-11A LO 2 3 5 6 7

Counterpoint Studios has completed all the entries for the month of November 2019, except the monthly adjusting entries. The following information is available to make the adjustments.

Nov 30	Annual depreciation on equipment totals $9,000
Nov 30	Interest accrued on the bank loan is $500
Nov 30	Services were performed for $8,100 to be received next month
Nov 30	The annual insurance policy was purchased on December 1, 2018, for $21,900

Complete the six-column worksheet for Counterpoint Studios.

Counterpoint Studios Worksheet November 30, 2019						
	Unadjusted Trial Balance		Adjustments		Adjusted Trial Balance	
Account Title	**DR**	**CR**	**DR**	**CR**	**DR**	**CR**
Cash	$52,250					
Accounts Receivable	24,800					
Prepaid Insurance	1,825					
Equipment	295,400					
Accumulated Depreciation—Equipment		$96,850				
Accounts Payable		31,500				
Bank Loan		140,000				
Wu, Capital		96,750				
Wu, Withdrawals	60,000					
Service Revenue		382,500				
Advertising Expense	100,000					
Salaries Expense	185,000					
Insurance Expense	20,075					
Depreciation Expense	8,250					
Total	<u>$747,600</u>	<u>$747,600</u>				

AP-12A LO 3 4 5 6 7

Swordfish Programming is owned by Mark Kulak and provides computer solutions to the security industry. At the end of April 2019, Swordfish had the following adjustments.

Apr 30	Interest of $250 had accrued on the bank loan
Apr 30	The balance of prepaid insurance is for a 12-month policy; one month of insurance has been used
Apr 30	During April, Swordfish Programming earned $900 of unearned revenue
Apr 30	The computers were purchased on April 1, 2019, and have an expected useful life of five years, after which they will have no residual value; record the depreciation for April

Using the following trial balance, complete the adjustments and the adjusted trial balance in the worksheet.

Swordfish Programming Worksheet April 30, 2019						
	Unadjusted Trial Balance		Adjustments		Adjusted Trial Balance	
Account Title	DR	CR	DR	CR	DR	CR
Cash	$4,200					
Accounts Receivable	2,300					
Prepaid Insurance	1,800					
Computers	9,600					
Accumulated Depreciation—Computers		$0				
Accounts Payable		1,640				
Interest Payable		0				
Unearned Revenue		1,950				
Bank Loan		2,400				
Kulak, Capital		10,235				
Kulak, Withdrawals	1,500					
Service Revenue		4,750				
Depreciation Expense	0					
Insurance Expense	0					
Interest Expense	0					
Rent Expense	1,300					
Telephone Expense	275					
Total	$20,975	$20,975				

AP-13A LO 3 4 5 6 7

High Flying Biplane has completed all its journal entries for the month of June 2019 and posted them to the general ledger. Based on the ledger balances, an unadjusted trial balance has been prepared.

High Flying Biplane Trial Balance June 30, 2019		
Account Title	**DR**	**CR**
Cash	$8,800	
Accounts Receivable	6,800	
Prepaid Insurance	1,200	
Equipment	64,000	
Accounts Payable		$7,700
Unearned Revenue		4,700
Bank Loan		19,000
Singh, Capital		48,800
Singh, Withdrawals	1,200	
Service Revenue		2,400
Advertising Expense	400	
Telephone Expense	200	
Total	**$82,600**	**$82,600**

The following adjustments must be made at the end of June.

Jun 30   One month of insurance worth $100 has been used

Jun 30   Depreciation on the equipment was $450 this month

Jun 30   Of the unearned revenue amount, $4,080 still remains unearned

Jun 30   Interest accrued on the bank loan was $75

Required

a) Fill in the unadjusted trial balance on the worksheet and complete the rest of the worksheet.

Account Title	Unadjusted Trial Balance		Adjustments		Adjusted Trial Balance	
	DR	CR	DR	CR	DR	CR
Cash	8800				8800	
Accounts receivable	6800				6800	
Prepaid insurance	1200			100	1100	
Equipment	64000				64000	
Account Payable		4700				4700
Unearned revenue		4700	620			4080
Bank loan		19000				19000
Singh, capital		48800				48800
Singh, withdrawals	1200				1200	
Service revenue		2400		620		3020
Advertising Expense	400				400	
Telephone Expense	200				200	
Depreciation Expense			450		450	
Interest expense			75		75	
Insurance, expense			100		100	
Accumulated dep-equip				450		450
Interest payable				75		75
Total	82600	82600	1245	1245	83125	83125

b) Create the journal entries for the adjustments from the worksheet.

Date	Account Title and Explanation	PR	Debit	Credit
2019				
June 30	Insurance expense		100	
	Prepaid insurance			100
June 30	Depreciation expense		450	
	Accumulated depreciation			450
June 30	Unearned revenue		620	
	Service Revenue			620
June 30	Interest expense		75	
	Interest payable			75

AP-14A LO 2 4 5 6 7

Limbo Lower has completed all its journal entries for the month of September 2019 and posted them to the general ledger. Based on the ledger balances, an unadjusted trial balance has been prepared.

Limbo Lower Trial Balance September 30, 2019		
Account Title	**DR**	**CR**
Cash	$5,800	
Accounts Receivable	1,450	
Prepaid Insurance	1,800	
Equipment	10,400	
Accounts Payable		$3,050
Unearned Revenue		1,400
Bank Loan		4,640
Patel, Capital		11,450
Patel, Withdrawals	1,600	
Service Revenue		1,900
Interest Expense	40	
Rent Expense	1,350	
Total	**$22,440**	**$22,440**

The following adjustments must be made at the end of September.

Sep 30   The amount of prepaid insurance is for 12 months; one month has been used

Sep 30   Depreciation for the month on equipment was $120

Sep 30   Unearned revenue of $360 has now been earned

Sep 30   Work was performed for $450, which will be paid for next month

Required

a) Fill in the unadjusted trial balance on the worksheet and complete the rest of the worksheet.

	Unadjusted Trial Balance		Adjustments		Adjusted Trial Balance	
Account Title	**DR**	**CR**	**DR**	**CR**	**DR**	**CR**

b)   Create the journal entries for the adjustments from the worksheet.

Date	Account Title and Explanation	PR	Debit	Credit

AP-15A LO 3.4 5 6 7

Zig Zag Robotics has the following adjustments to make at the end of September 2019, the end of its fiscal year.

Sep 30   Unearned revenue of $850 has now been earned

Sep 30   A review of the insurance policies shows that $430 worth of insurance is still prepaid

Sep 30   Salaries accrued but not yet paid amount to $2,430

Sep 30   Monthly depreciation on equipment was $600

The chart of accounts is shown below.

Account Description	Account #
ASSETS	
Cash	101
Accounts Receivable	105
Prepaid Insurance	110
Equipment	120
Accumulated Depreciation—Equipment	130

Account Description	Account #
LIABILITIES	
Accounts Payable	200
Unearned Revenue	210
Salaries Payable	220

Account Description	Account #
OWNER'S EQUITY	
Rizzo, Capital	300
Rizzo, Withdrawals	310

Account Description	Account #
REVENUE	
Service Revenue	400

Account Description	Account #
EXPENSES	
Salaries Expense	530
Depreciation Expense	535
Insurance Expense	540

Required

a) Complete the six-column worksheet.

	Zig Zag Robotics Worksheet September 30, 2019					
	Unadjusted Trial Balance		Adjustments		Adjusted Trial Balance	
Account Title	**DR**	**CR**	**DR**	**CR**	**DR**	**CR**
Cash	$3,000					
Accounts Receivable	950					
Prepaid Insurance	830					
Equipment	5,500					
Accumulated Depreciation—Equipment		$1,800				
Accounts Payable		1,250				
Unearned Revenue		1,700				
Rizzo, Capital		4,030				
Rizzo, Withdrawals	500					
Service Revenue		4,200				
Salaries Expense	2,200					
Total	$12,980	$12,980				

b) Journalize the adjustments.

Date	Account Title and Explanation	PR	Debit	Credit

c)   Post the transactions to the general ledger accounts provided.

Account: Prepaid Insurance					GL No: 110
Date:	Description	PR	DR	CR	Balance
	Opening Balance				

Account: Accumulated Depreciation—Equipment					GL No: 130
Date:	Description	PR	DR	CR	Balance
	Opening Balance				

Account: Unearned Revenue					GL No: 210
Date:	Description	PR	DR	CR	Balance
	Opening Balance				

Account: Salaries Payable					GL No: 220
Date:	Description	PR	DR	CR	Balance
	Opening Balance				

Account: Service Revenue					GL No: 400
Date:	Description	PR	DR	CR	Balance
	Opening Balance				

Account: Salaries Expense					GL No: 530
Date	Description	PR	DR	CR	Balance
	Opening Balance				

Account: Depreciation Expense					GL No: 535
Date	Description	PR	DR	CR	Balance
	Opening Balance				

Account: Insurance Expense					GL No: 540
Date	Description	PR	DR	CR	Balance
	Opening Balance				

Analysis

What is the purpose of preparing a worksheet before journalizing and posting adjusting entries, and before preparing financial statements?

_____

_____

_____

AP-16A LO 4 5 6 7

Sigmund Services has completed all its journal entries for the month of April 2019 and posted them to the general ledger. Based on the ledger balances, an unadjusted trial balance has been prepared.

Sigmund Services Trial Balance April 30, 2019		
Account Title	**DR**	**CR**
Cash	$32,050	
Accounts Receivable	9,000	
Prepaid Insurance	1,200	
Equipment	15,000	
Accounts Payable		$25,550
Unearned Revenue		4,500
Bank Loan		1,500
Sigmund, Capital		18,000
Service Revenue		25,000
Interest Expense	50	
Rent Expense	1,000	
Salaries Expense	8,000	
Telephone Expense	250	
Travel Expense	8,000	
Total	$74,550	$74,550

The following adjustments must be made at the end of April.

Apr 30   The balance of prepaid insurance represents a 12-month policy; one month has been used
Apr 30   Depreciation of equipment for the month is $120
Apr 30   Sigmund Services has earned $1,300 that was previously unearned

Required

a)   Fill in the unadjusted trial balance on the worksheet and complete the rest of the worksheet.

	Unadjusted Trial Balance		Adjustments		Adjusted Trial Balance	
Account Title	**DR**	**CR**	**DR**	**CR**	**DR**	**CR**

b)   Create the journal entries for the adjustments from the worksheet.

Date	Account Title and Explanation	PR	Debit	Credit

Application Questions Group B

AP-1B LO 2

Enlightenment Tutoring provides in-home tutoring services to elementary school students. In December 2019, it provided four tutoring sessions to a client, who agreed to pay $400 after every 10 sessions. The company has a December 31 year end.

Required

a) Assume that Enlightenment Tutoring Services will provide six more sessions to the client in January 2020, when the client will pay $400. Record any adjusting entries required on December 31, 2019.

Date	Account Title and Explanation	PR	Debit	Credit

b) Assume that Tutoring Services provided the other six sessions to the client in January and the client paid in full at the end of the month. Record the entry required on January 31, 2020.

Date	Account Title and Explanation	PR	Debit	Credit

AP-2B LO 3

Sugoi Manufacturing borrowed $75,000 from the bank on November 1, 2019, and must repay the loan principal and interest on February 1, 2020. The bank charges an annual interest rate of 6% on the loan.

Required

a) Prepare the adjusting entry to accrue the interest on December 31, which is Sugoi Manufacturing's year end. Sugoi Manufacturing has not accrued any interest before December 31, 2019.

Date	Account Title and Explanation	PR	Debit	Credit

b) Record the payment of loan principal and interest on February 1, 2020.

Date	Account Title and Explanation	PR	Debit	Credit

AP-3B LO 4

Meyers Office owns a number of offices for rent. The following information pertains to Meyers Office from October to December of 2019.

Oct 30   Collected $24,000 cash from Kawalin Inc. for 12 months of rent in advance; Kawalin Inc. moved in on November 1

Dec 1   Collected $9,000 cash from Zand Company for three months of rent in advance; Zand Company occupied the office immediately on December 1

Journalize the above transactions and any necessary adjusting entries for Meyers Office's year end on December 31, 2019.

Date	Account Title and Explanation	PR	Debit	Credit

AP-4B LO 5

On January 1, 2019, Rainer Company purchased a 12-month insurance policy. It paid $2,400 covering the 2019 calendar year. Prepare journal entries related to the purchase of the policy on January 1, 2019, and the January 31, 2019, adjusting entry related to the insurance.

Date	Account Title and Explanation	PR	Debit	Credit

AP-5B LO 6

On January 1, 2019, Hackerton purchased a new machine for $60,000. The machine is expected to last six years and will have no residual value. Hackerton has a December 31 year end. Prepare the table below showing the yearly depreciation, accumulated depreciation and net book value of the machine.

Year	Original Cost of Machine	Depreciation Expense	Accumulated Depreciation	Net Book Value
2019				
2020				
2021				
2022				
2023				
2024				

AP-6B LO 6

On November 1, 2019, Gregory Accounting refurnished the entire office for $25,000. The furniture is expected to last four years and has an estimated residual value of $1,000. Gregory Accounting has a December 31 year end. Prepare the table below showing the yearly depreciation, accumulated depreciation and net book value of the furniture.

Year	Original Cost of Furniture	Depreciation Expense	Accumulated Depreciation	Net Book Value
2019	25000	1000	1000	24000
2020	25000	6000	7000	18000
2021	25000	6000	13000	12000
2022	25000	6000	19000	6000
2023	25000	5000	24000	1000

AP-7B LO 8

Enza Martinez is the owner of Menza Consulting, which operates as a sole proprietorship. On December 27, 2019, Rose Hill Inc. signed a $12,000 contract to hire Menza Consulting for a project, starting in January 2020 and ending in March 2020. Rose Hill Inc. paid a $2,000 deposit on December 27, 2019, and agreed to pay the remaining amount to Menza Consulting at the end of the project on March 31, 2020. To avoid reporting a net loss for the fiscal year 2019, Enza decided to record the transaction related to Rose Hill Inc.'s contract as follows.

Date	Account Title and Explanation	PR	Debit	Credit
2019				
Dec 27	Cash		2,000	
	Service Revenue			2,000
	Received deposit from Rose Hill Inc.			
Dec 31	Accounts Receivable		10,000	
	Service Revenue			10,000
	Accrued revenue from Rose Hill Inc.			

Was it ethical for Enza to record the above journal entries? Why or why not? If you believe that Enza's action is unethical, describe how the transaction related to Rose Hill Inc.'s contract should be recorded in the fiscal year 2019.

_____

_____

_____

_____

_____

_____

_____

_____

_____

_____

_____

AP-8B LO 2 3 4 5

Yeesom Properties rented out a retail space to Ziphant Gift Shop for $3,300 per month. Ziphant Gift Shop prepaid $3,300 on September 15, 2019, for October's rent and started its occupancy on October 1, 2019. Unfortunately, Ziphant Gift Shop experienced short-term cash flow problems and could not afford to pay November's rent on time. Yeesom Properties agreed to let Ziphant Gift Shop pay for both November and December rent on December 31. Ziphant Gift Shop paid $6,600 cash to Yeesom Properties on December 31. Both Yeesom Properties and Ziphant Gift Shop record adjusting entries at the end of every month.

Required

a) Record all necessary journal entries for Yeesom Properties from September 15 to December 31, 2019.

Date	Account Title and Explanation	PR	Debit	Credit

b) Record all necessary journal entries for Ziphant Gift Shop from September 15 to December 31, 2019.

Date	Account Title and Explanation	PR	Debit	Credit

AP-9B LO 2 3 4 5 6

Spring Gardening Service provides seasonal gardening services. At the end of August 2019, the company must make the following adjustments.

Aug 31   Depreciation for equipment is $120

Aug 31   Interest due on a bank loan is $50; it will be paid next month

Aug 31   Accrued salary expense for an employee at the end of the month; the company owes the employee $450

Aug 31   One month of prepaid insurance at $70 per month has been used

Aug 31   Gardening services were provided for $300, which will be billed and paid for in September

Aug 31   Spring Gardening earned $670 that was previously unearned

Prepare the adjusting journal entries.

Date	Account Title and Explanation	PR	Debit	Credit

AP-10B LO 2 3 4 5 6

Speak Up provides hearing tests for clients. At the end of March 2019, it had the following account balances.

Speak Up Trial Balance March 31, 2019		
Account Title	**DR**	**CR**
Cash	$6,380	
Accounts Receivable	3,590	
Prepaid Insurance	999	
Equipment	16,290	
Accumulated Depreciation—Equipment		$400
Accounts Payable		2,120
Unearned Revenue		1,570
Bank Loan		4,930
Jones, Capital		12,659
Jones, Withdrawals	2,930	
Service Revenue		12,570
Rent Expense	1,920	
Salaries Expense	2,140	
Total	**$34,249**	**$34,249**

The following adjustments have to be made at the end of March.

Mar 31   Accrued $43 interest on the bank loan
Mar 31   The balance of the prepaid insurance is for the remaining nine months of the insurance policy; the insurance coverage for March has not been recorded
Mar 31   Speak Up completed $942 of work that was previously unearned
Mar 31   One month of depreciation is $250
Mar 31   Speak Up provided services for $448, which will be paid for in April

Complete the adjusting entries.

Date	Account Title and Explanation	PR	Debit	Credit

AP-11B LO 2 3 4 5 6.7

Chirp Hearing is owned by Christina Howell and provides hearing aids and other auditory services. At the end of November 2019, the company had the following adjustments.

Nov 30   Interest on the bank loan is set at 10%; one month of interest has accrued

Nov 30   The balance of the prepaid insurance is for the remaining 10 months of the insurance policy; one month of insurance has been used

Nov 30   The equipment was purchased on September 1, 2019, and will have a useful life of seven years, after which it will have a residual value of $1,140; depreciation is recorded every month; record depreciation for November

Nov 30   Chirp Hearing completed $650 of work that was previously unearned

Using the following trial balance, complete the adjustments and the adjusted trial balance in the worksheet.

	Chirp Hearing Worksheet November 30, 2019					
	Unadjusted Trial Balance		Adjustments		Adjusted Trial Balance	
Account Title	**DR**	**CR**	**DR**	**CR**	**DR**	**CR**
Cash	$6,250					
Accounts Receivable	3,440					
Prepaid Insurance	2,200					
Equipment	16,260					
Accumulated Depreciation—Equipment		$360				
Accounts Payable		2,260				
Interest Payable		0				
Unearned Revenue		1,240				
Bank Loan		4,800				
Howell, Capital		12,640				
Howell, Withdrawals	2,100					
Service Revenue		12,500				
Depreciation Expense	0					
Insurance Expense	0					
Interest Expense	0					
Rent Expense	1,650					
Salaries Expense	1,900					
Total	**$33,800**	**$33,800**				

AP-12B LO 4 5 6 7

Decodely Programming provides custom computer programming and web design. At the end of December 2019, it had four adjustments.

Dec 31   During December, Decodely Programming earned $830 of unearned revenue

Dec 31   Interest expense of $250 had accrued on the bank loan

Dec 31   The balance of prepaid insurance represents 11 months remaining on the policy; one month of insurance has been used

Dec 31   Equipment depreciated $110 during December

Using the following trial balance, complete the adjustments and the adjusted trial balance in the worksheet.

	Decodely Programming Worksheet December 31, 2019					
	Unadjusted Trial Balance		Adjustments		Adjusted Trial Balance	
Account Title	DR	CR	DR	CR	DR	CR
Cash	$4,000					
Accounts Receivable	2,620					
Prepaid Insurance	2,750					
Equipment	9,400					
Accumulated Depreciation—Equipment		$400				
Accounts Payable		1,900				
Interest Payable		0				
Unearned Revenue		4,500				
Bank Loan		1,620				
Singh, Capital		9,930				
Singh, Withdrawals	1,560					
Service Revenue		4,090				
Depreciation Expense	0					
Insurance Expense	0					
Interest Expense	0					
Rent Expense	1,970					
Utilities Expense	140					
Total	$22,440	$22,440				

AP-13B LO 3 4 5 6 7

Floating Speed Boat has completed its journal entries for the month of September and posted them to the general ledger. Based on the ledger balances, an unadjusted trial balance has been prepared.

The following adjustments must be made at the end of September.

Sep 30   Depreciation on equipment for the month is $390

Sep 30   Prepaid insurance of $250 has been used up this month

Sep 30   Interest of $150 has accrued on the bank loan

Sep 30   Unearned revenue of $570 has now been earned

Required

a) Complete the worksheet.

	Floating Speed Boat Worksheet September 30, 2019					
	Unadjusted Trial Balance		Adjustments		Adjusted Trial Balance	
Account Title	**DR**	**CR**	**DR**	**CR**	**DR**	**CR**
Cash	$8,800					
Accounts Receivable	7,900					
Prepaid Insurance	1,500					
Equipment	64,000					
Accumulated Depreciation—Equipment		$870				
Accounts Payable		9,900				
Interest Payable		0				
Unearned Revenue		6,500				
Bank Loan		15,500				
Murray, Capital		49,000				
Murray, Withdrawals	1,200					
Service Revenue		3,400				
Advertising Expense	430					
Depreciation Expense	0					
Insurance Expense	0					
Interest Expense	0					
Rent Expense	1,340					
Total	**$85,170**	**$85,170**				

b) Create the journal entries for the adjustments from the worksheet.

Date	Account Title and Explanation	PR	Debit	Credit

AP-14B LO 3 4 5 6 7

Space Jam Storage offers storage space and transportation services for customers. Space Jam Storage has already completed the transactions for the month and posted them to the general ledger. The following adjustments for December 2019 have not yet been prepared.

Dec 31	Provided services worth $1,500 to a customer who had paid in advance
Dec 31	One month of insurance of $1,000 was used
Dec 31	Depreciation for the month was $500
Dec 31	Salaries accrued at the end of December amounted to $3,370

Required

a) Prepare the six-column worksheet.

Space Jam Storage Worksheet December 31, 2019						
	Unadjusted Trial Balance		Adjustments		Adjusted Trial Balance	
Account Title	DR	CR	DR	CR	DR	CR
Cash	$3,250					
Accounts Receivable	2,750					
Prepaid Insurance	13,000					
Equipment	285,000					
Accumulated Depreciation—Equipment		$45,000				
Accounts Payable		5,500				
Salaries Payable		0				
Unearned Revenue		3,600				
Bank Loan		191,680				
Bugs, Capital		46,200				
Bugs, Withdrawals	13,500					
Service Revenue		78,000				
Maintenance Expense	5,200					
Depreciation Expense	4,000					
Interest Expense	1,280					
Insurance Expense	11,000					
Salaries Expense	31,000					
Total	$369,980	$369,980				

b) Record the journal entries for the adjusting entries.

Date	Account Title and Explanation	PR	Debit	Credit

AP-15B LO 3 4 5 6 7

Presto Chango has the following adjustments to make at the end of December 2019, the end of its fiscal year.

Dec 31   Salaries accrued but not yet paid amount to $750

Dec 31   Unearned revenue of $620 has now been earned

Dec 31   A review of the rental agreement indicates that $320 worth of rent is still prepaid

Dec 31   Interest accrued on the bank loan but not yet paid amounts to $70

Dec 31   Monthly depreciation on equipment was $400

Presto Chango Chart of Accounts (GL No.)

Account Description	Account #
ASSETS	
Cash	101
Accounts Receivable	105
Prepaid Rent	110
Equipment	120
Accumulated Depreciation—Equipment	130

Account Description	Account #
OWNER'S EQUITY	
Presto, Capital	300
Presto, Withdrawals	310

Account Description	Account #
REVENUE	
Service Revenue	400

Account Description	Account #
LIABILITIES	
Accounts Payable	200
Unearned Revenue	205
Interest Payable	210
Salaries Payable	220
Bank Loan	225

Account Description	Account #
EXPENSES	
Salaries Expense	520
Depreciation Expense	525
Interest Expense	530
Rent Expense	535

Required

a) Complete the six-column worksheet.

| Presto Chango Worksheet December 31, 2019 | | | | | | |
| Account Title | Unadjusted Trial Balance | | Adjustments | | Adjusted Trial Balance | |
	DR	CR	DR	CR	DR	CR
Cash	$4,200					
Accounts Receivable	1,350					
Prepaid Rent	680					
Equipment	14,500					
Accumulated Depreciation—Equipment		$800				
Accounts Payable		1,300				
Unearned Revenue		1,250				
Bank Loan		6,000				
Presto, Capital		4,880				
Presto, Withdrawals	800					
Service Revenue		8,700				
Salaries Expense	1,400					
Total						

b) Journalize the adjustments.

Date	Account Title and Explanation	PR	Debit	Credit

c)   Post the transactions to the general ledger accounts.

Account:					GL No:	
Date	**Description**	**PR**	**DR**	**CR**	**Balance**	
	Opening Balance					

Account:					GL No:	
Date	**Description**	**PR**	**DR**	**CR**	**Balance**	
	Opening Balance					

Account:					GL No:	
Date	**Description**	**PR**	**DR**	**CR**	**Balance**	
	Opening Balance					

Account:					GL No:	
Date	**Description**	**PR**	**DR**	**CR**	**Balance**	
	Opening Balance					

Account:					GL No:	
Date	**Description**	**PR**	**DR**	**CR**	**Balance**	
	Opening Balance					

Account:					GL No:	
Date	**Description**	**PR**	**DR**	**CR**	**Balance**	
	Opening Balance					

Account:					GL No:	
Date	**Description**	**PR**	**DR**	**CR**	**Balance**	
	Opening Balance					

Account:					GL No:	
Date	**Description**	**PR**	**DR**	**CR**	**Balance**	
	Opening Balance					

Account:					GL No:	
Date	Description	PR	DR	CR	Balance	
	Opening Balance					

Account:					GL No:	
Date	Description	PR	DR	CR	Balance	
	Opening Balance					

AP-16B LO 4 5.6 7

Thomas Topology has completed journal entries for the month of October and posted them to the general ledger. Based on the ledger balances, an unadjusted trial balance has been prepared.

The following adjustments must be made at the end of October.

Oct 31   One month of prepaid rent worth $720 has been used

Oct 31   Depreciation on equipment for the month was $340

Oct 31   Unearned revenue worth $1,330 has now been earned

Required

a)   Fill in the unadjusted trial balance on the worksheet and complete the rest of the worksheet.

Thomas Topology Worksheet October 31, 2019						
	Unadjusted Trial Balance		Adjustments		Adjusted Trial Balance	
Account Title	DR	CR	DR	CR	DR	CR
Cash	$32,000					
Accounts Receivable	9,500					
Prepaid Rent	5,760					
Equipment	15,000					
Accumulated Depreciation—Equipment		$950				
Accounts Payable		27,800				
Unearned Revenue		5,800				
Bank Loan		1,960				
Edwards, Capital		9,330				
Service Revenue		30,000				
Depreciation Expense						
Insurance Expense	570					
Interest Expense	150					
Rent Expense	0					
Salaries Expense	6,400					
Supplies Expense	360					
Utilities Expense	6,100					
Total	**$75,840**	**$75,840**				

b) Create the journal entries for the adjustments from the worksheet.

Date	Account Title and Explanation	PR	Debit	Credit

Case Study

CS-1 LO 2 3 4 5 6 8

One Stop Consulting is preparing year-end financial statements dated December 31, 2019, and has to make several adjustments before the financial statements can be prepared. The owner has approached the accountant with the following information.

1. A large contract worth a lot of money was started in November of this year that will be completed in early January. The customer will not pay until the contract is completed in January. The owner does not want to include any work already completed in revenue and would rather record the entire amount earned in January when the contract is complete.

2. Interest, utilities and salaries expense will be accrued on December 31, 2019. Utility bills are usually received on the 15th of the month and are usually the same amount each month. The owner wants to accrue the full amount of the utilities on December 31, 2019, instead of just half that would normally be accrued.

3. An insurance policy was purchased in September covering one year. The owner wants to include the entire amount of the policy as an expense for the 2019 year end.

4. A customer paid a deposit in October for work to be completed in December and January. The initial receipt of cash was recorded in unearned revenue. The majority of the work was completed by December 31, 2019. The owner wants to wait until the work is 100% complete in January before recording any of it as revenue.

5. Equipment and furniture are depreciated using the straight-line method over five years. The owner wants to change the estimate from five years to three years for the depreciation calculation on December 31, 2019.

Required

a) For each action the owner wants, identify if there is any violation of financial statement foundations or qualitative characteristics.

_____

_____

_____

_____

_____

_____

_____

b) For each action the owner wants, identify how it affects the financial statements.

_____

_____

_____

_____

_____

_____

_____

_____

c) What are some possible reasons the owner would want to make these changes to the adjustment process?

_____

_____

_____

_____

_____

Chapter 6

THE ACCOUNTING CYCLE: STATEMENTS AND CLOSING ENTRIES

LEARNING OBJECTIVES

LO 1 Prepare financial statements using the adjusted trial balance

LO 2 Prepare closing journal entries and post them to the general ledger

LO 3 Prepare the post-closing trial balance to complete the accounting cycle

LO 4 Prepare the classified balance sheet

LO 5 Analyze the financial statements using liquidity measures

LO 6 Describe the benefits of a computerized accounting system over a manual system

Appendix

LO 7 Prepare a 10-column worksheet

AMEENGAGE™ *Access **ameengage.com** for integrated resources including tutorials, practice exercises, the digital textbook and more.*

——— Assessment Questions ———

AS-1 LO 1

What does the income statement report?

_____

_____

AS-2 LO 1

Which statement is prepared after the income statement but before the balance sheet?

_____

_____

AS-3 LO 1

What does the statement of owner's equity report?

_____

_____

AS-4 LO 1

What two items cause owner's equity to increase and what two items cause owner's equity to decrease?

_____

_____

_____

AS-5 LO 1

Which categories of accounts are reported on the balance sheet?

_____

_____

AS-6 ⬚LO⬛1

How does accumulated depreciation affect the value of property, plant and equipment?

_____

_____

AS-7 ⬚LO⬛2

What does it mean to close the books?

_____

_____

_____

AS-8 ⬚LO⬛2

What are the three steps to close directly to owner's capital?

_____

_____

_____

_____

AS-9 ⬚LO⬛2

What are the four steps to close the accounts using the income summary?

_____

_____

_____

_____

_____

_____

AS-10 ⬚LO⬛2

If a company has a net income for the period and closes its books using the income summary account, will the income summary account have a debit or credit balance before it is closed to the capital account?

_____

_____

_____

AS-11 ⬚LO⬛3

Which categories of accounts appear on the post-closing trial balance?

_____

_____

_____

AS-12 LO 4

Define operating cycle.

_____

_____

_____

AS-13 LO 4

Define current assets.

_____

_____

_____

_____

AS-14 LO 4

Define long-term assets.

_____

_____

_____

_____

_____

AS-15 LO 4

What are current liabilities? Provide two examples of current liabilities.

_____

_____

_____

_____

AS-16 LO 4

What are long-term liabilities? Provide two examples of long-term liabilities.

_____

_____

_____

AS-17 LO 4

What is one difference between a non-classified balance sheet and a classified balance sheet?

_____

_____

_____

AS-18 `LO 5`

How do you calculate the working capital? What does negative working capital mean?

_____

_____

_____

_____

AS-19 `LO 5`

How do you calculate the current ratio and what does it measure?

_____

_____

_____

_____

AS-20 `LO 5`

How do you calculate the quick ratio and what does it measure?

_____

_____

_____

_____

AS-21 `LO 6`

Identify two benefits of a computerized accounting system.

_____

_____

_____

_____

AS-22 `LO 6`

Why is it important to understand a manual accounting system before using a computerized accounting system?

_____

_____

_____

_____

Application Questions Group A

AP-1A LO 1

Floating Speed Boat has completed all its journal entries and adjusting entries for the month of September 2019. The adjusted trial balance is shown below.

Note: During the month of September, the owner of Floating Speed Boat invested $6,900 into the business.

Floating Speed Boat Adjusted Trial Balance September 30, 2019		
Account Title	**DR**	**CR**
Cash	$8,800	
Accounts Receivable	7,900	
Prepaid Insurance	1,150	
Equipment	64,000	
Accumulated Depreciation—Equipment		$1,260
Accounts Payable		9,900
Interest Payable		150
Unearned Revenue		5,930
Bank Loan		15,400
Murray, Capital		49,000
Murray, Withdrawals	1,200	
Service Revenue		3,970
Advertising Expense	430	
Depreciation Expense	390	
Insurance Expense	250	
Interest Expense	150	
Rent Expense	1,340	
Total	**$85,610**	**$85,610**

Required

a) Prepare the income statement from the adjusted trial balance.

Floating Speed Boat Income Statement For the Month Ended Sep 30		
Service Revenue		3970
Expenses: Adv. exp		
Advertising expense	430	
Depreciation	390	
Insurance	250	
Interest	150	
Rent	1340	
Total		2560
Net income		1410

b) Prepare the statement of owner's equity from the adjusted trial balance.

Floating Speed Boat		
Statement of owner's equity		
Murray's on September 30, 2019		
Murray's capital at Sep 1		42160 → 49000 = 6900
Add: additional investment	6900	
Net income	1410	8310
Subtotal		50410
less: Murray Withdrawals		1200
Murray, Capit Sep 30		49210

c) Prepare the balance sheet from the adjusted trial balance.

Floating Speed Boat		
Balance Sheet		
Sep 30, 2019		
Assets		
cash		8800
Accounts receivable		4900
Prepaid insurance		1150
Equipment	64000	
Accumulated dep - equip m	(1260)	62740
Total Assets		80590
liabilities		
Accounts payable	9900	
Interest payable	150	
Unearned revenue	5930	
Bank loan	15400	
Total		31380
Owner's equity		
Murray, Capital		49210
total liabilities and owner's equity		80590

AP-2A LO 1

Regina Consulting has completed all its journal entries and adjusting entries for the month of October 2019. The adjusted trial balance is shown below.

Regina Consulting Adjusted Trial Balance October 31, 2019		
Account Title	**DR**	**CR**
Cash	$32,000	
Accounts Receivable	9,500	
Prepaid Rent	4,680	
Equipment	15,000	
Accumulated Depreciation—Equipment		$1,290
Accounts Payable		27,800
Unearned Revenue		4,470
Bank Loan		1,600
Regina, Capital		9,330
Service Revenue		31,330
Depreciation Expense	340	
Insurance Expense	570	
Interest Expense	150	
Rent Expense	720	
Salaries Expense	6,400	
Supplies Expense	360	
Utilities Expense	6,100	
Total	**$75,820**	**$75,820**

Required

a) Prepare the income statement from the adjusted trial balance.

b) Prepare the statement from the adjusted trial balance.

c)   Prepare the balance sheet from the adjusted trial balance.

AP-3A LO 2

Frank's Custom Framing has journalized its adjusting entries and prepared its adjusted trial balance.

Frank's Custom Framing Adjusted Trial Balance October 31, 2019		
Account Title	**DR**	**CR**
Cash	$8,620	
Accounts Receivable	2,340	
Prepaid Insurance	2,650	
Equipment	23,400	
Accumulated Depreciation—Equipment		$1,640
Accounts Payable		3,540
Interest Payable		120
Unearned Revenue		2,110
Bank Loan		5,500
Frank, Capital		24,080
Frank, Withdrawals	3,200	
Service Revenue		8,750
Depreciation Expense	260	
Insurance Expense	185	
Interest Expense	120	
Office Supplies Expense	1,840	
Rent Expense	1,200	
Salaries Expense	1,650	
Telephone Expense	275	
Total	**$45,740**	**$45,740**

Prepare the closing entries using the income summary account for October.

Date	Account Title and Explanation	PR	Debit	Credit
Oct 31	Service revenue		8750	
	Income Summary			8750
Oct 31	Income Summary		5550	
	Depreciation			260
	Insurance			185
	Interest			120
	Office supplies			1840
	Rent			1200
	Salaries			475
	Telephone			650
Oct 31	Income Summary		3220	
	Frank, Capital			3220
Oct 31	Frank, Capital		3200	
	Frank, Withdrawals			3200

AP-4A LO 2 3

Keynote Consulting has journalized its adjusting entries and prepared its adjusted trial balance.

Keynote Consulting Adjusted Trial Balance August 31, 2019		
Account Title	**DR**	**CR**
Cash	$6,200	
Accounts Receivable	1,750	
Prepaid Insurance	1,650	
Equipment	10,650	
Accumulated Depreciation—Equipment		$320
Accounts Payable		1,640
Interest Payable		50
Unearned Revenue		1,420
Bank Loan		3,000
Nichols, Capital		14,290
Nichols, Withdrawals	2,000	
Service Revenue		4,100
Depreciation Expense	150	
Insurance Expense	170	
Interest Expense	50	
Office Supplies Expense	1,150	
Rent Expense	800	
Telephone Expense	250	
Total	**$24,820**	**$24,820**

Required

a) Prepare the closing entries using the income summary account for August.

Date	Account Title and Explanation	PR	Debit	Credit

b)   Prepare the post-closing trial balance.

AP-5A LO 2 3

Home Protector has journalized its adjusting entries and prepared its adjusted trial balance.

Home Protector Adjusted Trial Balance December 31, 2019		
Account Title	**DR**	**CR**
Cash	$12,650	
Accounts Receivable	5,420	
Prepaid Insurance	2,820	
Equipment	25,600	
Accumulated Depreciation—Equipment		$2,340
Accounts Payable		6,250
Salaries Payable		650
Unearned Revenue		4,250
Bank Loan		7,500
Holmes, Capital		21,645
Holmes, Withdrawals	4,300	
Service Revenue		16,875
Depreciation Expense	320	
Insurance Expense	220	
Interest Expense	160	
Office Supplies Expense	2,240	
Rent Expense	1,890	
Salaries Expense	3,540	
Telephone Expense	350	
Total	**$59,510**	**$59,510**

Required

a) Prepare the closing entries directly to owner's capital for the month of December.

Date	Account Title and Explanation	PR	Debit	Credit
Dec 31	Service Revenue		16875	
	Holmes, Capital			16875
	Close revenue			
Dec 31	Capital, Holmes		8720	
	Depreciation expense			320
	Insurance expense			220
	Interest expense			160
	Office supplies Expense			2240
	Rent expense			1890
	Telephone			350
	Salaries			3540
Dec, 31	Holmes, Capi	.	4300	
	Holmes withdrawals			4300

b) Prepare the post-closing trial balance.

AP-6A LO 2 3

Luminary Electric has journalized its adjusting entries and prepared its adjusted trial balance.

Luminary Electric Adjusted Trial Balance March 31, 2019		
Account Title	**DR**	**CR**
Cash	$10,420	
Accounts Receivable	6,350	
Prepaid Insurance	2,350	
Equipment	32,500	
Accumulated Depreciation—Equipment		$5,480
Accounts Payable		4,870
Salaries Payable		840
Unearned Revenue		5,340
Bank Loan		9,000
Watts, Capital		23,745
Watts, Withdrawals	5,200	
Service Revenue		17,850
Depreciation Expense	410	
Insurance Expense	195	
Interest Expense	210	
Office Supplies Expense	2,530	
Rent Expense	2,150	
Salaries Expense	4,360	
Telephone Expense	450	
Total	**$67,125**	**$67,125**

Required

a) Prepare the closing entries directly to owner's capital for the month of March.

Date	Account Title and Explanation	PR	Debit	Credit

b)   Prepare the post-closing trial balance.

AP-7A LO 1 2 3

Thomas Topology has completed all its journal entries and adjusting entries for the month of April 2019. The chart of accounts and adjusted trial balance are shown below.

Account Description	Account #
ASSETS	
Cash	101
Accounts Receivable	105
Prepaid Insurance	110
Equipment	120
Accumulated Depreciation—Equipment	125
LIABILITIES	
Accounts Payable	200
Unearned Revenue	210
Bank Loan	215
OWNER'S EQUITY	
Edwards, Capital	300
Edwards, Withdrawals	310
Income Summary	315

Account Description	Account #
REVENUE	
Service Revenue	400
EXPENSES	
Depreciation Expense	510
Insurance Expense	515
Interest Expense	520
Rent Expense	540
Salaries Expense	545
Telephone Expense	550
Travel Expense	555

Thomas Topology Adjusted Trial Balance April 30, 2019		
Account Title	**DR**	**CR**
Cash	$32,050	
Accounts Receivable	9,000	
Prepaid Insurance	1,100	
Equipment	15,000	
Accumulated Depreciation—Equipment		$120
Accounts Payable		25,550
Unearned Revenue		3,200
Bank Loan		1,500
Edwards, Capital		18,000
Service Revenue		26,300
Depreciation Expense	120	
Insurance Expense	100	
Interest Expense	50	
Rent Expense	1,000	
Salaries Expense	8,000	
Telephone Expense	250	
Travel Expense	8,000	
Total	**$74,670**	**$74,670**

Required

a) Prepare the income statement for Thomas Topology.

b) Prepare the statement of owner's equity for Thomas Topology.

c) Prepare the balance sheet for Thomas Topology.

d) Create the closing entries using the income summary account and post the closing entries to the ledger accounts on the following pages.

Date	Account Title and Explanation	PR	Debit	Credit

e) Prepare the post-closing trial balance. Note: The daily transactions and adjustments for the month of April have already been posted in the general ledger. You are only responsible for posting the closing entries.

GENERAL LEDGER

Account: Cash — **GL No: 101**

Date	Description	PR	DR	CR	Balance	
2019						
Apr 1	Opening Balance				22,000	DR
Apr 2		J1	25,000		47,000	DR
Apr 3		J1		1,000	46,000	DR
Apr 4		J1		1,200	44,800	DR
Apr 10		J1		200	44,600	DR
Apr 14		J1		8,000	36,600	DR
Apr 20		J1		50	36,550	DR
Apr 30		J1		4,500	32,050	DR

Account: Accounts Receivable — **GL No: 105**

Date	Description	PR	DR	CR	Balance	
2019						
Apr 1	Opening Balance				9,000	DR

Account: Prepaid Insurance — **GL No: 110**

Date	Description	PR	DR	CR	Balance	
2019						
Apr 1	Opening Balance				0	DR
Apr 4		J1	1,200		1,200	DR
Apr 30	Adjustment	J2		100	1,100	DR

Account: Equipment — **GL No: 120**

Date	Description	PR	DR	CR	Balance	
2019						
Apr 1	Opening Balance				8,000	DR
Apr 1		J1	7,000		15,000	DR

Account: Accumulated Depreciation—Equipment — **GL No: 125**

Date	Description	PR	DR	CR	Balance	
2019						
Apr 30	Adjustment	J2		120	120	CR

Account: Accounts Payable — **GL No: 200**

Date	Description	PR	DR	CR	Balance	
2019						
Apr 1	Opening Balance				10,500	CR
Apr 1		J1		7,000	17,500	CR
Apr 10		J1	200		17,300	CR
Apr 22		J1		250	17,550	CR
Apr 24		J1		8,000	25,550	CR

Account: Unearned Revenue — **GL No: 210**

Date	Description	PR	DR	CR	Balance	
2019						
Apr 1	Opening Balance				4,500	CR
Apr 30	Adjustment	J2	1,300		3,200	CR

Account: Bank Loan — **GL No: 215**

Date	Description	PR	DR	CR	Balance	
2019						
Apr 1	Opening Balance				6,000	CR
Apr 30		J1	4,500		1,500	CR

Account: Edwards, Capital — **GL No: 300**

Date	Description	PR	DR	CR	Balance	
2019						
Apr 1	Opening Balance				18,000	CR

Account: Edwards, Withdrawals — **GL No: 310**

Date	Description	PR	DR	CR	Balance	

Account: Income Summary — **GL No: 315**

Date	Description	PR	DR	CR	Balance	

Account: Service Revenue — **GL No: 400**

Date	Description	PR	DR	CR	Balance	
2019						
Apr 2		J1		25,000	25,000	CR
Apr 30	Adjustment	J2		1,300	26,300	CR

Account: Depreciation Expense — **GL No: 510**

Date	Description	PR	DR	CR	Balance	
2019						
Apr 30	Adjustment	J2	120		120	DR

Account: Insurance Expense — **GL No: 515**

Date	Description	PR	DR	CR	Balance	
2019						
Apr 30	Adjustment	J2	100		100	DR

Account: Interest Expense					GL No: 520	
Date	Description	PR	DR	CR	Balance	
2019						
Apr 20		J1	50		50	DR

Account: Rent Expense					GL No: 540	
Date	Description	PR	DR	CR	Balance	
2019						
Apr 3		J1	1,000		1,000	DR

Account: Salaries Expense					GL No: 545	
Date	Description	PR	DR	CR	Balance	
2019						
Apr 14		J1	8,000		8,000	DR

Account: Telephone Expense					GL No: 550	
Date	Description	PR	DR	CR	Balance	
2019						
Apr 22		J1	250		250	DR

Account: Travel Expense					GL No: 555	
Date	Description	PR	DR	CR	Balance	
2019						
Apr 24		J1	8,000		8,000	DR

AP-8A LO 1 2 3

Limbo Lower has completed all its journal entries and adjusting entries for the month of September 2019. The chart of accounts and adjusted trial balance are shown below.

Account Description	Account #
ASSETS	
Cash	101
Accounts Receivable	105
Prepaid Insurance	110
Equipment	120
Accumulated Depreciation—Equipment	125

Account Description	Account #
LIABILITIES	
Accounts Payable	200
Unearned Revenue	210
Bank Loan	215

Account Description	Account #
OWNER'S EQUITY	
Patel, Capital	300
Patel, Withdrawals	310
Income Summary	315

Account Description	Account #
REVENUE	
Service Revenue	400

Account Description	Account #
EXPENSES	
Depreciation Expense	510
Insurance Expense	515
Interest Expense	520
Office Supplies Expense	530
Rent Expense	540

Limbo Lower Adjusted Trial Balance September 30, 2019		
Account Title	**DR**	**CR**
Cash	$6,450	
Accounts Receivable	1,450	
Prepaid Insurance	1,650	
Equipment	9,300	
Accumulated Depreciation—Equipment		$120
Accounts Payable		3,050
Unearned Revenue		1,040
Bank Loan		4,640
Patel, Capital		11,450
Patel, Withdrawals	1,600	
Service Revenue		2,260
Depreciation Expense	120	
Insurance Expense	150	
Interest Expense	40	
Office Supplies Expense	450	
Rent Expense	1,350	
Total	**$22,560**	**$22,560**

Note: The daily transactions and adjustments for the month of September have already been posted in the general ledger. You are only responsible for posting the closing entries.

Required

a) Prepare the income statement.

b) Prepare the statement of owner's equity.

c)   Prepare the balance sheet.

d)   Create the closing entries using the income summary account and post the closing entries to the ledger accounts on the following pages.

Date	Account Title and Explanation	PR	Debit	Credit

e)   Prepare the post-closing trial balance.

GENERAL LEDGER

Account: Cash GL No: 101

Date	Description	PR	DR	CR	Balance	
2019						
Sep 1	Opening Balance				7,850	DR
Sep 1		J1		1,800	6,050	DR
Sep 2		J1	1,900		7,950	DR
Sep 3		J1		1,350	6,600	DR
Sep 10		J1		40	6,560	DR
Sep 10		J1		960	5,600	DR
Sep 20		J1	2,200		7,800	DR
Sep 22		J1	850		8,650	DR
Sep 24		J1		600	8,050	DR
Sep 30		J1		1,600	6,450	DR

Account: Accounts Receivable GL No: 105

Date	Description	PR	DR	CR	Balance	
2019						
Sep 1	Opening Balance				2,300	DR
Sep 22		J1		850	1,450	DR

Account: Prepaid Insurance GL No: 110

Date	Description	PR	DR	CR	Balance	
2019						
Sep 1	Opening Balance				0	DR
Sep 1		J1	1,800		1,800	DR
Sep 30	Adjustment	J2		150	1,650	DR

Account: Equipment GL No: 120

Date	Description	PR	DR	CR	Balance	
2019						
Sep 1	Opening Balance				11,500	DR
Sep 20		J1		2,200	9,300	DR

Account: Accumulated Depreciation—Equipment					GL No: 125	
Date	**Description**	**PR**	**DR**	**CR**	**Balance**	
2019						
Sep 30	Adjustment	J2		120	120	CR

Account: Accounts Payable					GL No: 200	
Date	**Description**	**PR**	**DR**	**CR**	**Balance**	
2019						
Sep 1	Opening Balance				3,400	CR
Sep 4		J1		250	3,650	CR
Sep 24		J1	600		3,050	CR

Account: Unearned Revenue					GL No: 210	
Date	**Description**	**PR**	**DR**	**CR**	**Balance**	
2019						
Sep 1	Opening Balance				1,400	CR
Sep 30	Adjustment	J2	360		1,040	CR

Account: Bank Loan					GL No: 215	
Date	**Description**	**PR**	**DR**	**CR**	**Balance**	
2019						
Sep 1	Opening Balance				5,600	CR
Sep 10		J1	960		4,640	CR

Account: Patel, Capital					GL No: 300	
Date	**Description**	**PR**	**DR**	**CR**	**Balance**	
2019						
Sep 1	Opening Balance				11,450	CR

Account: Patel, Withdrawals					GL No: 310	
Date	**Description**	**PR**	**DR**	**CR**	**Balance**	
2019						
Sep 30		J1	1,600		1,600	DR

Account: Income Summary					GL No: 315	
Date	**Description**	**PR**	**DR**	**CR**	**Balance**	

Account: Service Revenue					GL No: 400	
Date	**Description**	**PR**	**DR**	**CR**	**Balance**	
2019						
Sep 2		J1		1,900	1,900	CR
Sep 30	Adjustment	J2		360	2,260	CR

Account: Depreciation Expense					GL No: 510	
Date	Description	PR	DR	CR	Balance	
2019						
Sep 30	Adjustment	J2	120		120	DR

Account: Insurance Expense					GL No: 515	
Date	Description	PR	DR	CR	Balance	
2019						
Sep 30	Adjustment	J2	150		150	DR

Account: Interest Expense					GL No: 520	
Date	Description	PR	DR	CR	Balance	
2019						
Sep 10		J1	40		40	DR

Account: Office Supplies Expense					GL No: 530	
Date	Description	PR	DR	CR	Balance	
2019						
Sep 30	Adjustment	J2	450		450	DR

Account: Rent Expense					GL No: 540	
Date	Description	PR	DR	CR	Balance	
2019						
Sep 3		J1	1,350		1,350	DR

AP-9A LO 4

The following information is taken from the records of Ginger Consulting.

Accounts Payable	$19,000
Short-Term Investment	12,000
Land	52,000
Cash	23,000
Factory Equipment	29,000
Bank Loan	30,000
Office Furniture	18,000
Prepaid Expense	9,000
Unearned Revenue	6,000

Required

a) Calculate total current assets.

_____

_____

_____

_____

b) Calculate total long-term assets.

_____

_____

_____

_____

c) Calculate total assets.

_____

_____

_____

_____

AP-10A [LO 4]

Suppose a business receives a $400,000 long-term bank loan on December 31, 2019. The borrowing arrangement requires the business to pay $100,000 of this debt by September 2020. Show how the business will report both current and long-term liabilities on its December 31, 2019, balance sheet.

_____

_____

_____

_____

_____

_____

AP-11A [LO 4]

Pelican Accounting took out a $1,000,000 interest-free bank loan on January 1, 2019. Payment will be made over four years in four equal annual installments. Calculate the current and long-term liabilities as at December 31 for the following years.

	As at December 31			
	2019	2020	2021	2022
Bank Loan, Current Portion				
Bank Loan, Long-Term Portion				

AP-12A [LO 4]

Renegade Landscaping's general ledger includes the following account balances on December 31, 2019.

Accounts Payable	$12,000
Interest Payable	3,000
Salaries Payable	2,000
Bank Loan	
Current Portion	10,000
Long-Term Portion	20,000

Required

a) Calculate current liabilities.

_____

_____

_____

_____

_____

b) Calculate long-term liabilities.

AP-13A LO 4

For the following independent transactions, determine the amount of current and long-term liabilities.

Transaction	Current Liability	Long-Term Liability
1. On December 31, 2019, Frankie Flowershop borrowed $300,000 from the bank. The entire amount is due on December 30, 2020.		
2. KLM Company purchased a small building at a cost of $190,000. The down payment is $100,000. The remaining balance is payable in three years with an annual payment of $30,000, starting next year.		
3. During June 2019, a business owner obtained an interest-free loan from a financing company. The loan amount was $60,000. The agreed terms of payment are four annual installments of $15,000.		
4. A business owner borrowed $20,000 from his close friend for a business expansion. They both signed an agreement that the full payment will be made after two years.		

AP-14A LO 4 5

Empowered Solutions has the following balances as at May 31, 2019.

Cash	$22,000
Accounts Receivable	15,000
Merchandise Inventory	12,000
Equipment	73,000
Accounts Payable	13,000
Unearned Revenue	8,000
Bank Loan, Current Portion	10,000
Bank Loan, Long-Term Portion	20,000
Powers, Capital	71,000

Required

a) Prepare a classified balance sheet using the balances listed.

b) Calculate the working capital for Empowered Solutions.

c) Calculate the current ratio for Empowered Solutions.

d) Calculate the quick ratio for Empowered Solutions.

AP-15A LO 4 5

Preston Services' financial accounting information for the year ending September 30, 2019, is presented below. Assume all accounts have a normal balance.

Cash	$7,500
Accounts Receivable	2,400
Merchandise Inventory	6,000
Prepaid Insurance	1,800
Equipment	35,000
Accumulated Depreciation—Equipment	800
Accounts Payable	5,100
Unearned Revenue	1,100
Bank Loan	18,000
Presto, Capital	27,700

The bank loan is payable over three years and $6,000 will be paid by September 30, 2020.

Required

a) Prepare a classified balance sheet.

b) Calculate the working capital for Preston Services.

Working capital = Current assets − current liabilities   17 700 − 12 200 = 5500

c) Calculate the current ratio for Preston Services.

Current ratio = $\dfrac{current\ assets}{current\ liab}$ = $\dfrac{17\ 700}{12\ 200}$ = 1.45

d) Calculate the quick ratio for Preston Services.

$\dfrac{Cash + ST\ investment + A/R}{current\ liabilities}$ = $\dfrac{7500 + 0 + 2400}{12\ 200}$ = 0.81

AP-16A LO 4

An alphabetical list of the adjusted trial balance of Sally Shill's Bookkeeping Services at September 30, 2019, after its first month of operations, is presented below. The capital balance represents investments made by Sally personally to the business during the month. Assume all amounts have a normal balance.

Accounts Payable	13,500
Accounts Receivable	20,650
Accumulated Depreciation—Furniture	1,500
Cash	21,000
Depreciation Expense—Furniture	350
Furniture	17,000
Insurance Expense	2,625
Interest Expense	50
Interest Income	350
Prepaid Insurance	1,050
Sally Shill, Capital	38,767
Sally Shill, Withdrawals	5,350
Service Revenue	73,000
Unearned Revenue	9,800
Wages Expense	69,850
Wages Payable	1,008

Prepare a classified balance sheet.

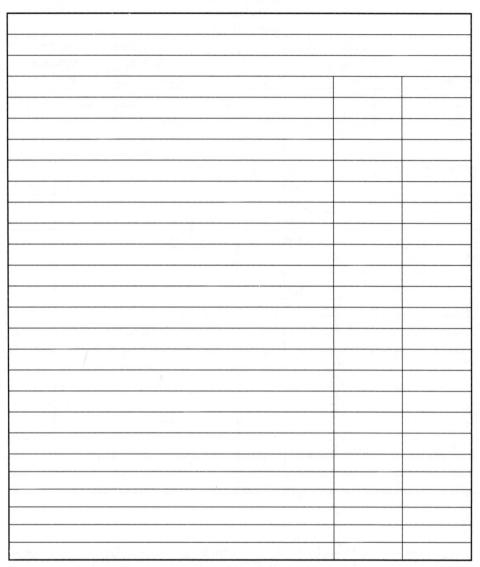

AP-17A LO 7

Coleson Services' unadjusted trial balance at the end of December 2019 is presented below. Adjusting entries have not yet been made. Use the trial balance and the information below to complete the worksheet.

Dec 31   Services were provided worth $480, to be paid for next month.

Dec 31   The equipment was purchased at the beginning of the year and is expected to last four years with no residual value.

Dec 31   Of the balance of unearned revenue, $600 has been earned.

Dec 31   The amount in prepaid insurance is for an annual policy that was paid on September 1, 2019.

	Unadjusted Trial Balance		Adjustments		Adjusted Trial Balance		Income Statement		Balance Sheet	
Account Title	DR	CR	DR	CR	DR	CR	DR	CR	DR	CR
Cash	$1,500									
Accounts Receivable	3,800									
Prepaid Insurance	1,800									
Equipment	6,000									
Accumulated Depreciation—Equipment		$0								
Accounts Payable		4,000								
Unearned Revenue		1,000								
Bank Loan		2,500								
Coleson, Capital		2,850								
Coleson, Withdrawals	1,200									
Service Revenue		8,000								
Depreciation Expense	0									
Insurance Expense	0									
Interest Expense	0									
Maintenance Expense	900									
Rent Expense	1,900									
Salaries Expense	150									
Telephone Expense	700									
Travel Expense	400									
Total	$18,350	$18,350								
Net Income										
Total										

Coleson Services
Worksheet
December 31, 2019

AP-18A LO 7

The August 31, 2019, unadjusted trial balance for Fraser Consulting, after the first month of operations, is shown below. Adjusting entries have not yet been made. Use the trial balance and the information below for the month of September to complete the 10-column worksheet.

- It was determined that $1,500 of the prepaid rent had been used during August.

- Depreciation on the automobile for the month of August was $1000.

- Salaries of $1,200 had been incurred but not yet paid.

- $1,500 of the unearned revenue was earned during the month.

- Interest of $600 on the bank loan had been incurred but had not been paid.

	Fraser Consulting									
	Worksheet									
	September 30, 2019									
	Unadjusted Trial Balance		Adjustments		Adjusted Trial Balance		Income Statement		Balance Sheet	
Account	DR	CR	DR	CR	DR	CR	DR	CR	DR	CR
Cash	$7,500									
Accounts Receivable	24,000									
Prepaid Rent	6,000									
Automobile	60,000									
Accumulated Depreciation—Automobile		0								
Accounts payable		$5,000								
Interest Payable		0								
Salaries Payable		0								
Unearned Revenue		8,000								
Bank Loan		15,000								
Fraser, Capital		45,000								
Fraser, Withdrawals	5,000									
Consulting Service Revenue		36,000								
Depreciation Expense—Automobile	0									
Equipment Rental Expense	3,000									
Interest Expense	500									
Rent Expense	2,000									
Salaries Expense	$1,000									
Total	$109,000	$109,000								
Net Income										
Total										

AP-19A LO 2 3

Tyler's Dry Cleaning showed the following trial balance at the end of the year. The trial balance was created after the posting of the closing entries on December 31, 2019.

Tyler's Dry Cleaning Trial Balance December 31, 2019		
Account Title	DR	CR
Cash	$13,200	
Accounts Receivable	1,200	
Prepaid Rent	600	
Equipment	32,000	
Accumulated Depreciation—Equipment		$6,400
Building	75,000	
Accumulated Depreciation—Building		3,000
Accounts Payable		2,200
Tyler Johnson, Capital		133,000
Advertising Expense	1,600	
Wage Expense	21,000	
Total	$144,600	$144,600

Required

a) List the error(s) in the above post-closing trial balance.

_____

_____

b) What entry should be made to correct the error(s) at year end? Assume Tyler's Dry Cleaning uses the direct method for closing accounts.

Date	Account Title and Explanation	PR	Debit	Credit

Application Questions Group B

AP-1B LO 1

Below is Caprio Services' adjusted trial balance for the year ending December 31, 2019. Note that during the year, the owner contributed $20,000 to the business. This is already included in Caprio, Capital.

Caprio Services Adjusted Trial Balance December 31, 2019		
Account Title	**DR**	**CR**
Cash	$90,200	
Accounts Receivable	47,800	
Prepaid Insurance	32,000	
Equipment	415,000	
Accumulated Depreciation—Equipment		$145,000
Accounts Payable		26,000
Unearned Revenue		15,800
Bank Loan		260,000
Caprio, Capital		108,200
Caprio, Withdrawals	40,000	
Service Revenue		545,000
Advertising Expense	100,000	
Insurance Expense	40,000	
Maintenance Expense	5,900	
Rent Expense	78,000	
Salaries Expense	228,500	
Telephone Expense	3,200	
Travel Expense	19,400	
Total	**$1,100,000**	**$1,100,000**

a) Using the information provided, prepare the income statement for the year ended December 31, 2019.

b) Prepare the statement of owner's equity for the year ended December 31, 2019.

c)   Prepare the balance sheet as at December 31, 2019.

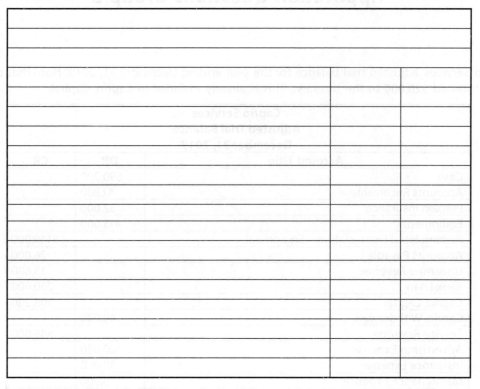

Analysis

In the accounting cycle, why is the income statement prepared first, then the statement of owner's equity, and finally the balance sheet?

_____

_____

_____

_____

AP-2B LO 1

Counterpoint Studios has completed all the entries for the fiscal year ending November 30, 2019, except the month of November's adjusting entries. The following information is available to make the adjustments.

- Annual depreciation on equipment totals $9,000.

- Interest accrued on the bank loan is $500.

- Unbilled services for the month were $8,100.

- The annual insurance policy was purchased December 1, 2018, for $21,900.

- The balance of owner's equity at the beginning of the year was $86,750.

Required

a) Complete the six-column worksheet for Counterpoint Studios.

Account Title	Unadjusted Trial Balance		Adjustments		Adjusted Trial Balance	
	DR	CR	DR	CR	DR	CR
Cash	$52,250					
Accounts Receivable	24,800					
Prepaid Insurance	1,825					
Equipment	305,800					
Accumulated Depreciation—Equipment		$107,250				
Accounts Payable		31,500				
Bank Loan		140,000				
Wu, Capital		96,750				
Wu, Withdrawals	60,000					
Service Revenue		382,500				
Advertising Expense	100,000					
Salaries Expense	185,000					
Insurance Expense	20,075					
Depreciation Expense	8,250					
Total	$758,000	$758,000				

b) Prepare the income statement for the year ended November 30, 2019.

c) Prepare the statement of owner's equity for the year ended November 30, 2019.

d) Prepare the balance sheet as at November 30, 2019.

AP-3B LO 2

Portal Delivery Services has prepared its income statement and statement of owner's equity.

Portal Delivery Services Income Statement For the Year Ended October 31, 2019		
Service Revenue		$500,000
Expenses		
Transportation Expense	$95,000	
Salaries Expense	240,000	
Maintenance Expense	70,000	
Depreciation Expense	45,000	
Total Expenses		450,000
Net Income (Loss)		$50,000

Portal Delivery Services Statement of Owner's Equity For the Year Ended October 31, 2019		
Jones, Capital at November 1, 2018		$120,000
Add:		
Additional Investments	$30,000	
Net Income (Loss)	50,000	80,000
Subtotal		200,000
Less:		
Jones, Withdrawals		100,000
Jones, Capital at October 31, 2019		$100,000

Prepare the closing entries using the income summary method for Portal Delivery Services.

Date	Account Title and Explanation	PR	Debit	Credit

Analysis

What is the purpose of preparing closing entries at the end of each period? Explain.

_____
_____
_____
_____
_____
_____
_____
_____
_____
_____
_____
_____
_____
_____
_____
_____

AP-4B LO 2 3

Jim's Custom Painting has journalized its adjusting entries and prepared its adjusted trial balance.

Jim's Custom Painting Adjusted Trial Balance August 31, 2019		
Account Title	DR	CR
Cash	$8,400	
Accounts Receivable	5,300	
Prepaid Rent	2,100	
Equipment	20,700	
Accumulated Depreciation—Equipment		$2,700
Accounts Payable		3,200
Interest Payable		300
Unearned Revenue		2,900
Mortgage Payable		5,400
Gordon, Capital		22,360
Gordon, Withdrawals	4,000	
Service Revenue		7,600
Depreciation Expense	150	
Insurance Expense	240	
Interest Expense	300	
Rent Expense	1,420	
Supplies Expense	350	
Travel Expense	1,500	
Total	$44,460	$44,460

Required

a) Prepare the closing entries using the income summary account for August.

Date	Account Title and Explanation	PR	Debit	Credit

b)   Prepare the post-closing trial balance.

AP-5B LO 2 3

Home Protector has journalized its adjusting entries and prepared its adjusted trial balance.

Home Protector Adjusted Trial Balance January 31, 2019		
Account Title	**DR**	**CR**
Cash	$14,200	
Accounts Receivable	6,900	
Prepaid Services	6,000	
Equipment	37,700	
Accumulated Depreciation—Equipment		$5,700
Accounts Payable		4,800
Salaries Payable		950
Unearned Revenue		4,800
Mortgage Payable		8,800
Sherlock, Capital		32,750
Sherlock, Withdrawals	4,900	
Service Revenue		18,200
Depreciation Expense	350	
Insurance Expense	290	
Maintenance Expense	470	
Rent Expense	1,500	
Telephone Expense	490	
Utilities Expense	3,200	
Total	**$76,000**	**$76,000**

Required

a) Prepare the closing entries directly to owner's capital for the month of January.

Date	Account Title and Explanation	PR	Debit	Credit

b) Prepare the post-closing trial balance.

AP-6B LO 2 3

Health Foods has journalized its adjusting entries and prepared its adjusted trial balance.

Health Foods Adjusted Trial Balance May 31, 2019		
Account Title	**DR**	**CR**
Cash	$14,800	
Accounts Receivable	7,600	
Prepaid Rent	5,600	
Equipment	39,300	
Accumulated Depreciation—Equipment		$5,200
Accounts Payable		4,200
Salaries Payable		980
Unearned Revenue		4,800
Mortgage Payable		11,000
Schmitt, Capital		34,820
Schmitt, Withdrawals	4,400	
Service Revenue		17,000
Depreciation Expense	140	
Insurance Expense	140	
Maintenance Expense	160	
Office Supplies Expense	880	
Rent Expense	1,400	
Telephone Expense	280	
Utilities Expense	3,300	
Total	**$78,000**	**$78,000**

Required

a) Prepare the closing entries directly to owner's capital for the month of May.

Date	Account Title and Explanation	PR	Debit	Credit

b)   Prepare the post-closing trial balance.

AP-7B LO 1 2 3

High Flying Biplane has completed all its journal entries and adjusting entries for the month of June 2019. The chart of accounts and adjusted trial balance are shown below.

Account Description	Account #
ASSETS	
Cash	101
Accounts Receivable	105
Prepaid Insurance	110
Equipment	120
Accumulated Depreciation—Equipment	125
LIABILITIES	
Accounts Payable	200
Interest Payable	205
Unearned Revenue	210
Bank Loan	215
OWNER'S EQUITY	
Singh, Capital	300
Singh, Withdrawals	310
Income Summary	315

Account Description	Account #
REVENUE	
Service Revenue	400
EXPENSES	
Advertising Expense	500
Depreciation Expense	510
Insurance Expense	515
Interest Expense	520
Telephone Expense	550

High Flying Biplane Adjusted Trial Balance June 30, 2019		
Account Title	**DR**	**CR**
Cash	$8,800	
Accounts Receivable	6,800	
Prepaid Insurance	1,100	
Equipment	64,000	
Accumulated Depreciation—Equipment		$450
Accounts Payable		7,700
Interest Payable		75
Unearned Revenue		4,080
Bank Loan		19,000
Singh, Capital		48,800
Singh, Withdrawals	1,200	
Service Revenue		3,020
Advertising Expense	400	
Depreciation Expense	450	
Insurance Expense	100	
Interest Expense	75	
Telephone Expense	200	
Total	**$83,125**	**$83,125**

Note: The daily transactions and adjustments for the month of June have already been posted in the general ledger. You are only responsible for posting the closing entries. Included in the capital account is a $5,000 investment by the owner during the month.

Required

a) Prepare the income statement.

b)   Prepare the statement of owner's equity.

c)   Prepare the balance sheet.

d)   Create the closing entries using the income summary account and post the closing entries to the ledger accounts on the following pages.

Date	Account Title and Explanation	PR	Debit	Credit

Date	Account Title and Explanation	PR	Debit	Credit

e)   Prepare the post-closing trial balance.

GENERAL LEDGER

Account: Cash					GL No: 101	
Date	**Description**	**PR**	**DR**	**CR**	**Balance**	
2019						
Jun 1	Opening Balance				8,000	DR
Jun 1		J1	5,000		13,000	DR
Jun 2		J1	1,500		14,500	DR
Jun 4		J1		200	14,300	DR
Jun 14		J1		4,000	10,300	DR
Jun 20		J1	1,600		11,900	DR
Jun 22		J1		900	11,000	DR
Jun 24		J1		1,000	10,000	DR
Jun 30		J1		1,200	8,800	DR

Account: Accounts Receivable					GL No: 105	
Date	**Description**	**PR**	**DR**	**CR**	**Balance**	
2019						
Jun 1	Opening Balance				6,000	DR
Jun 10		J1	2,400		8,400	DR
Jun 20		J1		1,600	6,800	DR

Account: Prepaid Insurance   **GL No: 110**

Date	Description	PR	DR	CR	Balance	
2019						
Jun 1	Opening Balance				1,200	DR
Jun 30	Adjustment	J2		100	1,100	DR

Account: Equipment   **GL No: 120**

Date	Description	PR	DR	CR	Balance	
2019						
Jun 1	Opening Balance				60,000	DR
Jun 14		J1	4,000		64,000	DR

Account: Accumulated Depreciation—Equipment   **GL No: 125**

Date	Description	PR	DR	CR	Balance	
2019						
Jun 30	Adjustment	J2		450	450	CR

Account: Accounts Payable   **GL No: 200**

Date	Description	PR	DR	CR	Balance	
2019						
Jun 1	Opening Balance				8,200	CR
Jun 3		J1		400	8,600	CR
Jun 22		J1	900		7,700	CR

Account: Interest Payable   **GL No: 205**

Date	Description	PR	DR	CR	Balance	
2019						
Jun 30	Adjustment	J2		75	75	CR

Account: Unearned Revenue   **GL No: 210**

Date	Description	PR	DR	CR	Balance	
2019						
Jun 1	Opening Balance				3,200	CR
Jun 2		J1		1,500	4,700	CR
Jun 30	Adjustment	J2	620		4,080	CR

Account: Bank Loan   **GL No: 215**

Date	Description	PR	DR	CR	Balance	
2019						
Jun 1	Opening Balance				20,000	CR
Jun 24		J1	1,000		19,000	CR

Account: Singh, Capital   **GL No: 300**

Date	Description	PR	DR	CR	Balance	
2019						
Jun 1	Opening Balance				43,800	CR
Jun 1		J1		5,000	48,800	CR

Account: Singh, Withdrawals | | | | | **GL No: 310**

Date	Description	PR	DR	CR	Balance	
2019						
Jun 30		J1	1,200		1,200	DR

Account: Income Summary | | | | | **GL No: 315**

Date	Description	PR	DR	CR	Balance	

Account: Service Revenue | | | | | **GL No: 400**

Date	Description	PR	DR	CR	Balance	
2019						
Jun 10		J1		2,400	2,400	CR
Jun 30	Adjustment	J2		620	3,020	CR

Account: Advertising Expense | | | | | **GL No: 500**

Date	Description	PR	DR	CR	Balance	
2019						
Jun 3		J1	400		400	DR

Account: Depreciation Expense | | | | | **GL No: 510**

Date	Description	PR	DR	CR	Balance	
2019						
Jun 30	Adjustment	J2	450		450	DR

Account: Insurance Expense | | | | | **GL No: 515**

Date	Description	PR	DR	CR	Balance	
2019						
Jun 30	Adjustment	J2	100		100	DR

Account: Interest Expense | | | | | **GL No: 520**

Date	Description	PR	DR	CR	Balance	
2019						
Jun 30	Adjustment	J2	75		75	DR

Account: Telephone Expense					GL No: 550	
Date	Description	PR	DR	CR	Balance	
2019						
Jun 4		J1	200		200	DR

AP-8B LO 1 2 3

Space Jam Storage offers storage space and delivery services for customers. Space Jam Storage has already completed most of the transactions for the month and posted them to the general ledger. The following transactions during December 2019 have not yet been prepared.

Dec 2   Prepaid $12,000 for one year of insurance in advance

Dec 5   Paid $1,400 cash for regular maintenance on delivery vehicles

Dec 12   The owner, Stephen Bugs, withdrew $3,500 cash from the business for personal use

Dec 18   Received $2,200 cash payment from a customer for future storage services

Dec 23   Paid $1,000 to reduce the bank loan, of which $870 was principal and the rest was interest

Dec 28   Received $450 cash from a customer who owed money for previous services

Required

a) Prepare the journal entries for the transactions for the month of December. The chart of accounts is on the next page.

Date	Account Title and Explanation	PR	Debit	Credit

b) Post the journal entries from part a) to the general ledger. The chart of accounts is shown below for your reference.

Account Description	Account #
ASSETS	
Cash	101
Accounts Receivable	105
Prepaid Insurance	110
Equipment	120
Accumulated Depreciation—Equipment	125
LIABILITIES	
Accounts Payable	200
Salaries Payable	210
Unearned Revenue	220
Bank Loan	250

Account Description	Account #
OWNER'S EQUITY	
Bugs, Capital	300
Bugs, Withdrawals	310
Income Summary	315
REVENUE	
Service Revenue	400
EXPENSES	
Maintenance Expense	500
Depreciation Expense	520
Interest Expense	540
Insurance Expense	560
Salaries Expense	570

GENERAL LEDGER

Account: Cash					GL No: 101	
Date	Description	PR	DR	CR	Balance	
2019	Opening Balance				18,500	DR

Account: Accounts Receivable					GL No: 105	
Date	Description	PR	DR	CR	Balance	
2019	Opening Balance				3,200	DR

Account: Prepaid Insurance					GL No: 110	
Date	Description	PR	DR	CR	Balance	
2019	Opening Balance				1,000	DR

Account: Equipment					GL No: 120	
Date	Description	PR	DR	CR	Balance	
2019	Opening Balance				285,000	DR

Account: Accumulated Depreciation—Equipment					GL No: 125	
Date	Description	PR	DR	CR	Balance	
2019	Opening Balance				45,000	CR

Account: Accounts Payable					GL No: 200	
Date	Description	PR	DR	CR	Balance	
2019	Opening Balance				5,500	CR

Account: Salaries Payable   **GL No: 210**

Date	Description	PR	DR	CR	Balance	
2019	Opening Balance				0	CR

Account: Unearned Revenue   **GL No: 220**

Date	Description	PR	DR	CR	Balance	
2019	Opening Balance				1,400	CR

Account: Bank Loan   **GL No: 250**

Date	Description	PR	DR	CR	Balance	
2019	Opening Balance				192,550	CR

Account: Bugs, Capital   **GL No: 300**

Date	Description	PR	DR	CR	Balance	
2019	Opening Balance				46,200	CR

Account: Bugs, Withdrawals   **GL No: 310**

Date	Description	PR	DR	CR	Balance	
2019	Opening Balance				10,000	DR

Account: Income Summary   **GL No: 315**

Date	Description	PR	DR	CR	Balance	
2019	Opening Balance				0	CR

Account: Service Revenue   **GL No: 400**

Date	Description	PR	DR	CR	Balance	
2019	Opening Balance				78,000	CR

Account: Maintenance Expense   **GL No: 500**

Date	Description	PR	DR	CR	Balance	
2019	Opening Balance				3,800	DR

Account: Depreciation Expense   **GL No: 520**

Date	Description	PR	DR	CR	Balance	
2019	Opening Balance				4,000	DR

Account: Interest Expense						GL No: 540	
Date	Description	PR	DR	CR	Balance	
2019	Opening Balance				1,150	DR

Account: Insurance Expense						GL No: 560	
Date	Description	PR	DR	CR	Balance	
2019	Opening Balance				11,000	DR

Account: Salaries Expense						GL No: 570	
Date	Description	PR	DR	CR	Balance	
2019	Opening Balance				31,000	DR

c) Prepare a six-column worksheet, starting with the account balances from the general ledger in part b). Space Jam Storage had the following year-end adjustments.

Dec 31   Provided $1,500 worth of services to customer who had previously paid in advance

Dec 31   One month of insurance worth $1,000 has been used

Dec 31   One month of depreciation is $500

Dec 31   Accrued salaries owed to employees worth $3,370

	Unadjusted Trial Balance		Adjustments		Adjusted Trial Balance	
Account Title	DR	CR	DR	CR	DR	CR

d) Prepare the income statement for Space Jam Storage.

e) Prepare the statement of owner's equity for Space Jam Storage.

f) Prepare the balance sheet for Space Jam Storage.

g) Record the journal entries for the adjusting and closing transactions. Use the income summary method. Post these entries in the general ledger above from part b).

Date	Account Title and Explanation	PR	Debit	Credit

h) Prepare the post-closing trial balance for Space Jam Storage.

Analysis

The accountant for Space Jam Storage found that a journal entry back in November had been entered incorrectly. The account that should have been debited was credited and vice versa. Why wasn't this error detected during the preparation of trial balances and financial statements?

_____

_____

_____

_____

_____

AP-9B LO 4

The following information is taken from the records of Basil Cleaning.

Accounts Payable	$18,000
Merchandise Inventory	14,000
Land	55,000
Cash	31,000
Factory Equipment	20,000
Bank Loan, Current Portion	21,000
Office Furniture	18,000
Prepaid Insurance	13,000
Unearned Revenue	8,000

Required

a)   Calculate total current assets.

_____

_____

b)   Calculate total long-term assets.

_____

_____

_____

c)   Calculate total assets.

_____

_____

AP-10B LO 4

Manuel Consulting took out a $1,180,000 interest-free bank loan on January 1, 2019. Payment will be made in four years in four equal annual installments (paid on each subsequent January 1). Calculate the current and long-term liabilities as at December 31 before the annual installments are made for the following years.

	December 31			
	2019	**2020**	**2021**	**2022**
Bank Loan, Current Portion				
Bank Loan, Long-Term Portion				

AP-11B LO 4

On July 1, 2019, Bryte Services took out a $200,000 bank loan. The loan will be repaid in equal annual installments over the next 10 years. Show how the bank loan will appear on Bryte Services' classified balance sheet on June 30, 2025.

Analysis

Show the journal entries required to record the receipt of the loan and the first principal payment.

Date	Account Title and Explanation	PR	Debit	Credit

AP-12B LO 4

On January 1, 2019, Detmore Consulting took out a $100,000 bank loan. The loan will be repaid in two equal payments; one on December 31, 2020, and the other on December 31, 2022. Complete the table below with the correct balances for the accounts at the dates listed.

	Bank Loan	
	Current	Long-Term
December 31, 2019		
December 31, 2020		
December 31, 2021		
December 31, 2022		

Analysis

Why is it helpful to split some liabilities into current and long-term portions for reporting purposes?

_____

_____

_____

_____

_____

_____

_____

_____

_____

AP-13B LO 4

Identify the following accounts as either current or long-term, and as either assets or liabilities.

Account Name	Current or Long-Term	Asset or Liability
Accounts Receivable		
Salaries Payable		
Equipment		
Cash		
Bank Loan due in six months		
Office Furniture		
Accounts Payable		
Prepaid Rent		
Bank Loan due in two years		
Merchandise Inventory		

AP-14B LO 4 5

Below is Bravolo's adjusted trial balance for the year ending September 30, 2019. Assume all accounts have a normal balance. The bank loan is payable over three years and $6,000 will be paid by September 30, 2020.

Cash	$17,400
Accounts Receivable	5,800
Prepaid Insurance	1,800
Equipment	23,000
Accumulated Depreciation—Equipment	1,100
Accounts Payable	7,600
Unearned Revenue	1,500
Bank Loan	18,000
Bravolo, Capital	19,800

Required

a) Prepare a classified balance sheet.

b) Calculate the working capital for Bravolo.

_____

_____

c) Calculate the current ratio for Bravolo.

_____

_____

d) Calculate the quick ratio for Bravolo.

_____

_____

AP-15B LO 4 5

Below is Canduro's financial information for the year ending June 30, 2019. Assume all accounts have a normal balance.

Accounts Payable	$8,900
Accounts Receivable	6,100
Accumulated Depreciation—Equipment	1,200
Bank Loan	21,000
Cash	19,000
Prepaid Insurance	3,250
Equipment	25,000
Canduro, Capital	20,550
Unearned Revenue	1,700

The bank loan is payable over five years and $4,200 will be paid by June 30, 2020.

Required

a) Prepare a classified balance sheet.

b) Calculate the working capital for Canduro.

_____

c) Calculate the current ratio for Canduro.

_____

d) Calculate the quick ratio for Canduro.

_____

AP-16B LO 4

An alphabetical list of the adjusted trial balance of Sam Green's Gardening Services at September 30, 2019, after its first month of operations, is presented below. The capital balance represents investments made by Sam personally to the business during the month. Assume all amounts have a normal balance.

Accounts Payable	40,500
Accounts Receivable	61,950
Accumulated Depreciation—Equipment	4,500
Cash	63,000
Depreciation Expense—Equipment	1,050
Equipment	51,000
Insurance Expense	7,875
Interest Expense	150
Interest Income	1,050
Prepaid Insurance	3,150
Sam Green, Capital	116,301
Sam Green, Withdrawals	16,050
Service Revenue	219,000
Unearned Revenue	29,400
Wages Expense	209,550
Wages Payable	3,024

Prepare a classified balance sheet.

AP-17B LO 7

Charles Ly is the owner of Gamma Services. He has hired you to prepare the financial statements for his company on April 30, 2019. As part of the process, you need to create the worksheet. Use the unadjusted trial balance and the adjustments to complete the worksheet.

Apr 30	Recognized prepaid insurance worth $100 for this month
Apr 30	Recorded $400 depreciation on equipment
Apr 30	Recognized $1,800 of unearned revenue that is now earned
Apr 30	Completed $1,000 of work for a client in April, which has not yet been invoiced

	Gamma Services Worksheet April 30, 2019									
	Unadjusted Trial Balance		Adjustments		Adjusted Trial Balance		Income Statement		Balance Sheet	
Account Title	**DR**	**CR**	**DR**	**CR**	**DR**	**CR**	**DR**	**CR**	**DR**	**CR**
Cash	$21,750									
Accounts Receivable	13,000									
Prepaid Insurance	1,200									
Equipment	17,500									
Accumulated Depreciation—Equipment		$2,000								
Accounts Payable		10,300								
Unearned Revenue		4,500								
Bank Loan		18,000								
Ly, Capital		14,000								
Service Revenue		9,000								
Insurance Expense	0									
Salaries Expense	4,000									
Telephone Expense	200									
Depreciation Expense	0									
Interest Expense	150									
Total	**$57,800**	**$57,800**								
Net Profit (Loss)										
Total										

AP-18B [LO 7]

The September 30, 2019, unadjusted trial balance for Valley Photo Inc. after the first month of operations is shown below. Adjusting entries have not yet been made. Use the trial balance and the information below for the month of September, to complete the 10-column worksheet.

- It was determined that $2,000 of the prepaid insurance had been used during September.

- Depreciation on the automobile for the month of September was $600.

- Interest on the bank loan of $500 accrued at the end of September.

- $1,500 of the unearned revenue was earned during the month.

- Completed $2,500 of work for a client in September, which has not yet been invoiced.

	Unadjusted Trial Balance		Adjustments		Adjusted Trial Balance		Income Statement		Balance Sheet	
Valley Photo Inc										
Worksheet										
September 30, 2019										
Account	**DR**	**CR**	**DR**	**CR**	**DR**	**CR**	**DR**	**CR**	**DR**	**CR**
Cash	$5,000									
Accounts Receivable	12,000									
Prepaid Insurance	4,000									
Automobile	50,000									
Accumulated Depreciation—Automobile		0								
Accounts Payable		$2,000								
Interest Payable		0								
Unearned Revenue		6,000								
Bank Loan		20,000								
Valley, Capital		45,000								
Valley, Withdrawals	4,000									
Service Revenue		9,000								
Depreciation Expense—Automobile	0									
Equipment Rental Expense	4,000									
Insurance Expense	1,000									
Interest Expense	2,000									
Total	**$82,000**	**$82,000**								
Net Income										
Total										

AP-19B LO 2 3

Joe's Auto Body showed the following post-closing trial balance. The trial balance was created after the posting of the closing entries on March 31, 2019.

Joe's Auto Body Trial Balance March 31, 2019		
Account Title	**DR**	**CR**
Cash	$13,200	
Accounts Receivable	1,200	
Prepaid Rent	600	
Equipment	32,000	
Accumulated Depreciation—Equipment		$6,400
Building	75,000	
Accumulated Depreciation—Building		3,000
Accounts Payable		2,200
Joe Long, Capital		47,200
Joe Long, Withdrawals	15,300	
Service Revenue		80,000
Other Expenses	1,500	
Total	**$138,800**	**138,800**

Required

a) List the error(s) in the above post-closing trial balance.

_____

_____

b) What entry should be made to correct the error(s) at year end? Assume Joe's Auto Body uses the direct method for closing accounts.

Date	Account Title and Explanation	PR	Debit	Credit

c) What is the correct amount of Joe's capital account at March 31, 2019?

Joe Long, Capital

Case Study

CS-1 LO 1 2 3 4 5

Grindstone Paving provides residential and commercial paving services. Its balance sheet at the end of June 2019 is shown below, along with its chart of accounts.

Grindstone Paving Balance Sheet As at June 30, 2019			
Assets		**Liabilities**	
Cash	$7,580	Accounts Payable	$15,800
Accounts Receivable	6,000	Unearned Revenue	6,200
Prepaid Insurance	1,800	Bank Loan	22,000
Equipment	55,000	**Total Liabilities**	44,000
		Owner's Equity	
		Stone, Capital	26,380
Total Assets	$70,380	**Total Liabilities and Owner's Equity**	$70,380

Account Description	Account #		Account Description	Account #
ASSETS			**REVENUE**	
Cash	101		Service Revenue	400
Accounts Receivable	105			
Prepaid Insurance	110		**EXPENSES**	
Equipment	120		Advertising Expense	500
Accumulated Depreciation—Equipment	125		Depreciation Expense	510
			Insurance Expense	515
LIABILITIES			Interest Expense	520
Accounts Payable	200		Salaries Expense	545
Interest Payable	205		Telephone Expense	550
Salary Payable	210			
Unearned Revenue	215			
Bank Loan	220			
OWNER'S EQUITY				
Stone, Capital	300			
Stone, Withdrawals	310			
Income Summary	315			

For the month of July 2019, Grindstone Paving had the following transactions.

Jul 1   The owner invested $8,000 cash into the business

Jul 2   Received $2,530 cash for work that will be provided in August

Jul 5   Received an advertising bill for $600, which will be paid next month

Jul 8   Paid the $350 telephone bill with cash

Jul 10   Provided $4,680 worth of services to customers who will pay later

Jul 14   Purchased equipment with $8,200 cash

Jul 20   Received $2,350 in payment from customers paying their accounts

Jul 22   Paid $1,970 toward accounts payable

Jul 24   Paid $1,300 toward principal of the bank loan

Jul 28   Paid salary of $2,400 to an employee

Jul 30   The owner withdrew $2,200 cash for personal use

At the end of July, the following adjustments had to be journalized to properly report the balances of the company's accounts.

Jul 31   One month of prepaid insurance worth $100 has been used
Jul 31   Monthly depreciation on the equipment was $450
Jul 31   Unearned revenue worth $620 has now been earned
Jul 31   Interest of $75 has accrued on the bank loan
Jul 31   Accrued salary expense of $500 for an employee

Note: Of the remaining balance of the bank loan, $5,000 will be paid within the next year.

Required

a) Enter the opening balances from the June 2019 balance sheet into the general ledger accounts (the ledger accounts are presented at the end of this question).

b) Prepare the journal entries for the month of July and post them to the appropriate general ledger accounts.

Date	Account Title and Explanation	PR	Debit	Credit

c) Create the trial balance in the worksheet and then complete the remaining section of the worksheet.

Account Title	Unadjusted Trial Balance		Adjustments		Adjusted Trial Balance	
	DR	CR	DR	CR	DR	CR

d) Prepare the income statement.

e) Prepare the statement of owner's equity.

f)   Prepare the classified balance sheet.

g)   Prepare the journal entries for the adjustments and post them to the appropriate general ledger accounts.

Date	Account Title and Explanation	PR	Debit	Credit

h) Prepare the journal entries to close the books for the month of July 2019 (use the income summary account), and post the journal entries to the appropriate general ledger accounts, which start on the next page.

JOURNAL				Page 3
Date	Account Title and Explanation	PR	Debit	Credit

i) Create the post-closing trial balance.

GENERAL LEDGER

Account:					GL No:	
Date	Description	PR	DR	CR	Balance	

Account:					GL No:	
Date	Description	PR	DR	CR	Balance	

Account:					GL No:	
Date	Description	PR	DR	CR	Balance	

Account:					GL No:	
Date	Description	PR	DR	CR	Balance	

Account:					GL No:	
Date	Description	PR	DR	CR	Balance	

Account:					GL No:	
Date	Description	PR	DR	CR	Balance	

Account:					GL No:	
Date	Description	PR	DR	CR	Balance	

Account:					GL No:	
Date	Description	PR	DR	CR	Balance	

Account:					GL No:	
Date	Description	PR	DR	CR	Balance	

Account:					GL No:	
Date	Description	PR	DR	CR	Balance	

Account:					GL No:	
Date	Description	PR	DR	CR	Balance	

Account:					GL No:	
Date	Description	PR	DR	CR	Balance	

Account:					GL No:	
Date	Description	PR	DR	CR	Balance	

Account:					GL No:	
Date	Description	PR	DR	CR	Balance	

Account:					GL No:	
Date	Description	PR	DR	CR	Balance	

Account:					GL No:	
Date	Description	PR	DR	CR	Balance	

Account:					GL No:	
Date	Description	PR	DR	CR	Balance	

Account:					GL No:	
Date	Description	PR	DR	CR	Balance	

Account:					GL No:	
Date	Description	PR	DR	CR	Balance	

Account:					GL No:	
Date	Description	PR	DR	CR	Balance	

j) Complete the chart below for Grindstone Paving and comment on the company's liquidity position at the end of July versus the prior month.

	July 31	June 30
Working capital		
Current ratio		

Chapter 7

INVENTORY: MERCHANDISING TRANSACTIONS

LEARNING OBJECTIVES

LO **1** Define a merchandising business

LO **2** Differentiate between the perpetual and the periodic inventory systems

LO **3** Record journal entries under the perpetual inventory system

LO **4** Calculate gross profit and gross profit margin percentages

LO **5** Prepare the income statement under the perpetual inventory system

LO **6** Prepare other adjustments and closing entries for a merchandising business under the perpetual inventory system

LO **7** Identify inventory controls

Appendix

LO **8** Record journal entries under the periodic inventory system

LO **9** Calculate cost of goods sold under the periodic inventory system

LO **10** Prepare a multi-step income statement under the periodic inventory system

LO **11** Prepare closing entries for a merchandising business under the periodic inventory system

AMEENGAGE™ Access **ameengage.com** for integrated resources including tutorials, practice exercises, the digital textbook and more.

Assessment Questions

AS-1 LO **1**

What is a merchandiser?

AS-2 LO **1**

Chai Canine Care operates several stores nationwide. They purchase one brand of pet food from Krong Company, who purchases this product line direct from the factory where it is produced by Mulo Pet Food. Explain which company (Chai Canine Care, Krong Company or Mulo Pet Food) acts as a manufacturer, wholesaler and retailer.

AS-3 LO **1**

What is merchandise inventory?

AS-4 `LO 1`

What does a merchandiser's operating cycle usually involve?

_____

_____

AS-5 `LO 1`

What is COGS and what type of account is it?

_____

_____

AS-6 `LO 1`

How is gross profit calculated?

_____

_____

AS-7 `LO 2`

In a perpetual inventory system, how often are inventory levels updated?

_____

_____

AS-8 `LO 2`

In a periodic inventory system, how often are inventory levels updated?

_____

_____

_____

AS-9 `LO 2`

What is the benefit to a company of using a perpetual inventory system?

_____

_____

_____

_____

_____

AS-10 `LO 3`

What are some reasons purchase returns occur?

_____

_____

AS-11 LO 3

When does a purchase allowance occur?

_____

_____

AS-12 LO 3

Indicate a possible incentive for a seller to give a sales discount.

_____

_____

AS-13 LO 3

What is a trade discount?

_____

_____

_____

AS-14 LO 3

If a cash discount term is written as 3/10, n/30, what does this mean?

_____

_____

AS-15 LO 3

Explain the difference between a sales allowance and a sales discount.

_____

_____

_____

_____

AS-16 LO 3

What are the two possible Freight on Board (FOB) points?

_____

_____

AS-17 LO 3

What does FOB shipping point indicate?

_____

_____

_____

AS-18 `LO 3`

What does FOB destination indicate?

_____

_____

AS-19 `LO 3`

What type of account is sales returns and allowances, and what is it used for?

_____

_____

AS-20 `LO 3`

In a perpetual inventory system, describe the transaction(s) required to record the sale of merchandise inventory.

_____

_____

AS-21 `LO 3`

What is inventory shrinkage? How is it journalized under the perpetual inventory system?

_____

_____

_____

AS-22 `LO 4`

What is the formula for gross profit margin?

_____

_____

AS-23 `LO 5`

Define operating expenses.

_____

_____

AS-24 `LO 5`

What is one difference between a single-step income statement and a multi-step income statement?

_____

_____

_____

AS-25 `LO 5`

What are selling expenses? What are some examples of selling expenses?

_____

_____

AS-26 LO 5

What are administrative expenses? What are some examples of administrative expenses?

_____

_____

_____

AS-27 LO 5

In a typical multi-step income statement, which category do items such as interest revenue and loss from a lawsuit fall under?

_____

_____

_____

AS-28 LO 5

What is the difference between the income statement under a periodic inventory system and the income statement under a perpetual inventory system?

_____

_____

_____

AS-29 LO 6

Explain why the inventory account is not debited or credited as a part of the closing entries when a perpetual inventory system is used.

_____

_____

_____

AS-30 LO 7

Provide an example of how an accountant can manage inventory to ensure the economical and efficient use of resources.

_____

_____

_____

_____

AS-31 LO 7

List two safety measures that can be taken to avoid inventory losses through theft.

_____

_____

_____

_____

AS-32 LO 8

In a periodic inventory system, describe the transaction(s) required to record the sale of merchandise inventory.

_____

_____

_____

AS-33 LO 9

Explain how cost of goods available for sale is calculated in a periodic inventory system.

_____

_____

_____

_____

_____

—————————————— **Application Questions Group A** ——————————————

AP-1A `LO 2`

Suppose that on March 15, 2019, both Company A and Company B sold inventory with a cost of $40,000. The updated balance of merchandise inventory as at March 1 for both companies was $90,000. Company A uses the perpetual inventory system. Company B uses the periodic inventory system and performs an inventory count at the end of each month. What is the value of merchandise inventory on record as at March 15 for each of Company A and Company B?

AP-2A `LO 3`

Super Shirt Wholesalers spent $10,000 to purchase 1,000 shirts from a shirt manufacturer as inventory. Hip Top Retailers paid $15,000 for the 1,000 shirts from Super Shirt Wholesalers on March 15, 2019. Payment is due on April 15. Both companies use the perpetual inventory system.

Required

a) Prepare the journal entry for Hip Top Retailers on March 15.

Date	Account Title and Explanation	Debit	Credit

b) Prepare the journal entries for Super Shirt Wholesalers on March 15.

Date	Account Title and Explanation	Debit	Credit

AP-3A `LO 3`

JB Supermarkets bought $3,000 worth of groceries on account from a produce supplier on May 10, 2019. On May 11, JB's bookkeeper was informed that $200 worth of tomatoes was substandard and returned to the supplier. Prepare the journal entry to record the purchase return using the perpetual inventory system.

Date	Account Title and Explanation	Debit	Credit

AP-4A LO 3

On January 12, 2019, Corner-Mart received a shipment of T-shirts from Promo Novelties for an event. The invoice amounted to $5,000 and was recorded in the accounting system. Soon after the delivery was made, the marketing manager discovered that the logo was printed incorrectly. The goods were returned to Promo Novelties on January 31. Prepare the journal entry for Corner-Mart to record the return using the perpetual inventory system.

Date	Account Title and Explanation	Debit	Credit

AP-5A LO 3

a) Beds Unlimited received a shipment of bed sheets on April 3, 2019. The value of the bed sheets was $8,000, and the sheets were shipped FOB shipping point. Freight charges came to $100. Prepare the journal entry to record the receipt of goods by Beds Unlimited, assuming payment will be made in May, using the perpetual inventory system.

Date	Account Title and Explanation	Debit	Credit

b) The bed sheets delivered to Beds Unlimited were the wrong material. After some negotiation, the manager agreed to keep the products with a 10% allowance. Prepare the entry on April 10, 2019, to record the purchase allowance. (Assume all bed sheets were still in inventory.) Allowances are not granted on freight charges.

Date	Account Title and Explanation	Debit	Credit

c) Journalize the transaction for Beds Unlimited when the payment is made on May 3, 2019.

Date	Account Title and Explanation	Debit	Credit

AP-6A LO 3

The following is written on an invoice relating to goods that were purchased: 5/10, n/30. What does it mean?

_____

_____

AP-7A LO 3

Shoe Retailers uses the perpetual inventory system. It purchased $10,000 worth of shoes from Runner Wear Supplies on March 1, 2019. Runner Wear's invoice shows terms of 2/10, n/30.

Required

a) What is the latest date Shoe Retailers can pay the bill and apply the discount?

b) As bookkeeper for Shoe Retailers, prepare the journal entry to record the March 1 purchase.

Date	Account Title and Explanation	Debit	Credit

c) Journalize the transaction for payment of the invoice, assuming the payment was made on March 5.

Date	Account Title and Explanation	Debit	Credit

d) Journalize the transaction for payment of the invoice, assuming the payment was made on April 3.

Date	Account Title and Explanation	Debit	Credit

AP-8A LO 3

On May 1, 2019, Food Wholesalers purchased $3,000 worth of dried fruit inventory plus $100 for freight charges on account. On May 15, Food Wholesalers sold all of the dried fruit inventory to Retail Grocers for $4,000 on account. As the bookkeeper for Food Wholesalers, journalize the transactions using the perpetual inventory system.

Date	Account Title and Explanation	Debit	Credit

AP-9A [LO 3]

Johnson is a maker of cotton garments that are sold to various retailers. On September 1, 2019, Craig's Retailers sent back a shipment of goods that were unsatisfactory. The goods had a cost of $4,620 and were sold on account for $7,700. Johnson returned the goods to inventory. Johnson uses a perpetual inventory system.

Required

a) As Johnson's bookkeeper, prepare the journal entries to reflect the return.

Date	Account Title and Explanation	Debit	Credit

b) Journalize the entry if Craig's only returned half of the shipment.

Date	Account Title and Explanation	Debit	Credit

AP-10A [LO 3]

The following information was presented by the bookkeeper for Switch Company for the month of January 2019.

Jan 5   Purchased merchandise for $12,000 on credit from Outdoor Pursuits, terms 1/10, n/30, FOB shipping point
Jan 5   Switch Company paid $25 to have the merchandise purchased from Outdoor Pursuits delivered
Jan 12   Purchased merchandise for $7,000 on credit from Cambleback, terms 2/10, n/30
Jan 14   Returned $300 of the merchandise purchased on January 5 from Outdoor Pursuits as it was defective
Jan 15   Paid for merchandise purchased from Outdoor Pursuits on January 5
Jan 26   Paid for merchandise purchased from Cambleback on January 12

Journalize the above transactions assuming that Switch Company uses a perpetual inventory system. Round all calculations to the nearest dollar.

Date	Account Title and Explanation	Debit	Credit
Jan 5	Merchandise inventory	12000	
	Accounts payable		12000
Jan 5	Merch inventory	25	
	Cash		25
Jan 12			

Date	Account Title and Explanation	Debit	Credit
Jan 14	Accounts payable		
	Merchandise inventory		
Jan 14	Accounts payable	11700	
	Merchandise inventory		117
	Cash		11583
	Accounts payable	7000	
	Cash		7000

AP-11A [LO 3]

The following transactions took place at Science Supplies during May 2019.

May 14   Sold merchandise on credit to Elements for $10,000, terms 2/10, n/30, FOB destination; cost of goods was $8,500

May 14   Science Supplies paid $50 to ship the goods to Elements

May 16   Elements returned $500 (sales price) worth of merchandise purchased on May 14; cost of goods was $375; goods were returned to inventory

May 17   Received payment from Elements for the May 14 sale

May 18   Sold merchandise on credit to Litmus for $6,000, terms 2/10, n/30; cost of goods was $3,600

May 26   Litmus kept the merchandise purchased on May 18; however, some of it was defective so Science Supplies agreed to a 50% allowance on the total sale

May 31   Received payment from Litmus for the May 18 sale

Journalize the above transactions assuming that Science Supplies uses a perpetual inventory system. Round all calculations to the nearest dollar.

Date	Account Title and Explanation	Debit	Credit

Date	Account Title and Explanation	Debit	Credit

AP-12A LO 3

Shirley's Wraps operates as a sandwich and wrap shop. Its customers can pay by cash, debit or credit card. For each debit transaction, Shirley pays $0.20. For credit cards, she pays 2% of the total of credit card transactions. On May 13, 2019, Shirley compiled the following summary for the work day.

Transaction Type	Total	Number of Transactions
Cash	$425	52
Debit Card	327	43
Credit Card	0	0

Required

a)   Calculate the total debit/credit card expense for May 13.

_____

b)   Record the journal entry for the day's sales. (Ignore COGS.)

Date	Account Title and Explanation	Debit	Credit

AP-13A LO 3

Tom's Bistro operates as a restaurant. Its customers can pay by cash, debit or credit card. For each debit transaction, Tom pays $0.15. For credit cards, he pays 3% of the total of credit card transactions. On March 22, 2019, Tom compiled the following summary for the work day.

Transaction Type	Total	Number of Transactions
Cash	$2,203	49
Debit Card	0	0
Credit Card	3,731	83

Required

a) Calculate the total debit/credit card expense for March 22.

_____

_____

b) Record the journal entry for the day's sales. (Ignore COGS.)

Date	Account Title and Explanation	Debit	Credit

AP-14A LO 3

Leslie and Ben run a dry cleaners together, called Pawny Cleaners. Their customers can pay by cash, debit or credit card. For each debit transaction, they pay $0.35. For credit cards, they pay 1.5% of the total of credit card transactions. On August 20, 2019, Ben compiled the following summary for the work day.

Transaction Type	Total	Number of Transactions
Cash	$741	35
Debit Card	4,376	120
Credit Card	2,883	68

Required

a) Calculate the total debit/credit card expense for August 20.

_____

_____

_____

_____

b) Record the journal entry for the day's sales. (Ignore COGS.)

Date	Account Title and Explanation	Debit	Credit

AP-15A LO 3

Assume you are the bookkeeper for Moira's Wholesalers, a distributor of kitchen furniture. Your sales manager informed you that Ted's Retailers is unhappy with the quality of some tables delivered on August 12, 2019, and will be shipping back all the goods. The original invoice amounted to $1,500 and the goods cost Moira's $1,000. Using a perpetual inventory system, complete the journal entries for Moira's Wholesalers for each of the following independent scenarios.

Required

a) Rather than taking back the tables, your sales manager allows Ted's Retailers a 10% discount if it agrees to keep the goods. Record Ted's payment in settlement of the invoice on September 12 assuming the allowance is not recorded until the settlement date.

Date	Account Title and Explanation	Debit	Credit

b) Suppose that Ted's shipped back all the goods on August 15 and the inventory was put back on the sales floor. Journalize the transactions.

Date	Account Title and Explanation	Debit	Credit

c)   Suppose that Ted's shipped back half the goods on August 15 and kept the other half with a 10% allowance. Journalize the transactions that took place on August 15.

Date	Account Title and Explanation	Debit	Credit

d)   Continue from part b). Since all the goods were sold and returned in the same period, what happened to Moira's gross profit? (Disregard the additional shipping and administration costs.) Explain your answer.

AP-16A LO 3 4

The following information pertains to Wicked Kitchen Supplies for March 2019.

Mar 1   Purchased merchandise for $16,000 on credit from Hotel Supplies, terms 1/20, n/30, FOB shipping point

Mar 1   Wicked paid $35 cash to have the merchandise from Hotel Supplies delivered

Mar 5   Sold merchandise on credit to Four Boars Restaurant for $8,000, terms 2/10, n/30; cost of goods was $5,500

Mar 5   Paid $25 cash to ship the goods to Four Boars Restaurant (FOB destination)

Mar 8   Four Boars returned $1,900 (sales price) worth of merchandise purchased on March 5; cost of goods was $800; there was nothing wrong with the merchandise and it will be resold

Mar 12   Returned $500 of the merchandise purchased on March 1 as it was the wrong design

Mar 15   Received payment from Four Boars Restaurant for the March 5 sale

Mar 15   Paid for merchandise purchased from Hotel Supplies on March 1

Mar 23   Sold merchandise on credit to Black Kettle Kitchen for $4,000, terms 2/10, n/30; cost of goods was $2,000

Mar 26   Black Kettle Kitchen returned $200 (sales price) of merchandise purchased on March 23; cost of goods was $50. Merchandise was returned to inventory

Mar 31   Received payment from Black Kettle Kitchen for the March 23 sale

Journalize the above transactions assuming that Wicked Kitchen Supplies uses a perpetual inventory system. Round all calculations to the nearest whole dollar.

Date	Account Title and Explanation	Debit	Credit

Date	Account Title and Explanation	Debit	Credit
Date	Account Title and Explanation	Debit	Credit

Date	Account Title and Explanation	Debit	Credit

Analysis

Calculate Wicked Kitchen Supplies' gross profit for the month.

_____

_____

_____

_____

_____

_____

_____

_____

_____

AP-17A LO 4

If net sales is $300,000 and cost of goods sold is $180,000, what is the gross profit and gross margin percentage?

_____

_____

_____

_____

_____

_____

_____

_____

AP-18A LO 4

If a computer company bought computers for $10,000 and sold them for $14,000, how much would the gross profit be on the entire shipment if the business took advantage of the early cash payment terms of 2/15, n/30 from its supplier?

_____

_____

_____

_____

_____

AP-19A LO 5

The following information is for Surplus Direct for the year ended September 30, 2019.

Cost of Goods Sold	$26,000
Interest Expense	780
Interest Revenue	550
Maintenance Expense	2,000
Rent Expense	4,000
Salaries Expense	6,000
Sales Discounts	5,000
Sales Returns & Allowances	50
Sales Revenue	90,000
Supplies Expense	600

Using the information provided, prepare a multi-step income statement. Assume that 60% of expenses are for selling and 40% are for administrative.

AP-19A LO 5

AP-20A LO 5

Glent Company prepared the following trial balance at its year end of September 30, 2019. The company is owned by Wayne Glent.

Glent Company Trial Balance September 30, 2019		
Account Title	DR	CR
Cash	$14,600	
Accounts Receivable	6,000	
Merchandise Inventory	6,600	
Prepaid Expenses	2,000	
Store Equipment	40,000	
Accumulated Depreciation—Store Equipment		$2,500
Accounts Payable		8,000
Unearned Revenue		6,000
Bank Loan		9,000
Glent, Capital		38,750
Glent, Withdrawals	1,000	
Sales Revenue		61,750
Gain on Sale of Equipment		4,000
Cost of Goods Sold	30,000	
Depreciation Expense—Store Equipment	500	
Interest Expense	600	
Advertising Expense	1,200	
Rent Expense—Retail Space	10,000	
Rent Expense—Office Space	5,000	
Sales Salaries Expense	8,000	
Office Salaries Expense	4,500	
Total	**$130,000**	**$130,000**

Notes:
1. Assume the balance of owner's equity is the opening balance.
2. The bank loan is payable over the next nine years in equal annual installments.

Required

a) Prepare a multi-step income statement using the trial balances.

b) Prepare a statement of owner's equity.

c) Prepare a classified balance sheet using the trial balances.

AP-21A LO 5 6

The following is Glueman Industries' adjusted trial balance **in account order** for the year ended September 30, 2019.

Glueman Industries Adjusted Trial Balance September 30, 2019		
Account Title	**DR**	**CR**
Cash	$3,800	
Accounts Receivable	2,800	
Prepaid Insurance	4,500	
Prepaid Rent	8,100	
Equipment	43,800	
Accumulated Depreciation—Equipment		$1,000
Accounts Payable		2,330
Unearned Revenue		2,000
Wages Payable		2,820
Kiefer, Capital		48,800
Sales Revenue		79,000
Sales Discounts	1,750	
Sales Returns & Allowances	430	
Cost of Goods Sold	36,780	
Rent Expense	9,300	
Utilities Expense	8,240	
Wages Expense	15,800	
Depreciation Expense	650	
Total	**$135,950**	**$135,950**

Required

a) Prepare a single-step income statement.

b) Prepare the journal entries to close the appropriate accounts using the income summary method.

Date	Account Title and Explanation	Debit	Credit

c) Prepare journal entries to close appropriate accounts directly to the capital account.

Date	Account Title and Explanation	Debit	Credit

AP-22A LO 5 7

A Bit of Fit operates several retail stores that specialize in products for a healthy lifestyle. Some of its financial information is shown below for its fiscal year ended December 31, 2019.

Cost of Goods Sold	$60,000
Depreciation Expense—Store Equipment	10,000
Gain on Sale of Equipment	3,000
Interest Expense	500
Insurance Expense	7,000
Office Salaries Expense	10,000
Sales Discounts	2,500
Sales Returns & Allowances	6,500
Sales Revenue	154,000
Sales Salaries Expense	40,000
Office Supplies Expense	2,000
Utilities Expense—Retail Space	6,750
Utilities Expense—Office Space	2,250

Required

a) Create a single-step income statement for A Bit of Fit.

b) Create a multi-step income statement for A Bit of Fit.

Analysis

Give a reason why income and expenses are categorized into "operating"—and further, by "selling" and "administrative"—and "other" on the multi-step income statement. Your response should consider impact on controls related to financial reporting.

AP-23A LO 3 7

CD Wholesalers had the following business transactions during the month of June 2019.

June 10   CD purchased $4,800 worth of towels from Taki Towels. The invoice showed payment terms of 2/10, n/30.

June 10   While unpackaging the above shipment, CD's receiving department noticed that some of the boxes of towels were damaged. The boxes were returned to the supplier. Total value was $800.

June 20   CD paid the balance of the invoice less the return and discount.

June 22   CD sold all of the towels to Metro Merchandise for $8,000 on terms of 3/10, n/45.

June 30   Metro paid CD for the goods purchased.

Required

a) Prepare the journal entries to record the above transactions. Assume CD Wholesalers uses a perpetual inventory system.

Date	Account Title and Explanation	Debit	Credit

b) Calculate June's ending inventory based on the above transactions. Assume that merchandise inventory at the beginning of June amounted to $2,500.

c) At the end of June, an inventory count was performed. The balance of inventory according to the count was $2,000. Management deemed that the difference between the ledger account and physical inventory count was due to theft (shrinkage). Prepare the journal entry to adjust the merchandise inventory balance on June 30.

Date	Account Title and Explanation	Debit	Credit

d) Explain how use of sales discounts and sales returns and allowances accounts supports internal controls for a merchandising type of business.

_____

_____

_____

_____

_____

_____

_____

_____

AP-24A LO 8

JB Supermarkets bought $3,000 worth of groceries on account from a produce supplier on May 10, 2019. On May 11, JB's bookkeeper was informed that $200 worth of tomatoes was substandard and returned to the supplier. Prepare the journal entry to record the purchase return using the periodic inventory system.

Date	Account Title and Explanation	Debit	Credit

AP-25A LO 8

On July 18, 2019, the Maple Trees received a shipment of jerseys from Norton Supplies for their hockey team. The invoice was for $6,000 and was recorded in the accounting system. When the box was opened, the team manager discovered the jerseys were the wrong colour. The goods were returned to Norton Supplies on July 31. Prepare the journal entry for the Maple Trees to record the return using the periodic inventory system.

Date	Account Title and Explanation	Debit	Credit

AP-26A LO 2 3 8

For each business transaction in the table below, identify which accounts are debited and credited. Do this for both the perpetual and periodic inventory systems.

Transaction	Perpetual Inventory System		Periodic Inventory System	
	DR	CR	DR	CR
1. Purchased inventory on account				
2. Returned a portion of the inventory purchased in transaction 1				
3. Paid for remaining invoice balance after taking advantage of the early payment discount				
4. Sold inventory on account				
5. Customer found that a portion of goods sold in transaction 4 were of lower quality; however, she agreed to keep them at a 10% discount				
6. Customer paid the remaining invoice balance after taking advantage of an early payment discount				

AP-27A LO 9 11

The following information was taken from the financial records of Redmond Distribution, owned by Marcus Redmond, at its year end of December 31, 2019. The company uses the periodic inventory system.

Freight-In	$1,400
Interest Expense	3,200
Merchandise Inventory, January 1, 2019	150,000
Merchandise Inventory, December 31, 2019	120,000
Purchase Returns & Allowances	13,800
Purchases	100,000
Rent Expense	30,000
Salaries Expense	44,000
Sales Discounts	9,200
Sales Revenue	250,000

Required

a) Calculate the cost of goods sold for Redmond Distribution for 2019.

b) Prepare the closing entries for Redmond Distribution for 2019 using the income summary method.

Date	Account Title and Explanation	Debit	Credit

AP-28A LO 8 9 10 11

Crystal Crockery, owned by Crystal Kleer, has provided you with the following information about the transactions occurring in March 2019.

Mar 2   Crystal Crockery received a shipment of gift mugs for resale from Cup Makers. The amount on the invoice is $7,000 and the stated terms are 2/15, n/45.

Mar 2   Crystal Crockery paid $400 cash for shipping charges.

Mar 5   The manager of Crystal Crockery checked the shipped cups and found that goods worth $700 were defective. The defective goods were returned to the supplier.

Mar 13   Crystal Crockery paid the remaining invoice balance and, in doing so, took advantage of the early payment discount.

Mar 20   Crystal Crockery sold the goods costing $6,174 to EatFresh Supermarket for $9,500.

Mar 22   EatFresh Supermarket found 10% worth of items to be defective and returned these to Crystal Crockery. The goods cannot be resold.

Mar 28   The invoice showed terms 2/10, n/60. EatFresh Supermarket paid the remaining invoice balance after taking advantage of the early settlement discount

The opening inventory balance was $500 and the closing inventory balance was $847.

Assume Crystal Crockery uses the periodic inventory system.

Required

a) Prepare the journal entries to record the purchase and sales transactions.

Date	Account Title and Explanation	Debit	Credit

Date	Account Title and Explanation	Debit	Credit

b) Prepare the journal entries to record the closing entries for the month using the income summary method. Assume that the accounting period for Crystal Crockery is one month.

Date	Account Title and Explanation	Debit	Credit

c) Prepare the net purchases section of the income statement.

d) Prepare the cost of goods sold section of the income statement.

AP-29A LO 9 10 11

The following information was taken from the records of Arc Suppliers on December 31, 2019. Assume all accounts have normal balances.

Accounts Payable	$6,000
Accounts Receivable	12,000
Beginning Inventory	22,500
Cash	34,500
Depreciation Expense	13,400
Ending Inventory	46,575
Freight-In	3,000
Insurance Expense	2,400
Interest Revenue	2,000
Purchase Discounts	11,000
Purchase Returns & Allowances	6,500
Purchases	142,545
Rent Expense	12,000
Sales Discounts	1,875
Sales Returns & Allowances	4,200
Sales Revenue	224,350
J. Arc, Withdrawals	15,000
J. Arc, Capital	35,600

Required

a) Prepare a partial multi-step income statement up to and including gross profit assuming a periodic inventory system is used.

b) Prepare a multi-step income statement up to and including gross profit assuming a perpetual inventory system is used.

c) Calculate net income.

_____

_____

d) Prepare the closing entries assuming a periodic inventory system was used.

Date	Account Title and Explanation	Debit	Credit

Application Questions Group B

AP-1B [LO 2]

A group of friends has just started a business selling computers. They are seeking advice regarding accounting for their inventory.

Required

a) Which inventory system should they use if they plan to track purchases and sales using a scanner and point of sale terminal?

_____

_____

_____

_____

b) Which inventory system should they use if they plan to keep costs down by using a manual accounting system to record transactions?

_____

_____

_____

AP-2B [LO 3]

On September 1, 2019, Fruit Wholesalers purchased $3,700 worth of dried fruit inventory and paid $120 for freight charges on account. On September 16, Fruit Wholesalers sold all of the dried fruit inventory to Retail Grocers for $5,920 on account. As the bookkeeper for Fruit Wholesalers, journalize the transactions under the perpetual inventory system.

Date	Account Title and Explanation	Debit	Credit

AP-3B LO 3

JB Supermarkets bought $2,140 worth of groceries on account from a produce supplier on December 8, 2019. On December 9, JB's bookkeeper was informed that 15% of the produce was substandard and returned to the supplier. Prepare the journal entry to record the purchase return using the perpetual inventory system.

Date	Account Title and Explanation	Debit	Credit

AP-4B LO 3

Top Mop Retailers bought $12,900 worth of mops from Super Mop Wholesalers Ltd. on March 15, 2019. Payment is due in April.

Required

a) Prepare the journal entry for Top Mop Retailers using the perpetual inventory system.

Date	Account Title and Explanation	Debit	Credit

b) Prepare the journal entry for Top Mop Retailers for the payment of $12,900 made to Super Mop Wholesalers Ltd. on April 15.

Date	Account Title and Explanation	Debit	Credit

AP-5B LO 3

a) Signs Unlimited received a shipment of plastic sheets on February 15, 2019. The sheets were shipped FOB shipping point. The value of the plastic was $9,000, and the shipping charges totalled $110. Prepare the journal entry to record the receipt of goods by Signs Unlimited, assuming the payments for the inventory and freight will be made in March, using the perpetual inventory system.

Date	Account Title and Explanation	Debit	Credit

b) The plastic sheets delivered to Signs Unlimited were the wrong colour. After some negotiation, the manager agreed to keep the products with a 6% allowance on the value of the inventory. Prepare the entry on February 22 to record the purchase allowance. (Assume all items were still in inventory.) Allowances are not granted on freight charges.

Date	Account Title and Explanation	Debit	Credit

c) Journalize the transaction for Signs Unlimited when the payment is made on March 15.

Date	Account Title and Explanation	Debit	Credit

AP-6B LO 3

a) Sandal Retailers purchased $8,100 worth of sandals from Comfy Wear Supplies on April 10, 2019. Comfy Wear's invoice shows terms of 2/15, n/30. What is the latest date Sandal Retailers can pay the bill to take advantage of the discount?

_____

_____

b) As the bookkeeper for Sandal Retailers, prepare the journal entry to record the purchase on April 10, using a perpetual inventory system.

Date	Account Title and Explanation	Debit	Credit

c) Journalize the transaction for payment of the invoice, assuming the payment was made on April 18.

Date	Account Title and Explanation	Debit	Credit

d) Journalize the transaction for payment of the invoice, assuming the payment was made on April 26.

Date	Account Title and Explanation	Debit	Credit

AP-7B LO 3

Rock Retailers purchased $11,200 worth of shoes from Runner Wear Supplies on April 4, 2019. Runner Wear's invoice shows terms of 2/10, n/30. What is the latest date that Rock Retailers can pay the bill to take advantage of the discount? How much cash is exchanged if the full discount is taken advantage of?

AP-8B LO 3

On March 20, 2019, Cup-A-Java received a shipment of gift mugs for resale from Cup Makers in the amount of $5,000. The terms stated on the invoice from Cup Makers were 3/15, n/60. Under a perpetual inventory system, journalize the following scenarios for Cup-A-Java.

Required

a) As the bookkeeper for Cup-A-Java, record the purchase of inventory.

Date	Account Title and Explanation	Debit	Credit

b) If Cup-A-Java decides to take advantage of the early payment cash discount, by when should the payment be made to qualify for the discount?

c) The payment by Cup-A-Java to Cup Makers was made on March 31. Prepare the journal entry for the payment of goods.

Date	Account Title and Explanation	Debit	Credit

d) Journalize the entry if payment had instead been made on May 20.

Date	Account Title and Explanation	Debit	Credit

e) On March 25, 20% of the shipment was returned because the mugs were the wrong size. The invoice has not yet been paid. Prepare the journal entry for this transaction.

Date	Account Title and Explanation	Debit	Credit

f) Continue from e). Journalize the entry if Cup-A-Java took advantage of the early payment cash discount when paying for the balance of the mugs on March 31.

Date	Account Title and Explanation	Debit	Credit

AP-9B LO 3

Macks makes garments that are sold to retailers. On June 1, 2019, Cory's Retailers sent back a shipment of goods. The goods sold on account for $6,000 and cost Macks $4,000 to make. Macks put the returned goods back into inventory for resale. Macks uses a perpetual inventory system.

Required

a) As Macks' bookkeeper, prepare the journal entries to reflect the return.

Date	Account Title and Explanation	Debit	Credit

b) Journalize the entry if Cory's only returned half of the shipment.

Date	Account Title and Explanation	Debit	Credit

c) What happened to the value of Macks' owner's equity when Cory's returned the merchandise? Did it increase, decrease or stay the same? Explain your answer.

_____

_____

_____

_____

d) Explain the logic behind debiting the sales returns and allowances as a contra account instead of debiting the revenue account directly.

_____

_____

AP-10B LO 3

Pete's Wholesalers imports and distributes towels. It sells products to various retailers throughout the country and offers payment terms of 2/10, n/30. On October 1, 2019, Pete's sold Ernie's Bathroom Retailers $15,000 of goods, which cost Pete's $9,000. Pete's uses a perpetual inventory system. Complete the following.

Required

a) Journalize the sale that was made on account for Pete's Wholesalers.

Date	Account Title and Explanation	Debit	Credit

b) By what date must Ernie's pay the invoice to qualify for the early cash payment discount?

_____

_____

c) Assume Ernie's paid the bill on October 5. Record the journal entry for Pete's Wholesalers.

Date	Account Title and Explanation	Debit	Credit

d) If Ernie's had returned half the shipment and paid for the balance owing on October 5, how would the transactions be journalized by Pete's Wholesaler's? Assume the inventory was restocked by Pete's Wholesalers.

Date	Account Title and Explanation	Debit	Credit

e) Suppose instead that Ernie's found the goods unsatisfactory and agreed to keep the goods with a 10% allowance. Prepare the journal entries for Pete's Wholesalers to record the sales allowance and Ernie's payment on October 20.

Date	Account Title and Explanation	Debit	Credit

AP-11B LO 3

The folowing transactions took place at Art Supplies during March 2019.

Mar 14   Sold merchandise on credit to Graphic Arts for $15,000; terms 3/15, n/30; cost of goods sold was $12,000

Mar 14   Art Supplies paid $75 to ship the goods to Graphic Arts (FOB destination)

Mar 16   Graphic Arts returned $1,000 (sales price) worth of merchandise purchased on March 14; cost of goods was $650; goods were returned to inventory

Mar 17   Received payment from Graphic Arts for March 14 sale

Mar 18   Sold merchandise on credit to Canvas Retailers for $8,000, terms 2/10, n/30; cost of goods was $5,500

Mar 26   Canvas kept the merchandise purchased on March 18; however, some of it was defective so Art Supplies agreed to a 40% allowance on the total sale

Mar 31   Received payment from Canvas for the March 18 sale

Journalize the above transactions assuming that Art Supplies uses a perpetual inventory system. Round all calculations to the nearest dollar.

Date	Account Title and Explanation	Debit	Credit

Date	Account Title and Explanation	Debit	Credit

Analysis

What was the gross profit earned by Art Supplies during the month of March? Show calculations.

_____

AP-12B LO 3

Brad Chang runs his own restaurant. Customers can pay by cash, debit or credit card. For each debit transaction, Brad pays $0.25. For credit cards, he pays 2% of the total of credit card transactions. On May 9, 2019, Brad compiled the following summary for the work day.

Transaction Type	Total	Number of Transactions
Cash	$1,459	23
Debit Card	4,632	72
Credit Card	0	0

Required

a) Calculate the total debit/credit card expense for May 9.

_____

_____

b) Record the journal entry for the day's sales. (Ignore COGS.)

Date	Account Title and Explanation	Debit	Credit

AP-13B LO 3

Burt Mecklin operates a large pet store. Customers can pay by cash, debit or credit card. For each debit transaction, Burt pays $0.15. For credit cards, he pays 2% of the total of credit card transactions. On November 15, 2019, Burt compiled the following summary for the work day.

Transaction Type	Total	Number of Transactions
Cash	$2,640	33
Debit Card	0	0
Credit Card	5,440	68

Required

a) Calculate the total debit/credit card expense for November 15.

b) Record the journal entry for the day's sales. (Ignore COGS.)

Date	Account Title and Explanation	Debit	Credit

AP-14B LO 3

Ron runs his own butcher shop. His customers can pay by cash, debit or credit card. For each debit transaction, Ron pays $0.25. For credit cards, Ron pays 3% of the total of credit card transactions. On April 3, 2019, Ron compiled the following summary for the work day.

Transaction Type	Total	Number of Transactions
Cash	$836	27
Debit Card	1,298	40
Credit Card	1,366	32

Required

a) Calculate the total debit/credit card expense for April 3.

b) Record the journal entry for the day's sales. (Ignore COGS.)

Date	Account Title and Explanation	Debit	Credit

AP-15B [LO 1 3 4]

Suppose that SCOOP Pet Supplies' gross profit margin is 40% and that all sales are cash sales. Prepare any journal entries required to record sales for the year ended December 31, 2019, assuming that the company had $846,500 in sales revenue for the year and uses a perpetual inventory system.

Date	Account Title and Explanation	Debit	Credit

AP-16B [LO 3 4]

Wilde Wilderness Supplies had the following transactions during January 2019.

Jan 1   Sold merchandise on credit to Merril for $15,000, terms 2/10, n/30; cost of goods was $8,500

Jan 1   Wilde paid $50 to ship the goods to Merril

Jan 5   Purchased inventory for $12,000 on credit from Outdoor Experts, terms 1/10, n/30, FOB shipping point

Jan 5   Wilde paid $25 to have the merchandise from Outdoor Experts delivered

Jan 8   Merril returned $1,200 (sales price) of merchandise purchased on January 1; the cost of goods sold was $800. The inventory will be resold.

Jan 12   Some of the merchandise purchased on January 5 was the wrong size. Wilde decided to keep the merchandise in exchange for a 25% allowance on the purchase. Allowances are not granted on shipping charges.

Jan 15   Received payment from Merril for the January 1 sale

Jan 18   Sold merchandise on credit to Forest Outfitters for $5,000, terms 2/15, n/30; cost of goods was $2,600

Jan 23   Paid for merchandise purchased from Outdoor Experts on January 5

Jan 26   Wilde granted Forest Outfitters a 20% allowance on the January 18 sale due to defective products

Jan 31   Received payment from Forest Outfitters for the January 18 sale

Journalize the above transactions assuming that Wilde Wilderness Supplies uses a perpetual inventory system. Round all calculations to the nearest whole dollar.

Date	Account Title and Explanation	Debit	Credit

Date	Account Title and Explanation	Debit	Credit

Analysis

Calculate Wilde Wilderness Supplies' gross profit margin for the month.

_____

_____

_____

_____

_____

_____

_____

_____

_____

_____

_____

_____

AP-17B LO 4

If sales are $290,000 and cost of goods sold is $130,000, what are the gross profit and gross margin percentage?

_____

_____

_____

_____

_____

_____

_____

AP-18B LO 4

If a cell phone retail business bought cell phones for $10,800 and sold them for $14,500, how much would the gross profit be on the entire shipment, assuming the business took advantage of the early cash payment terms of 3/10, n/30 from its supplier?

_____

_____

_____

_____

_____

_____

AP-19B LO 5

Let's Talk Shop sells cell phone accessories. The following information is available for the year ending June 30, 2019.

Cost of Goods Sold	$11,200
Interest Expense	1,000
Advertising Expense	800
Office Salaries Expense	12,000
Sales Revenue	49,000
Sales Salaries Expense	26,000
Rent Expense—Retail Space	2,000
Rent Expense—Office Space	1,000

Prepare the multi-step income statement for June 2019.

Analysis

Let's Talk Shop sold 3,500 phone cases at an average price of $14 each during the year. The company buys phone case inventory at an average price of $3.20 each. If Let's Talk Shop had sold 4,000 phone cases instead, would it have a positive net income? Assume operating expenses would remain the same. Show your work.

AP-20B LO 5

Bugle News operates by selling newspaper and magazines to consumers. Peter has prepared the income statement and balance sheet for Bugle News as shown below.

The bank loan is due in annual payments of $50,000.

Bugle News		
Income Statement		
For the Year Ended December 31, 2019		
Revenues		
Sales Revenue	$975,000	
Interest Revenue	25,000	
Total Revenues		$1,000,000
Expenses		
Cost of Goods Sold	150,000	
Advertising Expense	50,200	
Rent Expense—Newsstand	50,000	
Rent Expense—Office Space	5,800	
Office Salaries Expense	125,000	
Sales Salaries Expense	160,000	
Loss on Property Damage	59,000	
Total Expenses		600,000
Net Income		$400,000

Bugle News		
Balance Sheet		
As at December 31, 2019		
Assets		
Cash	$121,000	
Accounts Receivable	5,000	
Prepaid Insurance	514,000	
Merchandise Inventory	310,000	
Equipment	800,000	
Accumulated Depreciation	(250,000)	
Total Assets		$1,500,000
Liabilities		
Accounts Payable	$15,000	
Unearned Revenue	530,000	
Bank Loan	300,000	
Total Liabilities		$845,000
Owner's Equity		
Parker, Capital		655,000
Total Owner's Equity		655,000
Total Liabilities and Owner's Equity		$1,500,000

Required

a)   Prepare the multi-step income statement for Bugle News.

b)   Prepare the classified balance sheet for Bugle News.

Analysis

Calculate and interpret the current ratio for Bugle News.

AP-21B LO 5 6

The following is the adjusted trial balance **in alphabetical order** for LCP Construction for the year ended December 31, 2019.

LCP Construction Adjusted Trial Balance December 31, 2019		
Account Title	DR	CR
Accounts Payable		$2,330
Accumulated Depreciation—Equipment		1,140
Cash	$10,800	
Cost of Goods Sold	28,660	
Depreciation Expense	9,080	
Equipment	27,766	
Insurance Expense	5,260	
Interest Revenue		7,650
Pohler, Capital		48,060
Prepaid Insurance	4,675	
Prepaid Rent	18,100	
Rent Expense	9,300	
Sales Discounts	440	
Sales Returns & Allowances	1,749	
Sales Revenue		60,945
Unearned Revenue		1,000
Utilities Expense	2,240	
Wages Expense	5,800	
Wages Payable		2,745
Total	**$123,870**	**$123,870**

Required

a) Prepare a multi-step income statement.

b) Prepare the journal entries to close the appropriate accounts using the income summary method.

Date	Account Title and Explanation	Debit	Credit

AP-22B LO 5 7

Rita Retail is a merchandising business. The store's building contains a large selling area with merchandise displays and shelves, and a smaller back office area where administrative tasks are performed, such as payroll, marketing and HR. Excess inventory is stored at the sales manager's house, which is located an hour's drive away from the main office. The following information is available.

- Salaries are for the salespeople, as well as the office staff. Office staff salaries totalled $80,000 for the year.
- The office area is allocated 20% of the utility costs.
- Depreciation is charged on the merchandise displays only.

Rita Retail Income Statement For the Year Ended December 31, 2019		
Sales Revenue		$1,400,000
Expenses		
Cost of Goods Sold	$890,000	
Salaries Expense	210,000	
Office Supplies Expense	12,000	
Insurance Expense	42,000	
Utilities Expense	7,000	
Depreciation Expense	5,000	
Total Expenses		1,166,000
Net Income		$234,000

Prepare a multi-step income statement for Rita Retail.

Analysis

a) Give a reason why it is useful to separate expenses into selling and administrative categories on the income statement.

_____

_____

_____

_____

b) Discuss the control implications of storing inventory at the manager's home instead of at the store's location.

_____

_____

_____

_____

_____

AP-23B LO 3 6 7

AB Retailers had the following business transactions during the month of April 2019.

Apr 10   AB Retailers bought $3,500 worth of T-shirts from Unique Designers. The invoice showed payment terms of 2/10, n/30.

Apr 10   Soon after AB Retailers received the products, it was discovered that $500 worth of T-shirts did not meet quality standards. These goods were returned to the supplier.

Apr 20   AB Retailers paid the remaining invoice balance.

Apr 22   AB Retailers sold *all* the goods for $4,500 to SK Stores on terms 3/10, n/45.

Apr 28   SK Stores paid for the goods purchased.

Required

a) Prepare the journal entries to record the above transactions. Assume AB Retailers uses the perpetual inventory system.

Date	Account Title and Explanation	Debit	Credit

b) Calculate April's ending inventory based on the above transactions. Assume that merchandise inventory at the beginning of April amounted to $1,500.

c) At the end of April, an inventory count was performed. The balance of inventory according to the count was $1,300. Management deemed that the difference between the ledger account and physical inventory count was due to theft (shrinkage). Prepare the journal entry to adjust the merchandise inventory balance on April 30.

Date	Account Title and Explanation	Debit	Credit

d) What are some controls used to safeguard inventory against shrinkage?

_____

_____

_____

_____

AP-24B LO 8

a) Boards Unlimited received a shipment of skateboards on April 3, 2019. The value of the skateboards was $8,000, and they were shipped FOB shipping point. Freight charges came to $100. Prepare the journal entry to record the receipt of goods by Boards Unlimited, assuming payment will be made in May, using the periodic inventory system.

Date	Account Title and Explanation	Debit	Credit

b) The skateboards delivered to Boards Unlimited were the wrong colour. After some negotiation, the manager agreed to keep the products with a 10% discount. Prepare the entry on April 10 to record the purchase allowance. (Assume all skateboards were still in inventory.)

Date	Account Title and Explanation	Debit	Credit

c) Journalize the transaction for Boards Unlimited when the payment is made on May 3.

Date	Account Title and Explanation	Debit	Credit

AP-25B LO 8

Footloose Retailers uses the periodic inventory system. It purchased $10,000 worth of shoes from Jogger Wear Supplies on March 1, 2019. Jogger Wear's invoice terms are 2/15, n/30.

Required

a) What is the latest date Footloose Retailers can pay the bill to apply the discount?

_____

_____

b) As Footloose Retailers' bookkeeper, prepare the journal entry to record the March 1 purchase.

Date	Account Title and Explanation	Debit	Credit

c) Journalize the transaction for payment of the invoice on March 5.

Date	Account Title and Explanation	Debit	Credit

d) Journalize the transaction for payment of the invoice on April 3.

Date	Account Title and Explanation	Debit	Credit

AP-26B LO 2 3 8

On January 1, 2019, a company purchases 1,000 units of inventory at $12 per unit on account. On January 5, the company sells 25 units for $50 per unit on account.

Required

a) Write the journal entries to record the transactions under the perpetual inventory system.

Date	Account Title and Explanation	Debit	Credit

Date	Account Title and Explanation	Debit	Credit

b) Write the journal entries to record the transactions under the periodic inventory system.

Date	Account Title and Explanation	Debit	Credit

AP-27B LO 9 11

The following information was taken from the financial records of Bluevale Wholesalers, owned by Betty Bond, at its year end of December 31, 2019. The company uses the periodic inventory system:

Freight-In	$1,200
Interest Expense	2,300
Merchandise Inventory, January 1, 2019	140,000
Merchandise Inventory, December 31, 2019	110,000
Purchase Discounts	2,500
Purchase Returns & Allowances	12,300
Purchases	120,000
Rent Expense	24,000
Salaries Expense	47,000
Sales Discounts	7,500
Sales Revenue	230,000

a) Calculate the cost of goods sold for Bluevale Wholesalers for 2019.

b) Prepare the closing entries for Bluevale Wholesalers for 2019 using the income summary method.

Date	Account Title and Explanation	Debit	Credit

AP-28B LO 9

Tommy Greggson, owner of Greggson Retail, prepared the following adjusted trial balance at its year end of October 31, 2019.

Greggson Retail Trial Balance October 31, 2019		
Account Title	**DR**	**CR**
Cash	$78,000	
Accounts Receivable	30,000	
Merchandise Inventory	165,000	
Prepaid Expenses	6,000	
Store Equipment	250,000	
Accumulated Depreciation—Store Equipment		$80,000
Accounts Payable		126,000
Unearned Revenue		8,000
Bank Loan		50,000
Greggson, Capital		300,000
Greggson, Withdrawals	20,000	
Sales Revenue		360,000
Purchase Returns & Allowances		12,000
Purchase Discounts		5,000
Sales Returns & Allowances	30,000	
Sales Discounts	3,000	
Purchases	235,000	
Freight-In	7,000	
Depreciation Expense—Store Equipment	4,000	
Interest Expense	1,000	
Sales Salaries Expense	62,000	
Office Salaries Expense	50,000	
Total	**$941,000**	**$941,000**

A year-end inventory count revealed that $210,000 of inventory is on hand.

Required

a) Prepare a multi-step income statement for Greggson Retail, assuming a periodic inventory system is used.

b) Prepare the closing entries for Greggson Retail using the income summary method.

Date	Account Title and Explanation	Debit	Credit

AP-29B LO 9 10 11

The following information was taken from the records of Greggs Interior Supplies on December 31, 2019. Assume all accounts have normal balances.

Accounts Payable	$8,000
Accounts Receivable	13,500
Beginning Inventory	34,500
Cash	12,345
Depreciation Expense	12,300
Ending Inventory	32,400
Freight-In	1,000
Insurance Expense	3,600
Interest Revenue	3,250
Purchase Discounts	9,000
Purchase Returns & Allowances	3,420
Purchases	154,000
Rent Expense	6,000
Sales Discounts	900
Sales Returns & Allowances	3,200
Sales Revenue	450,000
G. Stone, Withdrawals	30,000
G. Stone, Capital	46,900

Required

a) Prepare a multi-step income statement up to and including gross profit assuming a periodic inventory system is used.

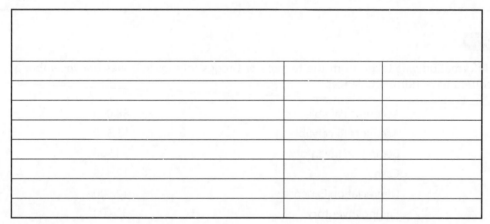

b) Prepare a multi-step income statement up to and including gross profit assuming a perpetual inventory system is used.

c) Calculate net income.

_____

_____

d) Prepare the closing entries using the income summary method and assuming a periodic inventory system was used.

Date	Account Title and Explanation	Debit	Credit

Case Study

CS-1 LO 3 4 5 7

George K. Connor is the owner and operator of Connor's Computers, a business that sells computers and other related merchandise using a perpetual inventory system. During its first month of operations, February 2019, the following transactions occurred.

Feb 1   Purchased inventory on account for $20,000, terms of 2/10, n/30

Feb 1   Received a deposit of $10,000 from a customer for products to be delivered later

Feb 1   Returned damaged inventory from the February 1 purchase worth $3,500

Feb 5   Sold products for cash of $13,000; the cost of goods was $6,000

Feb 10 Paid the balance owing to the supplier of inventory from February 1

Feb 16 Received an advertising bill for $3,000 which will be paid next month

Feb 21 Sold products on account for $31,000; the cost of goods was $10,000

Feb 22 Paid wages and benefits with $6,000 cash; this amount includes sales salaries of $4,000 and office salaries of $2,000

Feb 25 Purchased new computers on account for $4,000

Feb 26 A customer agreed to keep a defective product for a 30% allowance; the customer originally paid $1,000 on account for the product

Feb 27 A customer returned an incorrect product for cash; this product had a sales price of $500 and a cost of $300; the item was returned to the sales floor for resale

Feb 28 Incurred maintenance expense at the head office of $2,000 on account

The company uses the following chart of accounts to implement its accounting system.

Account Description	Account #
ASSETS	
Cash	101
Accounts Receivable	105
Merchandise Inventory	115
Computers	120
LIABILITIES	
Accounts Payable	200
Unearned Revenue	215
OWNER'S EQUITY	
Connor, Capital	300
Connor, Withdrawals	310

Account Description	Account #
REVENUE	
Sales Revenue	400
Sales Returns & Allowances	455
EXPENSES	
Cost of Goods Sold	500
Advertising Expense	505
Maintenance Expense	520
Salaries Expense	545

Required

a) Prepare the journal entries for the period.

Date	Account Title and Explanation	PR	Debit	Credit

Date	Account Title and Explanation	PR	Debit	Credit

b) Post the entries to the general ledger.

Account:					GL No:	
Date	Description	PR	DR	CR	Balance	

Account:					GL No:	
Date	Description	PR	DR	CR	Balance	

Account:					GL No:	
Date	Description	PR	DR	CR	Balance	

Account:					GL No:	
Date	Description	PR	DR	CR	Balance	

Account:					GL No:	
Date	Description	PR	DR	CR	Balance	

Account:					GL No:	
Date	Description	PR	DR	CR	Balance	

Account:					GL No:	
Date	Description	PR	DR	CR	Balance	

Account:					GL No:	
Date	Description	PR	DR	CR	Balance	

Account:					GL No:	
Date	Description	PR	DR	CR	Balance	

Account:					GL No:	
Date	Description	PR	DR	CR	Balance	

Account:						GL No:	
Date	**Description**	**PR**	**DR**	**CR**	**Balance**		

Account:						GL No:	
Date	**Description**	**PR**	**DR**	**CR**	**Balance**		

Account:						GL No:	
Date	**Description**	**PR**	**DR**	**CR**	**Balance**		

Account:						GL No:	
Date	**Description**	**PR**	**DR**	**CR**	**Balance**		

c) Prepare a trial balance.

d)   Prepare a multi-step income statement for the period.

e)   Prepare a statement of owner's equity for the period.

f)   Prepare a classified balance sheet for the period.

g)   Calculate the gross profit margin on product sales.

_____

_____

_____

_____

_____

h)   Calculate the current ratio at the end of the period.

_____

_____

_____

_____

_____

i)   What basic economic theory is related to proper management of inventory, and how would a business be impacted if it was not properly applied?

_____

_____

_____

_____

_____

_____

CS-2 LO 3 4 5 6 7

Freestyle Fashion, owned by Suzy Styles, is an urban clothing retailer using the perpetual inventory system. Its balance sheet as at January 1, 2019, is presented below.

Freestyle Fashion Balance Sheet As at January 1, 2019		
Current Assets		
Cash	$28,400	
Merchandise Inventory	50,000	
Prepaid Rent	12,000	
Total Current Assets		$90,400
Property, Plant & Equipment		
Equipment	32,000	
Total Property, Plant & Equipment		32,000
Total Assets		$122,400
Current Liabilities		
Accounts Payable	$20,500	
Unearned Revenue	12,000	
Total Current Liabilities		$32,500
Long-Term Liabilities		
Bank Loan	60,000	
Total Long-Term Liabilities		60,000
Total Liabilities		92,500
Owner's Equity		
Styles, Capital		29,900
Total Liabilities and Owner's Equity		$122,400

During January 2019, Freestyle Fashion had the following transactions.

Jan 2   Purchased 490 jackets at $50 each on account (with terms 2/10, n/30)

Jan 5   Sold $50,000 worth of inventory on account; this inventory cost $39,000

Jan 9   Purchased 100 pairs of jeans at $20 each on account (with terms 4/15, n/30)

Jan 11   Paid the balance owed to the supplier for all the jackets purchased on January 2

Jan 16   Paid wages of $2,000

Jan 18   A customer returned products for cash to the store due to a defect; these products were originally sold for $200 and cost $75

Jan 21   Paid the balance owed to the supplier for jeans purchased on January 9

Jan 24   Received $25,000 cash from sales previously made on account

Jan 26   Incurred $2,500 in utilities expenses, to be paid next month

Jan 30   Sold $20,000 worth of inventory for cash; this inventory cost $15,000

The company uses the following chart of accounts to implement its accounting system.

Account Description	Account #
ASSETS	
Cash	101
Accounts Receivable	105
Prepaid Rent	110
Merchandise Inventory	115
Equipment	120
Accumulated Depreciation—Equipment	125
LIABILITIES	
Accounts Payable	200
Interest Payable	205
Salary Payable	210
Unearned Revenue	215
Bank Loan	220
OWNER'S EQUITY	
Styles, Capital	300
Styles, Withdrawals	310
Income Summary	315

Account Description	Account #
REVENUE	
Sales Revenue	400
Sales Returns & Allowances	405
Sales Discounts	410
EXPENSES	
Cost of Goods Sold	500
Advertising Expense	505
Depreciation Expense	510
Insurance Expense	515
Interest Expense	520
Maintenance Expense	525
Office Supplies Expense	530
Professional Fees Expense	535
Rent Expense	540
Salaries Expense	545
Utilities Expense	550
Travel Expense	555

Required

Suzi is looking to expand her business and as such has arranged a meeting with private investors to review operating results for the month ended January 31, 2019. Knowing you are currently taking an accounting course, she has asked you to complete the following.

a)   Journalize the transactions for January 2019.

Date	Account Title and Explanation	PR	Debit	Credit

Date	Account Title and Explanation	PR	Debit	Credit

b) Journalize the following adjustments (to be recorded on January 31, 2019).

Jan 31   Prepaid rent represents one year of retail space rent; one month of prepaid rent has been used

Jan 31   Depreciation of store equipment for the month is $2,000

Jan 31 $1,000 of unearned revenue has now been earned

Jan 31 $100 of interest is accrued and owed on the bank loan

Date	Account Title and Explanation	PR	Debit	Credit

Date	Account Title and Explanation	PR	Debit	Credit

c) Post the transactions to the general ledger.

General Ledger

Account:						GL No:	
Date	Description	PR	DR	CR	Balance	

Account:						GL No:	
Date	Description	PR	DR	CR	Balance	

Account:						GL No:	
Date	Description	PR	DR	CR	Balance	

Account:						GL No:	
Date	Description	PR	DR	CR	Balance	

Account:					GL No:	
Date	Description	PR	DR	CR	Balance	

Account:					GL No:	
Date	Description	PR	DR	CR	Balance	

Account:					GL No:	
Date	Description	PR	DR	CR	Balance	

Account:					GL No:	
Date	Description	PR	DR	CR	Balance	

Account:					GL No:	
Date	Description	PR	DR	CR	Balance	

Account:					GL No:	
Date	Description	PR	DR	CR	Balance	

Account:					GL No:	
Date	Description	PR	DR	CR	Balance	

Account:					GL No:	
Date	Description	PR	DR	CR	Balance	

Account:					GL No:	
Date	Description	PR	DR	CR	Balance	

Account:					GL No:	
Date	Description	PR	DR	CR	Balance	

Account:					GL No:	
Date	Description	PR	DR	CR	Balance	

Account:					GL No:	
Date	Description	PR	DR	CR	Balance	

Account:					GL No:	
Date	Description	PR	DR	CR	Balance	

Account:					GL No:	
Date	Description	PR	DR	CR	Balance	

Account:					GL No:	
Date	Description	PR	DR	CR	Balance	

Account:					GL No:	
Date	Description	PR	DR	CR	Balance	

d) Prepare a multi-step income statement for January 2019. Assume that $2,000 of the utilities expense is for retail space and $500 is for head office. Assume that $1,200 of the salaries expense is for sales and $800 is for office staff.

e) Prepare a statement of owner's equity for January 2019.

f) Prepare a balance sheet for January 2019.

g) Prepare the month-end closing journal entries. Use the income summary account.

Date	Account Title and Explanation	PR	Debit	Credit

h) Suzi is concerned the investors will question why her inventory levels are less than half of that at the beginning of the month. Suggest some control measures she could implement to improve on this result in the future.

Chapter 8

INVENTORY VALUATION

LEARNING OBJECTIVES

LO 1 Determine the value of merchandise inventory under the perpetual inventory system

LO 2 Explain the impact of inventory errors

LO 3 Apply the lower of cost and net realizable value (LCNRV) rule to value merchandise inventory

LO 4 Measure a company's management of inventory using inventory ratios

LO 5 Describe ethics relating to inventory

Appendix

LO 6 Determine the value of merchandise inventory under the periodic inventory system

LO 7 Estimate the value of merchandise inventory under the periodic inventory system

AMEENGAGE *Access **ameengage.com** for integrated resources including tutorials, practice exercises, the digital textbook and more.*

Assessment Questions

AS-1 LO 1

List the three different inventory valuation methods allowed under GAAP.

_____

_____

AS-2 LO 1

In times of rising prices, which inventory valuation method results in the highest closing inventory? Explain your answer.

_____

_____

AS-3 LO 1

Different inventory valuation methods result in different inventory values. What factors may cause a company to select FIFO, weighted-average cost or specific identification?

_____

_____

_____

_____

_____

_____

_____

_____

AS-4 `LO 1`

Is a physical inventory count necessary for a company that uses the periodic inventory system? Why or why not?

_____

_____

_____

_____

AS-5 `LO 1`

Is a physical inventory count necessary for a company that uses the perpetual inventory system? Why or why not?

_____

_____

_____

_____

AS-6 `LO 1`

How does the actual flow of inventory affect the choice of inventory valuation method? How often can the inventory valuation method be changed?

_____

_____

_____

AS-7 `LO 1`

Which of the inventory valuation methods shows more ending inventory and less COGS in the case of rising prices?

_____

_____

_____

AS-8 `LO 2`

What is consigned inventory? Should it be recorded on the consignor's or the consignee's books?

_____

_____

_____

_____

_____

AS-9 `LO 2`

What does it mean for inventory errors to be self-correcting?

_____

_____

_____

AS-10 `LO 2`

Describe the impact of inventory errors on financial statement users.

_____

_____

_____

_____

_____

_____

_____

_____

_____

AS-11 `LO 3`

What is net realizable value?

_____

_____

_____

AS-12 `LO 3`

What does the lower of cost and net realizable value (LCNRV) rule refer to?

_____

_____

_____

_____

AS-13 `LO 4`

How do you calculate the inventory turnover ratio and what does it measure?

_____

_____

_____

AS-14 `LO 4`

How do you calculate days' sales in inventory and what does it measure?

_____

_____

_____

AS-15 LO 5

How can a company monitor and prevent inventory shrinkage?

_____

_____

_____

_____

_____

_____

AS-16 LO 2 5

What is the impact on financial statements of inflating inventory? What is the ethical responsibility of management in this regard?

_____

_____

_____

_____

_____

_____

AS-17 LO 1 6

Describe the differences between the specific identification method under the perpetual and the periodic inventory systems.

_____

_____

_____

AS-18 LO 7

Name two methods that can be used to estimate inventory for interim statement purposes under the periodic inventory system.

_____

_____

_____

_____

_____

_____

_____

_____

_____

Application Questions Group A

AP-1A LO **1**

The following purchases and sales took place at ZZZ Co. during the month of May 2019. The company had no inventory on hand on May 1. ZZZ Co. uses the perpetual inventory system. All sales are on account.

May 5   Purchased 200 units from AAA Co. for $10 per unit
May 7   Sold 100 units to SSS Co. for $30 each
May 13   Sold 50 units to TTT Co. for $30 each
May 15   Purchased 70 units from BBB Co. for $13 per unit
May 24   Sold 20 units to UUU Co. for $35 each
May 28   Purchased 80 units from CCC Co. for $15 per unit

Required

a) Fill in the inventory schedule using the weighted-average cost inventory valuation method.

Date	Purchases			Sales			Balance		
	Quantity	Unit Cost	Value	Quantity	Unit Cost	Value	Quantity	Unit Cost	Value

b) Fill in the inventory schedule using the FIFO (first-in, first-out) inventory valuation method.

Date	Purchases			Sales			Balance		
	Quantity	Unit Cost	Value	Quantity	Unit Cost	Value	Quantity	Unit Cost	Value

c) Fill in the inventory schedule using the specific identification inventory valuation method. Assume the units sold on May 7 and 13 were from the the purchase on May 5 and those sold on May 24 were from the purchase on May 15.

Date	Purchases			Sales			Balance		
	Quantity	Unit Cost	Value	Quantity	Unit Cost	Value	Quantity	Unit Cost	Value

d) Give the journal entries to record the May 24 sale using all three methods. Calculate the gross profit earned under each method for this sale.

Accounts	Weighted-Average Cost		FIFO		Specific Identification	

Method	Sales Revenue	Cost of Goods Sold	Gross Profit
Weighted Average Cost			
FIFO			
Specific Identification			

e) Which method results in the highest profit? Explain.

_____

_____

_____

AP-2A LO 1

Simplex Company has a fiscal year end on December 31. The company has only one product in inventory, and all units of that product are identical (homogenous). Complete the following schedule to calculate the value of ending inventory using the weighted-average cost method under the perpetual inventory system. Then calculate the cost of goods sold for the year 2019. Calculate unit cost to two decimal places. Round all value amounts to the nearest dollar.

Date	Purchases			Sales			Balance		
	Quantity	Unit Cost	Value	Quantity	Unit Cost	Value	Quantity	Unit Cost	Value
Jan 1							15	$10.00	$150
Feb 13	25	$12							
Mar 26	16	$13							
Apr 17				40					
Jul 25	34	$14							
Sep 28				14					
Nov 3				11					
Dec 31	75			65					

Cost of goods sold: _____

AP-3A LO 1

An inventory record card for item A-903 shows the following details in 2019.

Mar 1	60 units in opening inventory at a cost of $70 per unit
Mar 5	40 units sold
Mar 9	120 units purchased at a cost of $74 per unit
Mar 18	70 units sold
Mar 24	44 units purchased at a cost of $80 per unit
Mar 29	100 units sold
Mar 31	50 units purchased at a cost of $90 per unit

Required

The company uses the perpetual inventory method. Calculate the value of inventory at each of the above dates and determine the ending inventory at the end of March using the following methods.

a) FIFO

Date	Purchases			Sales			Balance		
	Quantity	Unit Cost	Value	Quantity	Unit Cost	Value	Quantity	Unit Cost	Value

b) Weighted-average cost

Date	Purchases			Sales			Balance		
	Quantity	Unit Cost	Value	Quantity	Unit Cost	Value	Quantity	Unit Cost	Value
							60	$70.00	$4,200.00

c) Which inventory valuation method should be used when merchandise includes perishable products (items with expiration dates) and why? Give an example of a type of merchandise inventory that would be perishable.

_____

_____

_____

_____

AP-4A LO 1

GB, a bookseller, had the following transactions during the month of August 2019 and uses a perpetual inventory system.

Aug 1   Bought 10 novels at $30 each
Aug 2   Bought 10 bags at $45 each
Aug 5   Sold 5 bags
Aug 10   Bought 15 pencil cases at $5 each
Aug 21   Sold 3 bags
Aug 25   Sold 12 pencil cases

Required

a) Calculate the value of inventory at each date using the specific identification method. Show the ending inventory for August 2019.

Date	Purchases			Sales			Balance		
	Quantity	Unit Cost	Value	Quantity	Unit Cost	Value	Quantity	Unit Cost	Value

b) Why would GB be more inclined to use the specific identification method for inventory valuation rather than either FIFO or weighted-average cost?

_____

_____

_____

_____

AP-5A LO 1

Poppy Company uses a perpetual inventory system. It reported the following data related to beginning inventory and inventory purchases and sales for the month of July 2019.

Jul 1	Beginning inventory consisted of 300 units at $13 per unit
Jul 9	Sold 200 units at $20 per unit
Jul 16	Purchased 120 units at $12 per unit
Jul 18	Purchased 300 units at $10 per unit
Jul 30	Sold 150 units at $20 per unit

Required

a) Fill in the inventory schedule and calculate the values of ending inventory, COGS and gross profit using the specific identification method. Assume that the 150 units sold on July 30 consist of 15 units from the beginning inventory, 35 units from the July 16 purchase and 100 units from the July 18 purchase.

Date	Purchases			Sales			Balance		
	Quantity	Unit Cost	Value	Quantity	Unit Cost	Value	Quantity	Unit Cost	Value
Jul 1							300	13	3900
Jul 9				200	13	2600	100	13	1300
Jul 16	120	12	1440				100	13	1300
							120	12	1440
Jul 18	300	10	3000				300	10	3000
Jul 30				15	13	195	85	13	1105
				35	12	420	85	12	1020
				100	10	1000	200	10	2000
	420		4400	3500		4215	370		4125

Ending inventory = 4125

COGS = 4215

Gross profit = 1200.

b) Fill in the inventory schedule and calculate the values of ending inventory, COGS and gross profit using the FIFO cost method.

Date	Purchases			Sales			Balance		
	Quantity	Unit Cost	Value	Quantity	Unit Cost	Value	Quantity	Unit Cost	Value

_____

_____

_____

c) Fill in the inventory schedule and calculate the values of ending inventory, COGS and gross profit using the weighted-average cost method.

Date	Purchases			Sales			Balance		
	Quantity	Unit Cost	Value	Quantity	Unit Cost	Value	Quantity	Unit Cost	Value

_____

_____

_____

Analysis

Which valuation method results in the lowest gross profit? Explain your answer.

_____

_____

AP-6A LO 2

A company reported ending inventory of $100,000 in Year 1. It was discovered in Year 2 that the correct value of the ending inventory was $90,000 for Year 1, and a correction was made. Complete the following table based on this information. Assume the company uses the perpetual inventory system.

Item	Reported	Correct Amount
Merchandise Inventory	$100,000	
Current Assets	$150,000	
Total Assets	$500,000	
Owner's Equity Year 1	$200,000	
Sales	$1,000,000	
Cost of Goods Sold	$500,000	
Profit (Loss) for Year 1	$6,000	

AP-7A LO 3

A company has three types of products: gadgets, widgets and gizmos. The cost and market price of each type is listed below. Complete the table by applying the lower of cost and net realizable value. The shaded areas do not require any entries.

Description	Category	Cost	NRV	LCNRV Applied to		
				Individual	Category	Total
Gadget Type 1	Gadgets	$1,000	$900			
Gadget Type 2	Gadgets	5,000	5,200			
Total Gadgets						
Widget A	Widgets	100	100			
Widget B	Widgets	20	200			
Total Widgets						
Gizmo 1	Gizmos	1,500	1,450			
Gizmo 2	Gizmos	1,750	2,000			
Total Gizmos						
Total						

AP-8A [LO 3]

Garden Company uses the perpetual inventory system and its inventory consists of four products as at December 31, 2019. Selected information is provided below.

Required

a) Calculate the inventory value that should be reported on December 31, 2019, using the lower of cost and net realizable value applied on an individual-item basis.

Product	Number of Units	Cost (per unit)	Net Realizable Value (per unit)	LCNRV (individual)
1	15	$80	$120	
2	20	$80	$60	
3	40	$60	$50	
4	5	$120	$180	

Inventory Value: _____

b) Using the results from a), prepare the journal entry to adjust merchandise inventory to LCNRV (at individual-item level).

Date	Account Title and Explanation	Debit	Credit

_____

_____

_____

_____

AP-9A [LO 3]

MJ Corporation sells three categories of products: shirts, socks and pants. The following information was available at the year end of December 31, 2019.

	Shirts	Socks	Pants
	$ per unit	$ per unit	$ per unit
Original Cost	10	13	15
Estimated Selling Price (Net Realizable Value)	15	12	14
Inventory: Number of Units Held	300	380	240

Required

a) Calculate the value of inventory (apply the LCNRV at the category level).

	Shirts	Socks	Pants
Inventory: Units Held			
Lower of Cost and Market			
Value of Inventory			

Total value of inventory: _____

_____

b) Using the results from a), prepare the journal entry to adjust merchandise inventory to LCNRV (at category level).

Date	Account Title and Explanation	Debit	Credit

_____

_____

_____

_____

AP-10A LO 4

Tanner Radio Company has an inventory turnover of 4.5, while its competitor, Deej Radio, has an inventory turnover ratio of 1.0.

Required

a) What do these ratios mean for each company? Which company has the better ratio?

_____

_____

_____

_____

b) Calculate the days' sales in inventory for each company and interpret their meaning.

_____

_____

_____

_____

AP-11A LO 4 5

The following are relevant merchandise inventory numbers from ABC Company for the 2019 fiscal year.

	$ Millions
Merchandise Inventory—December 31, 2018	$108.5
Merchandise Inventory—December 31, 2019	169.7
Cost of Goods Sold	$1,452.5

Relevant merchandise inventory numbers from XYZ Company for the 2019 fiscal year are shown below.

	$ Millions
Merchandise Inventory—December 31, 2018	$221.7
Merchandise Inventory—December 31, 2019	209.6
Cost of Goods Sold	$1,432.0

Required

a) Calculate the inventory turnover ratio and days' sales in inventory for ABC Company.

$$\frac{\text{Cost of goods Sold}}{\text{Average inventory}} = \frac{1452.5}{[108.5 + 169.71] : 2} = 10.4 \text{ times}$$

b) Calculate the inventory turnover ratio and days' sales in inventory for XYZ Company.

c) Compare the results between the two companies. What conclusion can we draw about the performance of these two companies comparatively?

d) Assume the two companies are in the same industry and competing for a contract for financing from private investors. Management at ABC Company was aware of an error in calculating the value of cost of goods sold that, if corrected, would have resulted in an inventory turnover of 4.8 instead of 10.4. Management was aware of the error. If unreported/not corrected, the investors may conclude that ABC does a better job of moving inventory than XYZ; however, if corrected, the investor may change their opinion and favour XYZ over ABC. As a manager for ABC, discuss the ethical implications related to reporting inventory.

AP-12A LO 5

In reviewing journal entries for the year ended December 31, 2019, the accountant for a flooring merchandiser noticed that errors were made in recording the cost of goods sold for several sales during the year. The bookkeeper had inadvertently applied FIFO instead of weighted-average cost method, which resulted in the total cost of goods sold being $10,000 lower than it should have been. Realizing the impact of this error on profit, the accountant alerted the manager to the errors. The manager thanked the accountant for the information but decided not to alert the owner, because he knew that the owner would not be pleased if he knew that the business was not doing as well as originally reported. The manager also knew that his performance bonus, which was accrued and paid in January of each year, was based on the profits reported for the previous year.

Discuss the ethical implications for the accountant and the manager in the above scenario.

AP-13A LO 6

Zipper Company has a fiscal year end of December 31. The company sells one kind of zipper called "The Z Plus." On January 1, Zipper had 20 units in inventory with a cost of $20 each. During the year, 65 units were sold. Zipper Company uses a periodic inventory system.

Required

a) Assuming weighted-average cost inventory valuation was used, calculate i) cost of goods sold and ii) ending inventory.

Round unit costs to two decimal places and total values to nearest dollar.

Date	Purchases and Opening Inventory				Sales			Balance		
	Quantity	Unit Cost	Value							
Jan 1	20	$20.00								
Feb 20	30	$22.00								
Mar 15	15	$25.00								
Jun 10	30	$27.00								
Sep 30	40	$30.00				Sales			Balance		
Nov 20	25	$32.00		Quantity	Unit Cost	Value		Quantity	Unit Cost	Value
Totals							i)			ii)

b) Assume FIFO inventory valuation method was used. Determine i) cost of goods sold and ii) ending inventory.

Date	Purchases and Opening Inventory				Sales			Balance		
	Quantity	Unit Cost	Value							
Jan 1	20	$20.00								
Feb 20	30	$22.00								
Mar 15	15	$25.00								
Jun 10	30	$27.00								
Sep 30	40	$30.00				Sales			Balance		
Nov 20	25	$32.00		Quantity	Unit Cost	Value		Quantity	Unit Cost	Value
Sales										
Totals							i)			ii)

c) Assume specific identification valuation method was used. The units sold were from the following purchases.

Jan 1	10
Feb 20	5
Mar 15	15
Jun 10	20
Sep 30	15
	65

Determine total i) cost of goods sold and ii) ending inventory.

Date	Purchases and Opening Inventory				Sales			Balance		
	Quantity	Unit Cost	Value		Quantity	Unit Cost	Value	Quantity	Unit Cost	Value
Jan 1	20	$20.00								
Feb 20	30	$22.00								
Mar 15	15	$25.00								
Jun 10	30	$27.00								
Sep 30	40	$30.00								
Nov 20	25	$32.00								
Sales										
Totals							i)			ii)

d) Which method will result in the highest profit? Lowest profit?

_____

_____

AP-14A LO 6

Marble Company uses a periodic inventory system. It reported the following data related to beginning inventory and inventory purchases and sales for the month of July 2019. Marble sold 350 units during the month of July for $25 each.

Jul 1	Beginning inventory consisted of 300 units at $13 per unit
Jul 9	Purchased 200 units at $12.50 per unit
Jul 16	Purchased 120 units at $12 per unit
Jul 18	Purchased 300 units at $10 per unit

Required

a) Fill in the inventory schedule and calculate the values of sales revenue, cost of goods sold, gross profit and ending inventory assuming the specific identification method for inventory valuation is used. Assume that, of the 350 units sold, 150 units were from the beginning inventory, 100 units from the July 9 purchase and 100 units from the July 18 purchase.

Date	Purchases and Opening Inventory		
	Quantity	Unit Cost	Value
Jul 1	300	$13.00	
Jul 9	200	$12.50	
Jul 16	120	$12.00	
Jul 18	300	$10.00	
Totals			

_____

_____

_____

_____

b)   FIFO method for inventory valuation

_____

_____

_____

_____

_____

_____

_____

_____

_____

_____

_____

_____

_____

_____

_____

_____

_____

_____

_____

_____

_____

_____

Analysis

Which method results in the higher gross profit? Why?

_____

_____

_____

AP-15A LO 7

Using the information provided from the general ledger, calculate the estimated closing inventory using the gross profit method.

Sales	$200,000
Opening Inventory	$67,000
Purchases	$90,000
Gross Profit Margin (from examination of prior years' statements)	30%

AP-16A LO 7

Use the following information to calculate the estimated closing inventory at cost by using the retail method.

	At Cost	At Retail
Cost of Goods Sold		
Opening Inventory	2,000	4,000
Purchases	42,000	90,000
Cost of Goods Available for Sale	44,000	94,000
Sales at Retail		50,000
Closing Inventory at Retail		44,000

_____

_____

_____

_____

_____

_____

_____

_____

_____

_____

_____

_____

Application Questions Group B

AP-1B LO 1

The following purchases and sales took place at Lock Co. during the month of January 2019. The company had 50 units of inventory on hand on Jan 1. Lock Co. uses the perpetual inventory system. All sales are on account.

Jan 1   Beginning inventory of 50 units that had a cost of $20 each

Jan 5   Purchased 200 units from Key Co. for $22 per unit

Jan 7   Sold 50 units to PSW Co. for $40 each

Jan 13   Sold 120 units to Ton Co. for $42 each

Jan 15   Purchased 70 units from LOL Co. for $25 per unit

Jan 24   Sold 40 units to SIM Co. for $45 each

Jan 28   Purchased 80 units from SOS Co. for $27 per unit

Required

a)   Fill in the inventory schedule using the weighted-average inventory valuation method.

Date	Purchases			Sales			Balance		
	Quantity	Unit Cost	Value	Quantity	Unit Cost	Value	Quantity	Unit Cost	Value

b)   Fill in the inventory schedule using the FIFO (first-in, first-out) cost inventory valuation method.

Date	Purchases			Sales			Balance		
	Quantity	Unit Cost	Value	Quantity	Unit Cost	Value	Quantity	Unit Cost	Value

c) Fill in the inventory schedule using the specific identification inventory valuation method. Assume the units sold on January 7 and 13 were from the beginning inventory and the January 5 purchase, respectively. Those sold on January 24 were from the purchase on January 15.

Date	Purchases			Sales			Balance		
	Quantity	Unit Cost	Value	Quantity	Unit Cost	Value	Quantity	Unit Cost	Value

d) Calculate the gross profit earned under each method of inventory valuation

Method	Sales Revenue	Cost of Goods Sold	Gross Profit
Weighted-Average Cost			
FIFO			
Specific Identification			

e) Give the journal entries to record the purchase on January 5 and the sale on January 7 assuming FIFO cost-flow method was used.

Date	Account/Explanation	Debit	Credit

f) Which method results in the highest value for ending inventory? Explain.

AP-2B LO 15

Oneway 3D Printers has a fiscal year end of December 31. The business has only one product in inventory and all units of that product are identical.

a) Complete the following schedule using the weighted-average cost inventory valuation method.
   (NOTE: Calculate unit cost to two decimal places and round total values to the nearest dollar.)

Date	Purchases			Sales			Balance		
	Quantity	Unit Cost	Value	Quantity	Unit Cost	Value	Quantity	Unit Cost	Value
Dec 1							5	$250.00	$1,250
Dec 5	20	$275.00							
Dec 7				8					
Dec 13	50	$290.00							
Dec 15				45					
Dec 23				10					
Dec 27	60	$300.00							
Dec 31									

b) What is the ending inventory and COGS based on the schedule in part a)?

_____

_____

c) Complete the following schedule using the FIFO inventory valuation method. Assume 8 units were sold on December 5, 45 units on December 15 and 10 units on December 23. (NOTE: Apply appropriate unit costs. Calculate unit cost to two decimal places and round total values to the nearest dollar.)

Date	Purchases			Sales			Balance		
	Quantity	Unit Cost	Value	Quantity	Unit Cost	Value	Quantity	Unit Cost	Value
Dec 1							5	$250.00	
Dec 5	20	$275.00							
Dec 7									
Dec 13	50	$290.00							
Dec 15									
Dec 23									
Dec 27	60	$300.00							
Dec 31									

Analysis

Suppose a manager receives a bonus based on profits earned during the period. Even though the weighted-average method has been used in the past, costs are increasing $250–$300 for this period. Which method would the manager most likely use to ensure the highest profit was reported? Discuss the ethical implications of using that method.

_____

_____

_____

_____

AP-3B LO 1

An inventory record card for item B-52 shows the following details in 2019.

Sep 1	40 units in opening inventory at a cost of $50 per unit
Sep 5	25 units sold
Sep 9	150 units purchased at a cost of $55 per unit
Sep 18	80 units sold
Sep 24	50 units purchased at a cost of $60 per unit
Sep 29	Sold 110 units
Sep 30	60 units purchased at a cost of $70 per unit

Required

The company uses the perpetual inventory method. Calculate the value of inventory at each of the above dates and determine the ending inventory at the end of September using the following methods.

a) FIFO

Date	Purchases			Sales			Balance		
	Quantity	Unit Cost	Value	Quantity	Unit Cost	Value	Quantity	Unit Cost	Value

b) Weighted-average cost

Date	Purchases			Sales			Balance		
	Quantity	Unit Cost	Value	Quantity	Unit Cost	Value	Quantity	Unit Cost	Value

c) Which inventory valuation method should be used if merchandise consists of identical items for which it doesn't matter which item is sold first? Why would this method be preferred over any other?

_____

_____

_____

AP-4B LO 1

Andy's Auto sells new and used cars. Andy started his business on October 1, 2019, with no beginning inventory.

Oct 2	Purchased 5 red cars for $25,000 each
Oct 5	Purchased 5 blue trucks for $30,000 each
Oct 6	Sold 2 blue trucks
Oct 7	Sold 2 red cars
Oct 12	Purchased 5 green SUVs for $35,000 each
Oct 15	Sold 1 green SUV

Required

a) Calculate the value of inventory at each date using the specific identification method. Show the ending inventory for October 2019.

Date	Purchases			Sales			Balance		
	Quantity	Unit Cost	Value	Quantity	Unit Cost	Value	Quantity	Unit Cost	Value

b) Assuming the red cars were sold for $30,000, the blue trucks for $40,000 and the green SUV for $40,000, which vehicle would yield the highest gross profit margin?

_____

_____

_____

_____

_____

AP-5B LO 1

Poppy Company uses a perpetual inventory system. It reported the following data related to beginning inventory and inventory purchases and sales for the month of August 2019.

Aug 1	Beginning inventory consisted of 180 units at $6 per unit
Aug 10	Purchased 400 units at $4 per unit
Aug 17	Sold 250 units at $10 per unit
Aug 23	Purchased 700 units at $3 per unit
Aug 27	Sold 500 units at $9.50 per unit

Required

a) Fill in the inventory schedule and calculate the values of ending inventory, COGS and gross profit using the specific identification method. Assume that the 250 units sold on August 17 consists of 100 units of beginning inventory and 150 units from the August 10 purchase. Also assume that the 500 units sold on August 27 consists of 50 units from the beginning inventory, 100 units from the August 10 purchase and 350 units from the August 23 purchase.

Date	Purchases			Sales			Balance		
	Quantity	Unit Cost	Value	Quantity	Unit Cost	Value	Quantity	Unit Cost	Value

_____

_____

_____

b) Fill in the inventory schedule and calculate the values of ending inventory, COGS and gross profit using the FIFO cost method.

Date	Purchases			Sales			Balance		
	Quantity	Unit Cost	Value	Quantity	Unit Cost	Value	Quantity	Unit Cost	Value

_____

_____

_____

c) Fill in the inventory schedule and calculate the values of ending inventory, COGS and gross profit using the weighted-average cost method.

Date	Purchases			Sales			Balance		
	Quantity	Unit Cost	Value	Quantity	Unit Cost	Value	Quantity	Unit Cost	Value

Analysis

In times of decreasing prices, which is the case in this question, which method results in the highest profit? Which method would result in the highest gross profit in times of rising prices? Explain.

AP-6B LO 2

Trevor and Arkady run Squash Stuff Company. The net income earned by their business during the year ended December 31, 2019, is $250,000. However, an inventory clerk realized that the ending inventory for 2019 was overstated by $10,000.

Required

a) If the error is not corrected, what is the effect on 2019 net income?

b) If the error is not corrected, what is the effect on the 2019 equity balance?

c) Record journal entries to correct the overstatement of merchandise inventory assuming the error was discovered on December 31, 2019.

Date	Account Title and Explanation	Debit	Credit

d) If the error is not corrected, how is the sum of 2019 and 2020 net income affected?

_____

_____

_____

_____

e) There have been cases where companies applying for bank loans have intentionally overstated their closing inventory. Why would companies overstate their closing inventory and what are some of the methods of overstating closing inventory?

_____

_____

_____

_____

_____

AP-7B LO 3

A company has three types of products: gadgets, widgets and gizmos. The cost and NRV of each type is listed below. Complete the table by applying the lower of cost and net realizable value. The shaded areas do not require entries.

Description	Category	Cost	NRV	LCNRV Applied to Individual	LCNRV Applied to Category	LCNRV Applied to Total
Gadget 1	Gadgets	$1,500	$1,390			
Gadget 2	Gadgets	4,830	5,430			
Total Gadgets		6,330	6,820			
Widget A	Widgets	890	470			
Widget B	Widgets	350	300			
Total Widgets		1,240	770			
Gizmo 1	Gizmo	1,350	1,960			
Gizmo 2	Gizmo	2,460	2,320			
Total Gizmos		3,810	4,280			
Total		$11,380	$11,870			

AP-8B LO 3

Patio Company uses the perpetual inventory system and its inventory consists of three types of products as at December 31, 2019. Selected information is provided below.

Required

a) Calculate the inventory value that should be reported on December 31, 2019, using the lower of cost and net realizable value applied on an individual-item basis.

Product	Number of Units	Cost (per unit)	Net Realizable Value (per unit)	LCNRV (individual)
1	5	110	115	
2	40	40	35	
3	20	60	75	

b) Using the results from part a), prepare the journal entry to adjust merchandise inventory to LCNRV (at individual-item level).

Date	Account Title and Explanation	Debit	Credit

_____

_____

_____

_____

AP-9B LO 3

On December 31, 2019, Kranky Bike Shop has three types of bikes: mountain bikes, road bikes and hybrid bikes. The cost and NRV of each type is listed below.

Required

a) Complete the table by applying the lower of cost and net realizable value. The shaded areas do not require entries.

Description	Category	Cost	NRV	LCNRV Applied to Individual	Category	Total
CCM	Mountain	$10,000	$8,000			
Mikado	Mountain	8,000	5,500			
Oryx	Mountain	2,000	3,100			
Total Mountain Bikes						
Giant	Road	7,000	12,500			
Norco	Road	6,000	8,100			
Total Road Bikes						
Electra	Hybrid	2,800	2,500			
Acquila	Hybrid	2,600	3,000			
Total Hybrid Bikes						
Total						

b) Prepare the adjusting entry, if required, if LCNRV was applied using
   i) individual products
   ii) category
   iii) total

	Date	Account Title and Explanation	Debit	Credit
i)				
ii)				
iii)				

AP-10B LO 7

A list of relevant inventory numbers from SI Company for the year ended December 31, 2019, is provided below.

Average Inventory—December 31, 2018	$90,000
Average Inventory—December 31, 2019	110,000
Cost of Goods Sold—2018	920,000
Cost of Goods Sold—2019	890,000

Required

a) Calculate the inventory turnover ratio and the days' sales in inventory for SI company for the two years.

	2019	2018
Inventory Turnover Ratio		
Days' Sales in Inventory		

b) Compare the results between two years. What conclusion can be drawn about the performance of the company regarding both years?

_____

_____

_____

_____

_____

_____

AP-11B LO 4 5

Delta Corporation reported the following amounts for ending inventory and cost of goods sold in the financial statements.

Ending Inventory		Cost of Goods Sold	
2019	$799,000	2019	$25,927,000
2018	$1,365,000	2018	$36,479,000
2017	$3,205,000	2017	$47,025,000

Required

a) Calculate the inventory turnover ratio and days' sales in inventory for 2019 and 2018.

_____

_____

_____

_____

b) Compare and discuss the results between the two years.

_____

_____

c) Delta Corporation is a software company in a rapidly changing industry. Evaluate the results from part a) by using this information and considering the amount of cost of goods sold.

_____

_____

_____

_____

_____

AP-12B LO 5

Casey's Computers, a local business owned by Casey Cameron, sells several makes and models of personal computers. Casey sells both lower and higher priced computers ranging in cost from $500 to $10,000. While price range varies, advances in manufacturing processes and technology have resulted in a decline in purchase costs for the retailer over the past few years. For example, a Dell Ultrabook laptop costing $2,500 at the beginning of the year is now priced at $2,150. Each computer has a serial number and other identifying features that distinguish one from another. Management uses a perpetual inventory system with FIFO method. Casey is aware that using specific identification would be the best matching of costs with revenues but finds that FIFO is easier to apply and also helps defer having to pay income tax on profits.

Explain the ethical issues related to the choice of inventory valuation method in the above scenario.

_____

_____

_____

_____

_____

_____

_____

AP-13B LO 6

Button Company has a fiscal year end of December 31. The company sells one kind of button called "The Button." On January 1, Button had 250 units in inventory with a cost of $3.25 each. During the year, 750 units were sold. Button Company uses a periodic inventory system.

Required

a) Assuming the weighted-average cost inventory valuation, calculate total i) cost of goods sold and ii) ending inventory. Round unit costs to two decimal places and totals to nearest dollar.

Date	Purchases and Opening Inventory				Sales			Balance		
	Quantity	Unit Cost	Value							
Jan 1	250	$3.25								
Feb 20	400	$3.00								
Mar 15	300	$2.60								
Jun 10	200	$2.50								
Sep 30	500	$2.25			**Sales**			**Balance**		
Nov 20	100	$2.00			Quantity	Unit Cost	Value	Quantity	Unit Cost	Value
Totals										
							i)			ii)

b) Assume FIFO inventory valuation method was used. Determine i) cost of goods sold and ii) ending inventory.

Date	Purchases and Opening Inventory			Sales			Balance		
	Quantity	Unit Cost	Value	Quantity	Unit Cost	Value	Quantity	Unit Cost	Value
Jan 1	250	$3.25							
Feb 20	400	$3.00							
Mar 15	300	$2.60							
Jun 10	200	$2.50							
Sep 30	500	$2.25							
Nov 20	100	$2.00							
Sales									
				400	$3.00	$1,200	200	$2.50	$500
				100	$2.60	$260	500	$2.25	$1,125
Totals									

i)   ii)

c) Assume specific identification valuation method was used and that units sold were from the following purchases.

Jan 1	100
Feb 20	50
Mar 15	250
Jun 10	200
Sep 30	150
	750

Determine total i) cost of goods sold and ii) ending inventory.

Date	Purchases and Opening Inventory			Sales			Balance		
	Quantity	Unit Cost	Value	Quantity	Unit Cost	Value	Quantity	Unit Cost	Value
Jan 1	250	$3.25							
Feb 20	400	$3.00							
Mar 15	300	$2.60							
Jun 10	200	$2.50							
Sep 30	500	$2.25							
Nov 20	100	$2.00							
Sales				100					
				50					
				250					
				200					
				150					
							100	$2.00	$200
Totals									

i)   ii)

d) Which method will result in the highest profit? Lowest profit?

_____

_____

AP-14B LO 6

Sparkle Company uses a periodic inventory system. It reported the following data related to beginning inventory and inventory purchases and sales for the month of September 2019. Sparkle sold 500 units during the month of September for $35 each.

Sep 1	Beginning inventory consisted of 200 units at $20 per unit
Sep 20	Purchased 320 units at $22 per unit
Sep 25	Purchased 400 units at $25 per unit

Required

a) Using weighted-average cost inventory valuation method, determine the cost of goods sold and value of ending inventory assuming 700 units were sold for $30 each during the month. Round unit costs to two decimal places and totals to nearest dollar.

| Date | Purchases and Opening Inventory | | |
	Quantity	Unit Cost	Value
Sep 1	200	$20.00	
Sep 20	320	$22.00	
Sep 25	400	$25.00	
Totals			

Analysis

Assume FIFO was used instead of weighted-average cost. What would be the effect on cost of goods sold and ending inventory? Would it be higher or lower than the amounts calculated above? Justify your answers.

AP-15B LO 7

During the month of January 2019, Fine Groceries lost inventory due to a fire. The following amounts have been extracted from the accounts of Fine Groceries Store.

Sales		$280,000
Beginning Inventory	$210,000	
Purchases	340,000	
Inventory in good condition after fire	300,000	
Gross Profit Margin		30%

Calculate the amount of inventory lost due to the fire by first calculating the amount of estimated ending inventory before the fire using the gross profit method.

Sales Revenue		
Cost of Goods Sold		
Opening Inventory	$210,000	
Purchases	340,000	
Cost of Goods Available for Sale		
Closing Inventory Before Fire		
Cost of Goods Sold		
Gross Profit		

AP-16B LO 7

The following information has been provided by AS Retailers for the month of August 2019. Calculate the estimated closing inventory at cost using the retail method.

	At Cost	At Retail
Cost of Goods Sold		
Opening Inventory	$3,000	$6,000
Purchases	32,000	80,000
Cost of Goods Available for Sale	$35,000	86,000
Sales at Retail		50,000
Closing Inventory at Retail		$36,000

Case Study

CS-1 [LO 1 3 7]

Monrose Park had the following transactions during the month of November 2019.

Nov 2   Purchased 1,000 widgets for $20 per unit on credit
Nov 5   Sold 900 widgets for $55 each for cash
Nov 10   Purchased 500 widgets for $25 per unit on credit
Nov 18   Sold 100 widgets for $60 each on credit
Nov 29   Sold 300 widgets for $50 each for cash

Monrose Park uses a perpetual inventory system and the FIFO inventory valuation method. There were no widgets in the company's opening inventory for November.

Required

a) Record the above transactions in the general journal.

Date	Account Title and Explanation	Debit	Credit

b) Prepare the schedule to calculate ending inventory after the above transactions.

Date	Purchases			Sales			Balance		
	Quantity	Unit Cost	Value	Quantity	Unit Cost	Value	Quantity	Unit Cost	Value

c) Calculate the value of merchandise inventory using the lower of cost and net realizable value (LCNRV).

Description	Category	Cost	NRV	LCNRV Applied to	
				Individual	Category
Widget A	Widgets	$3,000	$2,300		
Widget B	Widgets	2,000	3,300		
Total Widgets					
Total					

d) Record the journal entry to adjust the value of merchandise inventory to the lower of cost and net realizable value based on individual items using the results from c).

Date	Account Title and Explanation	Debit	Credit

e) Prepare an excerpt of the multiple-step income statement for the month showing sales revenue, cost of goods sold, and gross profit.

f)   Sales for December were $100,000 and purchases were $68,500. Using the gross profit method, estimate the closing value of inventory. Assume the gross profit margin from November will be the gross profit margin for December.

Sales Revenue		$100,000
Cost of Goods Sold		
Opening Inventory		
Purchases	68,500	
Cost of Goods Available for Sale		
Closing Inventory		
Cost of Goods Sold		
Gross Profit		

_____

_____

_____

_____

_____

g)   Using the following chart, show how the cost of goods sold and value of ending inventory would change using the weighted-average cost method for inventory.

Date	Purchases			Sales			Balance		
	Quantity	Unit Cost	Value	Quantity	Unit Cost	Value	Quantity	Unit Cost	Value

h)   Since there are two categories of widgets, A and B, which method of inventory valuation might Monrose consider using instead of FIFO? Explain.

_____

_____

_____

_____

_____

_____

Chapter 9

ACCOUNTING INFORMATION SYSTEMS

LEARNING OBJECTIVES

LO 1 Explain the flow of accounting information through the accounting paper trail

LO 2 Describe and record transactions in special journals and subsidiary ledgers

LO 3 Identify features of a computerized accounting system

Appendix

LO 4 Prepare special journals under a periodic inventory system

AMEENGAGE™ *Access **ameengage.com** for integrated resources including tutorials, practice exercises, the digital textbook and more.*

Assessment Questions

AS-1 LO 1

What is an accounting system?

AS-2 LO 1

What are the features of an effective accounting information system?

AS-3 LO 1

Describe the paper trail in a manual accounting system.

AS-4 LO 2

What are special journals used for?

_____

_____

_____

AS-5 LO 2

What type of information is found in the sales journal?

_____

_____

_____

AS-6 LO 2

What are general journals used for?

_____

_____

AS-7 LO 2

Why are subsidiary ledgers used?

_____

_____

_____

_____

AS-8 LO 2

What is the relationship between a controlling account and its corresponding subledgers?

_____

_____

_____

AS-9 LO 2

What type of information can be found in an accounts payable subsidiary ledger?

_____

_____

_____

AS-10 LO 2

At the end of the accounting period, what is done with the totals in the purchases special journal?

_____

_____

_____

AS-11 LO 2

When preparing a sales return in the general journal, what accounts are updated? How is the post reference column used to indicate the accounts are updated?

_____

_____

_____

_____

AS-12 LO 3

How do the elements in a computerized system differ from those in a manual system?

_____

_____

_____

AS-13 LO 3

Provide a few examples of reports that can be generated by QuickBooks.

_____

_____

_____

_____

AS-14 LO 3

What is cloud accounting?

_____

_____

_____

AS-15 LO 3

What are some advantages and disadvantages of cloud accounting?

_____

_____

_____

_____

_____

_____

_____

AS-16 LO 3

What are a few examples of cloud-based accounting services?

_____

_____

AS-17 LO 4

How is using special journals in the periodic inventory system different from using special journals in the perpetual inventory system?

_____

_____

_____

_____

_____

_____

_____

_____

_____

_____

_____

_____

_____

_____

_____

_____

_____

_____

_____

_____

_____

_____

_____

_____

_____

_____

_____

_____

_____

_____

_____

_____

_____

_____

_____

_____

_____

Application Questions Group A

AP-1A LO 1

An accounting system includes a "paper trail" of documents and processes used to record and report the financial results of the business for a given period of time.

Using numbers 1-8, list the order in which the following would occur.

_____ Record transaction in appropriate journal

_____ Prepare a trial balance

_____ Post to subsidary ledgers

_____ Complete the remaining steps in the accounting cycle

_____ Reconcile balances in subsidiary ledgers to general ledger control account

_____ Review source document to determine type of transaction and to which journal it needs to be recorded

_____ Post individual amounts to appropriate general ledger accounts as required

_____ Post column totals to appropriate accounts in general ledger

AP-2A LO 2

For each transaction, indicate in which journal it should be recorded.

- Sales Journal (SJ)
- Cash Receipts Journal (CR)
- Purchases Journal (PJ)
- Cash Payments Journal (CP)
- General Journal (GJ)

_____ Sold products for cash

_____ Received a loan from the bank

_____ Owner invested cash into the business

_____ Owner withdrew cash from the business

_____ Paid amount owing to a supplier

_____ Received a utility bill, which will be paid later

_____ Returned products to a supplier

_____ Recorded adjustment for depreciation

_____ Sold products on account

AP-3A LO 2

Hidson Inc. is a small retailer. The following is a list of sales transactions for the month of April.

Apr 2	Made a sale on account (Invoice #5703) to B. Fager for $450 (cost $300)
Apr 5	Made a sale on account (Invoice #5704) to J. Dryer for $1,150 (cost $900)
Apr 10	Made a sale on account (Invoice #5705) to T. Burton for $550 (cost $450)
Apr 12	Made a sale on account (Invoice #5706) to JB Inc. for $670 (cost $500)

Record these transactions in the sales journal. Assume all amounts are posted. Show posting references for customer accounts and for column totals.

Accounts Receivable	110
Inventory	120
Sales Revenue	400
Cost of Goods Sold	500

Sales Journal					Page 3
Date	Account	Invoice #	PR	Accounts Receivable/ Sales (DR/CR)	COGS/Merchandise Inventory (DR/CR)

AP-4A LO 2

F. Benjamin owns a small fabric store. The following is the list of prices he charges for different types of products.

Product	Price	Cost
Blue cotton	$6 per sheet	$4 per sheet
Black silk	$20 per yard	$15 per yard
White tape	$10 per roll	$6 per roll
Green felt	$4 per yard	$2 per yard

During the month of July, the company made the following sales.

Jul 1   Sold 3 rolls of white tape, 5 sheets of blue cotton and 1 yard of black silk to R. Grey, on account (Invoice #5739)

Jul 5   Sold 6 rolls of white tape and 30 yards of green felt to G. Abbott on account (Invoice #5740)

Jul 9   Sold 1 yard of black silk to E. Hines, on account (Invoice #5741)

Jul 11   Sold 10 rolls of white tape, 6 sheets of blue cotton, 3 yards of black silk and 11 yards of green felt to M. Allen, on account (Invoice #5742)

Jul 14   Sold 12 rolls of white tape, 14 sheets of blue cotton and 9 yards of green felt to B. Cooper, on account (Invoice #5743)

Record the above transactions in the sales journal. Show references, assuming all postings to the subsidiary and general ledger accounts were done. Use the following account numbers for general ledger accounts.

Accounts Receivable	110
Merchandise Inventory	120
Sales	400
Cost of Goods Sold	500

Sales Journal					Page 6
Date	Account	Invoice #	PR	Accounts Receivable/Sales (DR/CR)	COGS/Merchandise Inventory (DR/CR)

AP-5A LO 2

Riya Cosmetics has provided you with the following information about the transactions the company had during the month of June.

Jun 2   Received $2,000 from a cash sale to Faces Inc. (cost $1,500)

Jun 6   Received $840 from Beauty Breeze for outstanding accounts receivable

Jun 10   Received $650 for the cash sale of 5 facial scrubs (cost $540) to Seizers Salon

Jun 13   Received $325 in interest earned from Timberland Bank

Jun 25   Took out a loan of $3,000 from the bank

Record these transactions in the cash receipts journal. Assuming all amounts were posted to both the subsidiary and general ledger accounts, show proper referencing using the following account numbers.

Cash	100
Accounts Receivable	110
Merchandise Inventory	120
Bank Loan	220
Sales	400
Interest Revenue	410
Cost of Goods Sold	500

Cash Receipts Journal								Page 5
Date	Account	PR	Cash (DR)	Accounts Receivable (CR)	Sales (CR)	Interest Revenue (CR)	Other (CR)	COGS/ Merchandise Inventory (DR/CR)

AP-6A LO 2

Lin Z is an owner-operated sporting goods retailer. The following is a list of the company's transactions for the month of June.

Jun 2   The owner, Lin Zarra, invested $16,500 into the business

Jun 6   Received a loan of $1,000 from the bank

Jun 10   Received $150 of interest earned on the savings account with Allmount Bank

Jun 13   Received $2,000 from cash sales to Dawn Sports (sold sports items costing $1,500)

Jun 25   Received $800 from AD Sports regarding outstanding accounts receivable

Record the above transactions in the cash receipts journal. Using the following account numbers, enter the appropriate references for both individual and column totals, assuming all posting was completed.

Cash	100
Accounts Receivable	110
Merchandise Inventory	120
Bank Loan	220
Zarra, Capital	300
Sales	400
Interest Revenue	410
Cost of Goods Sold	500

Cash Receipts Journal								Page 4
Date	Account	PR	Cash (DR)	Accounts Receivable (CR)	Sales (CR)	Interest Revenue (CR)	Other (CR)	COGS/ Merchandise Inventory (DR/CR)

AP-7A LO 2

Peter's Pewter sells figurines. During the month of August 2019, the following transactions occurred.

Aug 3   Peter invested $4,000 into his business

Aug 7   Sold inventory to Joyce Fontane for $500 cash; the inventory had a cost of $240

Aug 16   Sold inventory to Carol Balsdon for $750 on account; the inventory had a cost of $310

Aug 17   Sold inventory to James Stewart for $820 on account; the inventory had a cost of $420

Aug 24   Received full payment from Carol Balsdon for the Aug 16 transaction

Assume zero opening balances for the subledger and general ledger accounts. Assume no entries were made directly to the accounts receivable general ledger from the general journal.

Use the following selected accounts to complete the posting references.

Account Description	Account #	Account Description	Account #
Cash	101	Pewter, Withdrawals	310
Accounts Receivable	110	Sales Revenue	400
Merchandise Inventory	120	Sales Discount	405
Accounts Payable	200	Interest Revenue	410
Bank Loan	220	Cost of Goods Sold	500
Pewter, Capital	300	Office Supplies Expense	510
		Salaries Expense	520
		Telephone Expense	525

Required

a) Record the above transactions in the sales journal and the cash receipts journal. Assume all postings were completed. Show referencing.

Sales Journal					Page 1
Date	Account	Invoice #	PR	Accounts Receivable/ Sales (DR/CR)	COGS/ Merchandise Inventory (DR/CR)

Cash Receipts Journal								Page 3
Date	Account	PR	Cash (DR)	Accounts Receivable (CR)	Sales (CR)	Bank Loan (CR)	Other (CR)	COGS/ Merchandise Inventory (DR/CR)

b) Show how the above were posted to the accounts receivable control and subsidiary ledger accounts.

Account: Accounts Receivable					GL No:
Date	Description	PR	DR	CR	Balance

Account: Carol Balsdon				
Date	PR	DR	CR	Balance

Account: James Stewart				
Date	PR	DR	CR	Balance

AP-8A LO 2

Ryan Manufacturing sells flat-pack bookcases to retailers. The following transactions occurred during the month of September 2019. All sales on account come with terms of 2/10, net 30.

Sep 1   Received a loan from the bank for $15,000

Sep 5   Sold products for cash to Brock Retailer for $8,400; the products had a cost of $4,620

Sep 8   Sold products on account to Furniture Outlet for $10,600; the products had a cost of $6,360

Sep 12   Furniture Outlet paid the amount owing from Sep 8

Sep 21   Sold products on account to Brock Retailer for $6,200; the products had a cost of $3,410

Required

a) Record the transactions in the appropriate journal. Assuming all amounts were properly posted, show references using the following account numbers.

Cash	100
Accounts Receivable	110
Inventory	120
Bank Loan	220
Sales	400
Sales Discounts	410
Cost of Goods Sold	500

Sales Journal					Page 1
Date	Account	PR	Invoice #	Accounts Receivable/ Sales (DR/CR)	COGS/Merchandise Inventory (DR/CR)

Cash Receipts Journal								Page 1
Date	Account	PR	Cash (DR)	Sales Discount (DR)	Accounts Receivable (CR)	Sales (CR)	Other (CR)	COGS/ Merchandise Inventory (DR/CR)

b) Where appropriate, update the accounts receivable subledgers, including referencing. At the end of the month, calculate the totals of the columns in the journals and update the controlling account. Also show references for column totals, assuming amounts were posted to all general ledger accounts.

Account:	Accounts Receivable				**GL No:** 110	
Date	**Description**	**PR**	**DR**	**CR**	**Balance**	

Account:	Furniture Outlet			
Date	**PR**	**DR**	**CR**	**Balance**

Account:	Brock Retailer			
Date	**PR**	**DR**	**CR**	**Balance**

AP-9A LO 2

J. Glen, a sports retailer, made the following purchases during the month of May.

May 2   Received a bill (Invoice #125) from F. Day for the purchase of 2 basketballs worth $100 each and 6 footballs worth $45 each

May 4   Received a bill (Invoice #135) from G. Smith for the purchase of 7 cricket bats worth $65 each, 5 pairs of ice skates worth $32 each and 4 rugby balls worth $32 each

May 10   Received a bill (Invoice #145) from L. Todd for the purchase of 6 cricket bats worth $55 each

May 12   Received a bill (Invoice #222) from M. Moore for the purchase of 9 packages of golf balls at $45 each

Record these transactions in the purchases journal.

Purchases Journal					**Page 3**
Date	**Account**	**Invoice #**	**PR**	**Merchandise Inventory (DR)**	**Accounts Payable (CR)**

AP-10A LO 2

Vina Duckworth has provided the following information relating to her activities in the month of June 2019.

Jun 2   Paid amount owing of $650 (Invoice #780) to SK Depot (Cheque #195)

Jun 6   Paid back loan of $800 to the bank (Cheque #196)

Jun 10   Paid $3,000 to Nektel Inc. for purchase of inventory (Cheque #197)

Jun 13   Received a telephone bill for $350 and paid the amount owing to CasTech Inc. (Cheque #198)

Jun 25   Paid $205 to SFC Inc. for general expenses (Cheque #199)

Record these transactions in the cash payments journal.

Cash Payments Journal							Page 7
Date	Account	Cheque #	PR	Other (DR)	Merchandise Inventory (DR)	Accounts Payable (DR)	Cash (CR)

AP-11A LO 2

Medicines World, a medical store, makes all transactions in cash only. It has provided you with the following information about the transactions for the month of May.

May 2   Paid $1,000 rent for the month of May to Mrs. Elizabeth (Cheque #23)

May 4   Paid $800 salary to James Jones for the month of April (Cheque #24)

May 6   Paid repair and maintenance charges of $300 to Building Services Inc. (Cheque #25)

May 10   Paid $200 for internet charges to Castech (Cheque #26)

May 12   Bought medicine costing $8,000 from Medicines Inc. (Cheque #27)

Record these transactions in the cash payments journal.

Cash Payments Journal							Page 3
Date	Account	Cheque #	PR	Other (DR)	Merchandise Inventory (DR)	Accounts Payable (DR)	Cash (CR)

AP-12A LO 2

Blossoming Gardens sells landscaping materials. During the month of May 2019, the following transactions occurred.

May 3   Purchased office supplies for $800 on account from Office Supply Shop

May 7   Purchased inventory for $1,200 cash from Rock Bottom with Cheque #456

May 10   Paid a telephone bill for $350 with Cheque #457

May 17   Paid the amount owing to Office Supply Shop with Cheque #458

May 24   Purchased inventory for $3,500 from Paving Stones on account

Assume zero opening balances for the subledger and general ledger accounts. Assume no entries were made directly to the accounts payable general ledger from the general journal.

Use the following selected accounts to complete the posting references.

Account Description	Account #	Account Description	Account #
Cash	101	Owner's Withdrawals	310
Accounts Receivable	110	Sales Revenue	400
Merchandise Inventory	120	Sales Discount	405
Accounts Payable	200	Interest Revenue	410
Bank Loan	220	Cost of Goods Sold	500
Owner's Capital	300	Office Supplies Expense	510
		Salaries Expense	520
		Telephone Expense	525

Required

a) Record the above transactions in the purchases journal and the cash payments journal.

Purchases Journal							Page 6
Date	Account	Invoice #	PR	Merchandise Inventory (DR)	Office Supplies Expense (DR)	Other (DR)	Accounts Payable (CR)

Cash Payments Journal							Page 4
Date	Account	Cheque #	PR	Accounts Payable (DR)	Other (DR)	Merchandise Inventory (DR)	Cash (CR)

b) Post the appropriate transactions from the journals to the subledger accounts. At the end of the month, total the journals and update the accounts payable controlling account.

Account: Accounts Payable					GL No:
Date	Description	PR	DR	CR	Balance

Account:	Office Supply Shop			
Date	**PR**	**DR**	**CR**	**Balance**

Account:	Paving Stones			
Date	**PR**	**DR**	**CR**	**Balance**

AP-13A LO 2

Cap It sells a variety of hats. The following is a list of transactions for the month of November 2019.

Nov 5   Received Invoice #2563 for $4,000 worth of office supplies from Office Outfitters
Nov 9   Received Invoice #8475 from Aqua for $180 for water
Nov 12   Paid amount on Invoice #2563 to Office Outfitters with Cheque #153
Nov 21   Purchased inventory from Fedora Company for $4,000 with Cheque #154
Nov 22   Paid amount on Invoice #8475 to Aqua with Cheque #155
Nov 25   Paid $260 to John Walker for repair expenses with Cheque #156
Nov 26   Received Invoice #563 from Total Hats for $3,700 worth of inventory

Required

a) Record the above entries in the appropriate journal. Assuming all amounts were properly posted, show references using the following account numbers.

Cash	100
Accounts Receivable	110
Merchandise Inventory	120
Accounts Payable	200
Bank Loan	220
Sales	400
Sales Discounts	410
Cost of Goods Sold	500
Office Supplies Expense	530
Repairs Expense	540
Water Expense	550

Purchases Journal							Page 1
Date	**Account**	**Invoice #**	**PR**	**Water Expense (DR)**	**Office Supplies Expense (DR)**	**Merchandise Inventory (DR)**	**Accounts Payable (CR)**

Cash Payments Journal							Page 1
Date	Account	Cheque #	PR	Other (DR)	Merchandise Inventory (DR)	Accounts Payable (DR)	Cash (CR)

b) Post the entries in the subledger accounts. At the end of the month, total the special journals and update the accounts payable controlling account.

Opening Balances

Office Outfitters	$400 (CR)
Aqua	$40 (CR)
Total Hats	$1,300 (CR)

Note that Cap It's accounts payable records consist of only these three subledgers. Assume no entries were made directly to accounts payable through the general journal. Update the PR columns in both the subledgers and special journals.

Account : Accounts Payable					GL No: 200	
Date	Description	PR	DR	CR	Balance	

Accounts Payable Subsidiary Ledger				
Office Outfitters				
Date	PR	DR	CR	Balance

Accounts Payable Subsidiary Ledger				
Aqua				
Date	PR	DR	CR	Balance

Accounts Payable Subsidiary Ledger				
Total Hats				
Date	PR	DR	CR	Balance

AP-14A LO 2

Gherry Shoe Store had the following account balances as at April 30, 2019.

Gherry's Shoe Store		
Trial Balance		
April 30, 2019		
Account Title	DR	CR
Cash	$8,660	
Accounts Receivable	2,340	
Merchandise Inventory	17,500	
Equipment	16,000	
Accumulated Depreciation—Equipment		$500
Furniture & Fixtures	12,500	
Accumulated Depreciation—Furniture & Fixtures		800
Accounts Payable		3,600
Interest Payable		400
Bank Loan		12,000
Gherry, Capital		10,000
Sales Revenue		45,810
Sales Discounts	350	
Sales Returns & Allowances	675	
Interest Revenue		200
Cost of Goods Sold	12,400	
Depreciation Expense	900	
Interest Expense	400	
Maintenance Expense	975	
Office Supplies Expense	235	
Telephone Expense	375	
Totals	$73,310	$73,310

Note: Gherry does not prepare monthly financial statements and prepares closing entries as a part of year end processing.

The following is a list of transactions for the month of May.

May 4   Received $6,000 from a cash sale to Teamster Inc. (sold sport shoes costing $700)

May 5   Received a bill (Invoice #5780) for $800 worth of office supplies from BZDepot Inc. (terms 2/10, n/30)

May 6   Received $800 from Jo-Ann regarding her outstanding accounts receivable, which includes a deduction of $40 as discount for early payment

May 9   Received $650 for the cash sale of 5 pairs of shoes (costing a total of $85) to Sgt. Pepper

May 9   Received a telephone bill from ComTech Inc. (Invoice #167) for $150

May 10   Received $25 in interest from Method Bank on bank account balance for past month

May 12   Paid amount owing (Invoice #5780) less discount to BZDepot Inc. (Cheque #201)

May 15	Received a loan of $1,000 from Method Bank
May 18	Made a sale on account (Invoice #2341) to Keith Ricardo, for $250 (with inventory costing $200)
May 21	Paid $2,000 to Nikel Inc. for the purchase of inventory (Cheque #202)
May 22	Paid amount owing (Invoice #167) to ComTech Inc. for telephone services with Cheque #203
May 25	Paid $205 to BFG Inc., for maintenance expenses (Cheque #204)
May 26	Received bill from Adibas Inc. (Invoice #113) for $5,500 worth of inventory
May 28	Made a sale on account (Invoice #2342), to Gary Lineker for $2,000 worth of shoes (costing $1,700)
May 30	Gary Lineker returned $500 worth of shoes (costing $300)
May 31	Record monthly depreciation of $125 for the equipment and $100 for the furniture and fixtures. The business uses one depreciation expense account and separate accumulated depreciation accounts for each asset.
May 31	Record $100 of accrued interest on the bank loan. Annual interest will be paid January 1, 2020.

Use the following selected accounts to complete the posting references.

Account Description	Account #	Account Description	Account #
Cash	100	Sales Revenue	400
Accounts Receivable	110	Sales Discounts	410
Merchandise Inventory	120	Sales Returns & Allowances	420
Equipment	150	Interest Revenue	430
Accumulated Depreciation—Equipment	155	Cost of Goods Sold	500
Furniture & Fixtures	160	Depreciation Expense	520
Accumulated Depreciation—Furniture & Fixtures	165	Interest Expense	530
Accounts Payable	200	Maintenance Expense	540
Interest Payable	210	Office Supplies Expense	550
Bank Loan	220	Telephone Expense	560
Gherry, Capital	300		

Required

a) Record the transactions in the relevant journal. Show referencing.

Cash Receipts Journal										Page 1
Date	Account	PR	Cash (DR)	Sales Discount (DR)	Accounts Receivable (CR)	Sales (CR)	Interest Revenue (CR)	Bank Loan (CR)	Other (CR)	COGS/ Merchandise Inventory (DR/CR)

Sales Journal					Page 1
Date	Account	Invoice #	PR	Accounts Receivable/ Sales (DR/CR)	COGS/Merchandise Inventory (DR/CR)

Purchases Journal							Page 1
Date	Account	Invoice #	PR	Telephone Expense (DR)	Office Supplies Expense (DR)	Merchandise Inventory (DR)	Accounts Payable (CR)

Cash Payments Journal								Page 1
Date	Account	Cheque #	PR	Other (DR)	Merchandise Inventory (DR)	Accounts Payable (DR)	Merchandise Inventory (CR)	Cash (CR)

General Journal				Page 1
Date	Account Title and Explanation	PR	Debit	Credit

b) Post from the special journals to the accounts receivable subledger. Assume the following opening subledger balances.

Jo-Ann	$940 (DR)
Keith Ricardo	$600 (DR)
Gary Lineker	$800 (DR)

Note that Gherry's accounts receivable records consist of only these three subledgers. Update the PR columns in the subledgers and special journals. Note there should be one entry from the general journal for a sales return that needs to be posted both to the accounts receivable control account in the general ledger and also to the customer's account in the subsidiary ledger. Also note that the column totals from the sales and cash receipts journals need to be posted and referenced to the appropriate accounts in the general ledger. Space is provided at the end of each journal to record the account number where the total was posted.

Accounts Receivable Subsidiary Ledger Jo-Ann				
Date	PR	DR	CR	Balance

Accounts Receivable Subsidiary Ledger Keith Ricardo				
Date	PR	DR	CR	Balance

Accounts Receivable Subsidiary Ledger Gary Lineker				
Date	PR	DR	CR	Balance

c) Post from the special journals to the individual accounts in the accounts payable subledger. Assume the following opening subledger balances.

BZDepot Inc.	$1,000 (CR)
ComTech Inc.	$1,200 (CR)
Adibas Inc.	$1,400 (CR)

Note that Gherry's accounts payable records consist of only these three subledgers. Assume no entries were made directly to accounts payable through the general journal. Update the PR columns in both the subledgers and special journals. Note that column totals for the purchases and cash payments journals should be posted and referenced at the end of the month to their appropriate general ledger accounts. Space has been provided for you to enter the account numbers, below the total amount, to which the amounts were posted in the general ledger accounts listed below.

Accounts Payable Subsidiary Ledger BZDepot Inc.				
Date	PR	DR	CR	Balance

Accounts Payable Subsidiary Ledger ComTech Inc.				
Date	PR	DR	CR	Balance

<table>
<tr><th colspan="6">Accounts Payable Subsidiary Ledger
Adibas Inc.</th></tr>
<tr><th>Date</th><th>PR</th><th>DR</th><th>CR</th><th colspan="2">Balance</th></tr>
<tr><td></td><td></td><td></td><td></td><td></td><td></td></tr>
<tr><td></td><td></td><td></td><td></td><td></td><td></td></tr>
</table>

Account: Cash   **GL No:** 100

Date	Description	PR	DR	CR	Balance	
Apr 30	Balance					

Account: Accounts Receivable   **GL No:** 110

Date	Description	PR	DR	CR	Balance	
Apr 30	Balance					

Account: Merchandise Inventory   **GL No:** 120

Date	Description	PR	DR	CR	Balance	
Apr 30	Balance					

Account: Equipment   **GL No:** 150

Date	Description	PR	DR	CR	Balance	
Apr 30	Balance					

Account: Accumulated Depreciation—Equipment   **GL No:** 155

Date	Description	PR	DR	CR	Balance	
Apr 30	Balance					

Account: Furniture & Fixtures   **GL No:** 160

Date	Description	PR	DR	CR	Balance	
Apr 30	Balance					

Account: Accumulated Depreciation—Furniture & Fixtures   **GL No:** 165

Date	Description	PR	DR	CR	Balance	
Apr 30	Balance					

Account: Accounts Payable					**GL No:** 165	
Date	**Description**	**PR**	**DR**	**CR**	**Balance**	
Apr 30	Balance					

Account: Interest Payable					**GL No:** 210	
Date	**Description**	**PR**	**DR**	**CR**	**Balance**	
Apr 30	Balance					

Account: Bank Loan					**GL No:** 220	
Date	**Description**	**PR**	**DR**	**CR**	**Balance**	
Apr 30	Balance					

Account: Gherry, Capital					**GL No:** 300	
Date	**Description**	**PR**	**DR**	**CR**	**Balance**	

Account: Sales Revenue					**GL No:** 400	
Date	**Description**	**PR**	**DR**	**CR**	**Balance**	
Apr 30	Balance					

Account: Sales Discounts					**GL No:** 410	
Date	**Description**	**PR**	**DR**	**CR**	**Balance**	
Apr 30	Balance					

Account: Sales Returns & Allowances					**GL No:** 420	
Date	**Description**	**PR**	**DR**	**CR**	**Balance**	
Apr 30	Balance					

Account: Interest Revenue					**GL No:** 430	
Date	**Description**	**PR**	**DR**	**CR**	**Balance**	
Apr 30	Balance					

Account: Cost of Goods Sold					**GL No:** 500	
Date	**Description**	**PR**	**DR**	**CR**	**Balance**	
Apr 30	Balance					

Account: Depreciation Expense					**GL No:** 520	
Date	Description	PR	DR	CR	Balance	
Apr 30	Balance					

Account: Interest Expense					**GL No:** 530	
Date	Description	PR	DR	CR	Balance	
Apr 30	Balance					

Account: Maintenance Expense					**GL No:** 540	
Date	Description	PR	DR	CR	Balance	
Apr 30	Balance					

Account: Office Supplies Expense					**GL No:** 550	
Date	Description	PR	DR	CR	Balance	
Apr 30	Balance					

Account: Telephone Expense					**GL No:** 550	
Date	Description	PR	DR	CR	Balance	
Apr 30	Balance					

d) Prepare a trial balance as at May 31, 2019, and a schedule of acccounts receivable and schedule of accounts payable. Prove the totals of each schedule agree with their related general ledger account balances.

Gherry's Shoe Store		
Trial Balance		
May 31, 2019		
Account Title	DR	CR

Gherry's Shoe Store	
Schedule of Accounts Receivable	
May 31, 2019	
Accounts Receivable (General Ledger)	

Gherry's Shoe Store	
Schedule of Accounts Payable	
May 31, 2019	
Accounts Payable (General Ledger)	

AP-15A LO 3

A computerized accounting system uses many of the steps found in a manual system.

Required

Using the Quickbooks illustration discussed in the chapter, list the steps involved in recording the following transactions.

Note: Assume Quickbooks is open and ready for you to enter transactions.

a)   "On account" sales to an existing customer

_____

_____

_____

_____

b)   Payment received from customer for previous "on account" sale

_____

_____

_____

_____

AP-16A LO 4

Blossoming Gardens sells landscaping materials. During the month of May 2019, the following transactions occurred. Blossoming Gardens uses the periodic inventory system.

May 3	Purchased office supplies for $800 on account from Office Supply Shop
May 7	Purchased inventory for $1,200 cash from Rock Bottom with Cheque #456
May 10	Paid a telephone bill for $350 cash with Cheque #457
May 17	Paid the amount owing to Office Supply Shop with Cheque #458
May 24	Purchased inventory for $3,500 from Paving Stones on account

Assume zero opening balances for the subledger and general ledger accounts. Assume no entries were made directly to the accounts payable general ledger from the general journal.

Use the following selected accounts to complete the posting references.

Account Description	Account #	Account Description	Account #
Cash	101	Owner's Withdrawals	310
Accounts Receivable	110	Sales Revenue	400
Merchandise Inventory	120	Sales Discount	405
Accounts Payable	200	Interest Revenue	410
Bank Loan	220	Purchases	500
Owner's Capital	300	Office Supplies Expense	510
		Salaries Expense	520
		Telephone Expense	525

Required

a) Record the above transactions in the purchases journal and the cash payments journal.

Purchases Journal							Page 6
Date	Account	Invoice #	PR	Purchases (DR)	Office Supplies Expense (DR)	Other (DR)	Accounts Payable (CR)

Cash Payments Journal							Page 4
Date	Account	Cheque #	PR	Accounts Payable (DR)	Other (DR)	Purchases (DR)	Cash (CR)

b) Post the appropriate transactions from the journals to the subledger accounts. At the end of the month, total the journals and udpate the accounts payable controlling account.

Account:	Accounts Payable				GL No:
Date	Description	PR	DR	CR	Balance

Account:	Office Supply Shop			
Date	PR	DR	CR	Balance

Account:	Paving Stones			
Date	PR	DR	CR	Balance

Application Questions Group B

AP-1B LO 1

Subsidiary ledgers are often used within an accounting information system where special journals are used. Explain why subsidiary ledgers are used.

_____

_____

_____

_____

_____

_____

_____

AP-2B LO 2

For each transaction, indicate in which journal it should be recorded.

- Sales Journal (SJ)
- General Journal (GJ)
- Cash Receipts Journal (CR)
- Cash Payments Journal (CP)
- Purchases Journal (PJ)

_____ Received payment from a customer
_____ Paid salaries to employees
_____ Sold products on account
_____ A customer returned unused product
_____ Purchased inventory on account
_____ Recorded adjustment for unearned revenue
_____ Paid interest on a bank loan
_____ Purchased office supplies on account

AP-3B LO 2

SmartWays has provided you with the following information about its sales transactions during the month of September.

Sep 1　　Made a sale on account (Invoice #1122) to Fatima Inc. for $1,450 (cost $1,200)

Sep 5　　Made a sale on account (Invoice #1123) to Charisma Ltd. for $2,150 (cost $1,900)

Sep 9　　Made a sale on account (Invoice #1124) to Hidendsa Inc. for $750 (cost $600)

Sep 11　　Made a sale on account (Invoice #1125) to Henry Inc. for $1,270 (cost $1,080)

Sep 14　　Made a sale on account (Invoice #1126) to Snoob Inc. for $970 (cost $800)

Sep 20　　Made a sale on account (Invoice #1127) to Lime&Lemon for $ 1,150 (cost $1,020)

Record these transactions in the sales journal.

				Accounts Receivable/Sales (DR/CR)	COGS/Merchandise Inventory (DR/CR)
Date	**Account**	**Invoice #**	**PR**		

Sales Journal — Page 6

AP-4B LO 2

Jane Fisher is selling the following items at the prices listed below.

Product	Price	Cost
Plastic tubing	$1 per yard	$0.50 per yard
Polythene sheeting	$2 per yard	$1 per yard
Vinyl padding	$5 per box	$3 per box
Foam rubber	$3 per sheet	$2 per sheet

She has provided you the following data about sales transactions during the month of August.

Aug 2   Sold 22 yards of plastic tubing, 6 sheets of foam rubber and 4 boxes of vinyl padding to A. Portsmouth, on account (Invoice #1240)

Aug 4   Sold 50 yards of polythene sheeting, 6 sheets of foam rubber and 4 boxes of vinyl padding to B. Butler, on account (Invoice #1241)

Aug 6   Sold 4 yards of plastic tubing to A. Gate, on account (Invoice #1242)

Aug 10   Sold 30 yards of plastic tubing to L. Makeson, on account (Invoice #1243)

Aug 12   Sold 32 yards of plastic tubing, 24 yards of polythene sheeting and 20 boxes of vinyl padding to M. Alison, on account (Invoice #1244)

Record these transactions in the sales journal.

				Accounts Receivable/Sales (DR/CR)	COGS/Merchandise Inventory (DR/CR)
Date	**Account**	**Invoice #**	**PR**		

Sales Journal — Page 3

AP-5B LO 2

Book World is a dealer for stationery items. The company has provided the following information about the transactions in the month of March.

Mar 2 Received $3,500 from cash sale to Books & Books (cost $3,000)
Mar 9 Received $300 in interest earned from Hooper Bank
Mar 14 Received bank loan of $500 from Hooper Bank
Mar 19 Received $700 from cash sale to Book Ocean (cost $500)
Mar 21 Received $900 from cash sale to Beacon Books (cost $700)

Record these transactions in the cash receipts journal.

Cash Receipts Journal								Page 2
Date	Account	PR	Cash (DR)	Sales (CR)	Accounts Receivable (CR)	Interest Revenue (CR)	Other (CR)	COGS/Merchandise Inventory (DR/CR)

AP-6B LO 2

Highway Interchange sells clothing to retailers. During the month of July 2019, the following transactions occurred.

Jul 7 Sold inventory to Fashion House (Invoice #526) for $5,600 cash; the inventory had a cost of $2,400
Jul 10 Received a loan from Kingsman Bank for $5,000
Jul 15 Sold inventory to Stella Lanes (Invoice #527) on account for $8,500; the inventory had a cost of $3,400
Jul 17 Sold inventory to Cover Me (Invoice #528) for $7,500 on account; the inventory had a cost of $3,100
Jul 24 Received full payment from Stella Lanes for the sale on July 15
Jul 31 Received $50 of interest earned on a savings account

Assume zero opening balances for the subledger and general ledger accounts. Assume no entries were made directly to the accounts receivable general ledger from the general journal.

Use the following selected accounts to complete the posting references.

Account Description	Account #	Account Description	Account #
Cash	101	Owner's Withdrawals	310
Accounts Receivable	110	Sales Revenue	400
Merchandise Inventory	120	Sales Discount	405
Accounts Payable	200	Interest Revenue	410
Bank Loan	220	Cost of Goods Sold	500
Owner's Capital	300	Office Supplies Expense	510
		Salaries Expense	520
		Telephone Expense	525

Required

a) Record the above transactions in the sales journal and the cash receipts journal.

				Sales Journal	Page 1
Date	Account	Invoice #	PR	Accounts Receivable/ Sales (DR/CR)	COGS/Merchandise Inventory (DR/CR)

					Cash Receipts Journal			Page 1
Date	Account	PR	Cash (DR)	Accounts Receivable (CR)	Sales (CR)	Bank Loan (CR)	Other (CR)	COGS/ Merchandise Inventory (DR/CR)

b) Post the appropriate transactions in the sales journal and the cash receipts journal. At the end of the month, total the journals and update the accounts receivable controlling account.

Account: Accounts Receivable					**GL No:**	
Date	Description	PR	DR	CR	Balance	

Account: Stella Lanes				
Date	PR	DR	CR	Balance

Account: Cover Me				
Date	PR	DR	CR	Balance

AP-7B LO 2

Blip Wholesalers provides wholesale pastries to supermarkets. Since most customers are large retailers, Blip Wholesalers sells a lot of products on account and provides discounts for early payment. The following transactions occurred during the month of July 2019. All sales on account come with terms of 2/10, net 30.

Jul 3   Sold products on account to Farmer's Market for $5,200; the products had a cost of $3,120
Jul 7   Sold products for cash to customers for $4,200; the products had a cost of $2,310
Jul 8   Received a loan from Stanley Bank for $3,000
Jul 10   Farmer's Market paid the amount owing from July 3
Jul 15   Sold products on account to Renfrew for $3,200; the products had a cost of $1,760

Use the following selected accounts to complete the posting references.

Account Description	Account #	Account Description	Account #
Cash	101	Sales Revenue	400
Accounts Receivable	110	Sales Discount	405
Merchandise Inventory	120	Interest Revenue	410
Accounts Payable	200	Cost of Goods Sold	500
Bank Loan	220	Office Supplies Expense	510
Silver, Capital	300	Salaries Expense	520
Silver, Withdrawals	310	Telephone Expense	525

Required

a) Record the transactions in the appropriate journal.

Sales Journal					Page 5
Date	Account	PR	Invoice #	Accounts Receivable/Sales (DR/CR)	COGS/Merchandise Inventory (DR/CR)

Cash Receipts Journal								Page 1
Date	Account	PR	Cash (DR)	Sales Discount (DR)	Accounts Receivable (CR)	Sales (CR)	Other (CR)	COGS/Merchandise Inventory (DR/CR)

b) Where appropriate, update the accounts receivable subledger accounts. At the end of the month, calculate the totals of the columns in the journals and update the accounts receivable controlling account.

Account:	Accounts Receivable				GL No: 110	
Date	Description	PR	DR	CR	Balance	

Account: Farmer's Market

Date	PR	DR	CR	Balance

Account: Renfrew

Date	PR	DR	CR	Balance

AP-8B LO 2

Bob123, a household items retailer, made the following purchases during the month of March.

Mar 2 Received a bill (Invoice #305) from D. Pope for the purchase of 4 DVDs, worth $240 each

Mar 4 Received a bill (Invoice #426) from F. Lloyd for the purchase of 2 washing machines worth $560 each and 5 vacuum cleaners worth $400 each

Mar 6 Received a bill (Invoice #765) from B. Sankey for the purchase of 1 wireless router worth $600 and 2 washing machines worth $320 each

Mar 10 Received a bill (Invoice #2132) from J. Wilson for the purchase of 6 blenders worth $45 each

Mar 12 Received a bill (Invoice #1234) from R. Freer for the purchase of 4 dishwashers worth $240 each

Record these transactions in the purchases journal.

Purchases Journal					Page 5
Date	Account	Invoice #	PR	Merchandise Inventory (DR)	Accounts Payable (CR)

AP-9B LO 2

Philips, a clothing store, made the following purchases for the month of September.

Sep 2 Received a bill (Invoice #723) from Smith Inc. for the purchase of $80 worth of silk and $100 worth of cotton

Sep 7 Received a bill (Invoice #657) from Grantley Store for the purchase of Lycra goods worth $38 and woolen items worth $64

Sep 12 Received a bill (Invoice #498) from Henry Inc. for the purchase of silk worth $45, cotton worth $130 and Lycra worth $135

Sep 17 Received a bill (Invoice #342) from Kelly Inc. for the purchase of $98 worth of cotton and $56 worth of Lycra goods

Sep 22 Received a bill (Invoice #290) of $380 from Hamilton Inc. for the purchase of Lycra goods

Record these transactions in the purchases journal.

		Purchases Journal				Page 4
Date	Account	Invoice #	PR	Merchandise Inventory (DR)	Accounts Payable (CR)	

AP-10B LO 2

Ambassador uses a cash payments journal to record all the payments made by the company. Ambassador has provided you with the following information about the transactions in the month of August.

Aug 2   Paid salary to Amanda Blythe, $1,600 cash (Cheque #241)

Aug 12   Paid $2,400 owing (Invoice #543) to Hargrave Inc. (Cheque #242)

Aug 14   Paid insurance premium of $300 (Cheque #243)

Aug 20   Paid newspaper bill of $150 to News & Paper (Cheque #244)

Aug 26   Paid $2,000 to JKL Company for the purchase of inventory (Cheque #245)

Record these transactions in the cash payments journal.

		Cash Payments Journal						Page 7
Date	Account	Cheque #	PR	Other (DR)	Merchandise Inventory (DR)	Accounts Payable (DR)	Cash (CR)	

AP-11B LO 2

Put-A-Wrench-In-It sells tools. During the month of October 2019, the following transactions occurred.

Oct 3   Purchased inventory for $6,300 on account from Block and Deck

Oct 7   Paid salary for $2,100 with Cheque #256

Oct 10   Purchased inventory for $4,100 cash from Malida Inc. with Cheque #257

Oct 17   Paid the full amount owing to Block and Deck from the Oct 3 transaction with Cheque #258

Oct 24   Purchased inventory for $7,700 on account from Debolt Inc.

Assume zero opening balances for the subledger and general ledger accounts. Assume no entries were made directly to the accounts payable general ledger from the general journal.

Use the following selected accounts to complete the posting references.

Account Description	Account #	Account Description	Account #
Cash	101	Owner's Withdrawals	310
Accounts Receivable	110	Sales Revenue	400
Merchandise Inventory	120	Sales Discount	405
Accounts Payable	200	Interest Revenue	410
Bank Loan	220	Cost of Goods Sold	500
Owner's Capital	300	Office Supplies Expense	510
		Salaries Expense	520
		Telephone Expense	525

Required

a) Record the above transactions in the purchases journal and the cash payments journal. Show posting references for supplier and individual accounts and column totals, assuming all amounts were posted.

		Purchases Journal						Page 6
Date	Account	Invoice #	PR	Merchandise Inventory (DR)	Office Supplies Expense (DR)	Other (DR)	Accounts Payable (CR)	

		Cash Payments Journal					Page 4
Date	Account	Cheque #	PR	Accounts Payable (DR)	Other (DR)	Merchandise Inventory (DR)	Cash (CR)

b) Post the appropriate transactions from the journals to the subledger accounts. At the end of the month, total the journals and update the accounts payable controlling account.

Account: Accounts Payable					**GL No:**	
Date	Description	PR	DR	CR	Balance	

Account: Block and Deck

Date	PR	DR	CR	Balance

Account: Debolt Inc.

Date	PR	DR	CR	Balance

AP-12B LO 2

Step On It is a small shoe retailer. The following is a list of transactions for the month of June 2019.

June 5   Received a bill (Invoice #5780) for $4,000 worth of office supplies from Runner

June 9   Received a telephone bill from Telly (Invoice #167) for $200

June 12   Paid amount owing (Invoice #5780) to Runner (Cheque #201)

June 21   Paid $3,500 to Jumper for purchase of inventory (Cheque #202)

June 22   Paid amount owing (Invoice #167) to Telly for telephone services with Cheque #203

June 25   Paid $300 to Daley Company for maintenance expenses (Cheque #204)

June 26   Received bill from The Walker (Invoice #113) for $4,200 worth of inventory

Required

a)   Record the above entries in the appropriate journal.

Purchases Journal							Page 1
Date	Account	Invoice #	PR	Telephone Expense (DR)	Office Supplies Expense (DR)	Merchandise Inventory (DR)	Accounts Payable (CR)

Cash Payments Journal							Page 1
Date	Account	Cheque #	PR	Other (DR)	Merchandise Inventory (DR)	Accounts Payable (DR)	Cash (CR)

b) Post the entries to the subledger accounts. At the end of the month, total the special journals and update the accounts payable controlling account. Assume a perpetual inventory is used.

Opening Balances

Runner	$1,000 (CR)
Telly	$1,200 (CR)
The Walker	$1,400 (CR)

Note that Step On It's accounts payable records consist of only these three subledgers. Assume no entries were made directly to accounts payable from the general journal. Update the PR columns in both the subledgers and special journals.

Account: Accounts Payable					**GL No:** 200
Date	**Description**	**PR**	**DR**	**CR**	**Balance**

Accounts Payable Subsidiary Ledger
Runner

Date	**PR**	**DR**	**CR**	**Balance**

Accounts Payable Subsidiary Ledger
Telly

Date	**PR**	**DR**	**CR**	**Balance**

Accounts Payable Subsidiary Ledger
The Walker

Date	**PR**	**DR**	**CR**	**Balance**

AP-13B LO 2

Horizon Company had the following transactions for the month of November 2019. They are recorded in the journals and posted to the ledger accounts. Assume a perpetual inventory is used.

Nov 1   Purchased inventory from Diagonal Company for $8,600 with Cheque #153
Nov 5   Received Invoice #2563 for $1,500 worth of office supplies from Max Supplies
Nov 9   Received Invoice #8475 from Vertical for $250 for hydro
Nov 10   Paid $320 to John Walker for repair expenses with Cheque #154
Nov 18   Paid amount owing to Vertical with Cheque #155
Nov 19   Paid amount owing to Max Supplies with Cheque #156
Nov 26   Received Invoice #563 from Total Hats for $4,600 worth of inventory

							Purchases Journal					Page 1
Date	Account	Invoice #	PR	Hydro Expense (DR)	Office Supplies Expense (DR)	Merchandise Inventory (DR)	Accounts Payable (CR)
Nov 1	Diagonal Company	153				8,600	8,600
Nov 5	Max Supplies	2563	✓			1,500	1,500
Nov 9	Vertical	8475	✓	250			250
Nov 26	Total Hats	563	✓			4,600	4,600
Nov 30	Total			250		14,700	14,950

				Cash Payments Journal			Page 1
Date	Account	Cheque #	PR	Other (DR)	Merchandise Inventory (DR)	Accounts Payable (DR)	Cash (CR)
Nov 10	Repair Expense	154		320			320
Nov 18	Vertical	155	✓			250	250
Nov 19	Max Supplies	156	✓	1,500			1,500
Nov 30	Total			1,820		250	2,070

Opening Balances

Max Supplies	$200 (CR)
Vertical	$60 (CR)
Total Hats	$1,400 (CR)

Account: Accounts Payable					**GL No: 200**	
Date	Description	PR	DR	CR	Balance	
Opening					1,660	CR
Nov 30		PJ1		14,950	16,610	CR
Nov 30		CP1	250		16,360	CR

Accounts Payable Subsidiary Ledger					
Max Supplies					
Date	PR	DR	CR	Balance	
Opening				200	CR
Nov 5	PJ1	1,500		1,300	DR
Nov 19	CP1		1,500	200	CR

Accounts Payable Subsidiary Ledger Vertical					
Date	PR	DR	CR	Balance	
Opening				60	CR
Nov 9	PJ1		250	310	CR
Nov 18	CP1	250		60	CR

Accounts Payable Subsidiary Ledger Total Hats					
Date	PR	DR	CR	Balance	
Opening				1,200	CR
Nov 26	PJ1		4,600	5,800	CR

Identify the errors made when the transactions were posted to the journals or when they were posted to the ledgers. What impact would these errors have on account balances?

_____

_____

_____

_____

_____

_____

_____

_____

_____

_____

_____

_____

_____

_____

AP-14B LO 3

As with a manual system that uses special journals, a computerized accounting system requires transactions that do not "fit" into one of the special journals be recorded in the general journal. Using the Quickbooks illustration discussed in the chapter, list the steps involved in recording transactions in the general journal.

Note: Assume Quickbooks is open and ready for you to enter transactions.

_____

_____

_____

AP-15B LO 4

Highway Interchange sells clothing to retailers. During the month of July 2019, the following transactions occurred. Highway Interchange uses the periodic inventory system.

Jul 7   Sold inventory to Fashion House for $5,600 cash. The inventory had a cost of $2,400. The invoice number was #526.

Jul 10   Received a loan from Goldman Bank for $5,000.

Jul 15   Sold inventory to Stella Lanes on account for $8,500. The inventory had a cost of $3,400. The invoice number was #527.

Jul 17   Sold inventory to Cover Me for $7,500 on account. The inventory had a cost of $3,100. The invoice number was #528.

Jul 24   Received full payment from Stella Lanes for the sale on July 15.

Jul 31   Received $50 of interest earned on a savings account.

Required

a) Record the above transactions in the sales journal and the cash receipts journal. Show all posting references as though all amounts were posted.

				Sales Journal		Page 1
Date	Account	Invoice #	PR	Accounts Receivable/Sales (DR/CR)

	Cash Receipts Journal							Page 1
Date	Account	PR	Cash (DR)	Accounts Receivable (CR)	Sales (CR)	Bank Loan (CR)	Other (CR)

b) Post the appropriate transactions from the journals to the subledger accounts. At the end of the month, total the journals and update the accounts receivable controlling account.

Assume zero opening balances for the subledger and general ledger accounts. Assume no entries were made directly to the accounts receivable general ledger from the general journal.

Account: Accounts Receivable					**GL No:** 110
Date	Description	PR	DR	CR	Balance

Account: Stella Lanes				
Date	**PR**	**DR**	**CR**	**Balance**

Account: Cover Me				
Date	**PR**	**DR**	**CR**	**Balance**

Case Study

CS-1 LO 2 3

Easy Riser sells pre-fabricated staircases to builders for new homes and renovations. Lately, the owner has been receiving calls from suppliers regarding late payments. The owner is aware of the late payments because he has been holding back payments due to a shortage of cash. The company is having excellent sales and earning a very good profit even though it has a cash shortfall.

When asked about the cash shortage problem, the bookkeeper informed the owner about the accounting process. All transactions are entered into the general journal and posted to the general ledger. The supplier invoices are stored in one folder and the sales invoices in another folder in the bookkeeper's desk. When the owner asked to see a sales invoice from last month (to see if the amount had been collected), the bookkeeper had trouble finding it. When it was finally found, it was determined that it had not been collected yet.

a)   What ethical and control issues does this company have?

b)   What would you suggest to improve the bookkeeping for this company?

Chapter 10

CASH AND INTERNAL CONTROLS

LEARNING OBJECTIVES

| LO 1 | Describe and apply internal controls for a business |
| LO 2 | Apply cash controls |

| LO 3 | Prepare a bank reconciliation and related journal entries |
| LO 4 | Prepare a petty cash fund and record related journal entries |

AMEENGAGE *Access **ameengage.com** for integrated resources including tutorials, practice exercises, the digital textbook and more.*

—————————————— **Assessment Questions** ——————————————

AS-1 LO 1

What are internal controls? Explain.

_____

_____

_____

_____

AS-2 LO 1

List three reasons for designing internal controls in a company.

_____

_____

_____

_____

AS-3 LO 1 2

List two general controls that can be used for petty cash.

_____

_____

_____

AS-4 LO 2

List two controls that can be used to prevent the misuse of cash.

_____

_____

_____

AS-5 LO 2

Define cash equivalents.

_____

_____

AS-6 LO 2

Briefly describe what it means to be in bank overdraft.

_____

_____

AS-7 LO 2

Describe the position of cash equivalents on the balance sheet.

_____

_____

AS-8 LO 2

List two reasons why cash equivalents are entered with cash on the balance sheet.

_____

_____

AS-9 LO 2

List three examples of cash equivalent items.

_____

_____

_____

AS-10 LO 2

Why would a business invest in cash equivalents?

_____

_____

AS-11 LO 2

What are the two different ways a business usually receives cash from customers?

_____

_____

_____

_____

AS-12 `LO 2`

Considering controls for a cash sale, what is important for the customer to do as part of the transaction?

_____

_____

AS-13 `LO 2`

Describe how a business can protect cash on its premises.

_____

_____

_____

_____

AS-14 `LO 2`

What is the overall goal of a business in managing its cash?

_____

_____

AS-15 `LO 2`

What is a voucher system for cash payments?

_____

_____

AS-16 `LO 2`

What is a remittance advice on an invoice?

_____

_____

_____

_____

AS-17 `LO 3`

What is a bank reconciliation?

_____

_____

AS-18 `LO 3`

List three typical reasons for a bank to make additional deductions from a company's cash account.

_____

_____

AS-19 LO 3

What are two typical reasons for a bank making additional deposits to a company's cash account?

_____

_____

AS-20 LO 3

In a typical bank reconciliation, what are the titles of the two column headers?

_____

_____

AS-21 LO 3

What are non-sufficient funds (NSF) cheques?

_____

_____

AS-22 LO 3

What is an outstanding deposit?

_____

_____

AS-23 LO 3

When is a journal entry required during a bank reconciliation?

_____

_____

AS-24 LO 3

How are outstanding cheques recorded on the bank reconciliation?

_____

_____

AS-25 LO 4

What is an imprest system for petty cash?

_____

_____

AS-26 LO 4

Briefly describe the responsibilities of the petty cash custodian.

_____

_____

AS-27 LO 4

What does an employee who requires petty cash need to present to the petty cash custodian?

_____

_____

AS-28 LO 4

What is a petty cash summary sheet?

_____

_____

AS-29 LO 4

Why do petty cash overages or shortages occur?

_____

_____

AS-30 LO 4

When does the cash over and short account behave like an expense account?

_____

_____

AS-31 LO 4

What are the only two times that the petty cash account in the ledger is debited or credited?

_____

_____

_____

Application Questions Group A

AP-1A

Gordon Green operates a golf ball driving range called Greenaway Golf, open from May 1 to November 1. Gordon employs two people, one who works from 6 a.m. until 2 p.m. and the other who works from 2 p.m. to close at 10 p.m., 7 days a week. The two employees are cousins of Gordon, so he saw no reason to have to bond them. The office and equipment are located in a trailer at the front of the property, close to the road and parking lot. Gordon takes pride in the fact that he accepts only cash and pays all his bills using cash. No cheques or credit cards may be used by customers for sales or by his staff when paying bills. Gordon keeps all cash on the premises until he counts it and prepares a bank deposit once per week.

List all of the internal control weaknesses with Gordon's business.

_____

_____

_____

_____

_____

_____

_____

_____

_____

_____

AP-2A LO 2

A business dealing with cash transactions needs to ensure adequate internals controls are in place to protect this asset from loss due to theft or error. Identify which control would be the most effective in preventing/detecting violations of internal controls over cash in each of the following scenarios.

Cash Control

1. Invest idle cash into highly liquid investments
2. Use EFT for cash payments
3. Allow customers to deposit cheques directly into company bank account
4. Provide each cashier with their own cash drawer with a predetermined amount of cash included at the beginning of their shift
5. Display sale amounts for customers to see while sale is being keyed into cash register
6. Provide customer with a remittance copy of their statement that can be sent with payment to ensure it is applied to the correct account
7. Have cashier prepare a duplicate bank deposit slip, where one copy goes with the deposit to the bank and is stamped as verified and then returned to the business for filing
8. Use a cash over and short account to account for differences due to rounding
9. Require that all cash payments are independently authorized
10. Prepare monthly bank reconciliation

Scenario

_____Customers claim they have been overcharged for items.

_____Customers have difficulty getting their payment to the business because of their remote location.

_____The business owner is concerned unauthorized payments are being made.

_____The balance of the business bank account at the end of the year does not agree with the balance reported in the general ledger cash account.

_____The account is used to track discrepancies in cash received for cash sales with actual amount of sales.

_____Customer payments received in the mail are not getting posted to their account properly.

_____The amount of a bank deposit does not agree with what was prepared by the cashier.

_____Errors are being made by one of the cashiers, but it is difficult to determine who, since four cashiers use the same cash register during the day.

_____The balance of cash is consistently the highest of all assets.

_____Monthly payments for things like insurance or utility bills are sometimes missed.

AP-3A LO 3

Quality Electronic is preparing a bank reconciliation and has identified the following potential reconciling items. For each item, indicate in the action column if it is (i) added to the balance of the ledger, (ii) deducted from the balance of the ledger, (iii) added to the balance of the bank statement, or (iv) deducted from the balance of the bank statement.

Item	Action
a) deposits that are not shown on the bank statement	+ bank
b) interest deposited to the company's account	+ book ledger
c) bank service charges	- ledger
d) outstanding cheques	- ~~ledger~~ bank
e) NSF cheques returned	- ledger

AP-4A LO 3

The following data represents information necessary to assist in preparing the June 30, 2019, bank reconciliation for Trimore Company.

- The June 30 bank balance was $5,300.
- The bank statement indicated a deduction of $20 for all bank service charges.
- A customer deposited $1,200 directly into the bank account to settle an outstanding accounts receivable bill.
- Cheque #850 for $600 and Cheque #857 for $420 have been recorded in the company ledger but did not appear on the bank statement.
- A customer paid an amount of $4,534 to Trimore on June 30, but the deposit did not appear on the bank statement.
- The accounting clerk made an error and recorded a $200 cheque as $2,000. The cheque was written to pay the outstanding accounts payable account.
- Cheque #9574 for $100 was deducted from Trimore's account by the bank. This cheque was not written by Trimore and needs to be reversed by the bank.
- The bank included an NSF cheque in the amount of $820 relating to a customer's payment. The NSF service fee was $10.
- The general ledger cash account showed a balance of $6,764 on June 30.

Required

a)   Complete the bank reconciliation for Trimore Company.

b)   Write the necessary journal entries to correct Trimore's records.

Date	Account Title and Explanation	Debit	Credit

AP-5A LO 3

Mike's Cleaning Service received its monthly bank statement for its business bank account, with a balance of $55,062 for the month of July 2019. The balance of the ledger account as at July 31, 2019, was $59,461.

After a comparison of the cheques written by the company and those deducted from the bank account, Mike's accountant determined that three cheques, totalling $2,806 (Cheque #256 for $606, Cheque #261 for $1,200, and Cheque #262 for $1,000), were outstanding on July 31. A review of the deposits showed that a deposit on July 1 for $12,610 was actually recorded in the company's ledger on June 30 and a July 31 deposit of $9,760 was recorded in the company's ledger but had not yet been recorded by the bank. The July bank statement showed a total service fee of $18, a customer's cheque in the amount of $70 that had been returned NSF, a loan payment of $857 that was deducted automatically by the bank, and a $3,500 payment from a customer that was deposited directly into the Mike's Cleaning bank account.

Required

a) Prepare the bank reconciliation as at July 31, 2019.

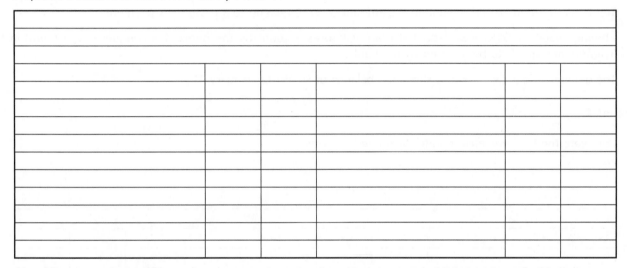

b) How much cash does Mike's Cleaning Service actually have in its cash account on July 31?

_____

c) Prepare journal entries to record all necessary adjustments to bring the cash account to its adjusted balance.

Date	Account Title and Explanation	Debit	Credit

AP-6A LO 3.

The following data represents information necessary to assist in preparing the January 31, 2019, bank reconciliation for Sellmore Company.

- The January 31 bank balance was $4,598.

- A customer deposited $900 directly into the bank account to settle an outstanding accounts receivable bill.

- The bank statement indicated a deduction of $33 for all bank service charges.

- Cheque #821 for $360 and Cheque #865 for $252 have been recorded in the company ledger but did not appear on the bank statement.

- A customer paid $4,589 to Sellmore on January 31 but the deposit did not appear on the bank statement.

- The accounting clerk made an error and recorded a $180 cheque as $1,800. The cheque was written to pay the outstanding accounts payable account.

- The bank included an NSF cheque in the amount of $710 relating to a customer's payment.

- Cheque #9504 for $153 was deducted from Sellmore's account by the bank. This cheque was not written by Sellmore and needs to be reversed by the bank.

- The general ledger cash account showed a balance of $6,951 on January 31.

Required

a) Complete the bank reconciliation for Sellmore Company.

b) Write the necessary journal entries to correct Sellmore's records.

Date	Account Title and Explanation	Debit	Credit

Date	Account Title and Explanation	Debit	Credit

AP-7A LO 3

Use the following information to prepare the bank reconciliation for Jeremiah Motors.

- The bank balance on March 31 was $13,500.
- The general ledger cash account showed a balance of $14,950 on March 31.
- Received Cheque #80 from a customer for $950, but it has not been deposited yet.
- The bank statement shows a charge of $110 for all bank service fees.
- A customer transferred $800 directly into the company's bank account to pay their account.
- Recorded Cheque #94 to pay for supplies in the journal as $480 instead of $840.
- The bank statement showed an NSF cheque from a customer for $830.

Required

a) Complete the bank reconciliation for Jeremiah Motors.

b) Prepare any necessary journal entries to update the company's records for March 2019.

Date	Account Title and Explanation	Debit	Credit

AP-8A LO 3

The following cash ledger contains information about RJ Cosmetics' cash account.

GENERAL LEDGER

Account: Cash				GL No: 101	
Date	Description	Debit	Credit	Balance	
Feb 1	Opening Balance			4,000	DR
Feb 3	Cheque #1		800	3,200	DR
Feb 12	Deposit	2,500		5,700	DR
Feb 21	Cheque #2		1,200	4,500	DR
Feb 26	Cheque #3		950	3,550	DR
Feb 27	Cheque #4		600	2,950	DR
Feb 28	Deposit	1,300		4,250	DR

RJ Cosmetics' bank statement for the month of February is shown below.

BANK STATEMENT				
Date	Description	Withdrawal	Deposit	Balance
Feb 01	Opening Balance			4,000
Feb 03	Cheque #1	800		3,200
Feb 12	Deposit		2,500	5,700
Feb 14	NSF Cheque	500		5,200
Feb 14	NSF Charge	15		5,185
Feb 21	Cheque #2	1,200		3,985
Feb 25	EFT—Monthly rent expense	1,000		2,985
Feb 28	Service charges	25		2,960
Feb 28	Interest on bank account		20	2,980

Required

a)   Prepare a bank reconciliation for RJ Cosmetics as at February 28, 2019.

b)   Prepare the required journal entries for the corrections made in the bank reconciliation.

Date	Account Title and Explanation	Debit	Credit

c) Prepare the full reconciled cash ledger account for the month of February.

GENERAL LEDGER

Account: Cash				GL No: 101	
Date	Description	Debit	Credit	Balance	

d) Using last month's data along with the bank statement and the general ledger provided, prepare a bank reconciliation for RJ Cosmetics for March 31, 2019.

GENERAL LEDGER

Account: Cash				GL No: 101	
Date	Description	Debit	Credit	Balance	
Mar 1	Opening Balance			2,730	DR
Mar 7	Cheque #5		920	1,810	DR
Mar 13	Deposit	850		2,660	DR
Mar 18	Cheque #6		450	2,210	DR
Mar 28	Deposit	2,135		4,345	DR
Mar 29	Cheque #7		1,100	3,245	DR

BANK STATEMENT				
Date	Description	Withdrawal	Deposit	Balance
Mar 1	Opening Balance			2,980
Mar 2	Deposit		1,300	4,280
Mar 3	Cheque #4	600		3,680
Mar 7	Cheque #5	920		2,760
Mar 13	Deposit		850	3,610
Mar 18	Cheque #6	450		3,160
Mar 25	EFT—Monthly rent expense	1,000		2,160
Mar 28	Deposit		2,135	4,295
Mar 31	Service charges	25		4,270
Mar 31	Interest on bank account		13.65	4,283.65

Please note that the deposit from March 28 contains a cheque from the customer who provided an NSF cheque from the month before. The customer paid for the original amount of $500, plus the $15 charge.

AP-9A LO 3

Consider the following general ledger and bank statement for Meena Salon.

GENERAL LEDGER

Account: Cash | | | | **GL No: 101**

Date	Description	Debit	Credit	Balance	
Apr 1	Opening Balance			8,000	DR
Apr 6	Jimmy Supplies—Cheque #101		500	7,500	DR
Apr 10	HitHit Supplies—Cheque #102		1,000	6,500	DR
Apr 11	Mary Malony	250		6,750	DR
Apr 14	Inner Beauty Inc.—Cheque #103		757	5,993	DR
Apr 19	Shona Care Ltd.—Cheque #104		840	5,153	DR
Apr 29	Deposit	2,500		7,653	DR

BANK STATEMENT				
Date	Description	Withdrawal	Deposit	Balance
Apr 1	Opening Balance			8,000
Apr 6	Cheque #101	500		7,500
Apr 10	Cheque #102	1,000		6,500
Apr 10	EFT—Monthly rent	800		5,700
Apr 11	Mary Malony		250	5,950
Apr 11	NSF Cheque	250		5,700
Apr 11	NSF charge	5		5,695
Apr 14	Cheque #103	575		5,120
Apr 21	Cheque #1520	3,000		2,120
Apr 30	Service charges	25		2,095
Apr 30	Interest on bank account		20	2,115

Additional Information

1. On April 14, Meena Salon purchased $575 worth of salon supplies from Inner Beauty Inc.

2. The salon's cheque numbers are always three digits in length.

Required

a)   Prepare a bank reconciliation for Meena Salon on April 30, 2019.

	Meena Salon					
	Bank reconciliation					
	April 30, 2019					
Cash Balance per ledger		7653	Cash Balance per bank			2115
Add:			Add:			
Ledger error	132		Outstanding deposit	2500		
Less:			Less: outstanding cheques			
EFT - Rent	800		Cheque #104			840
NSF Cheque	250					
NSF Fee	25					

b)   Prepare the necessary journal entries.

Date	Account Title and Explanation	Debit	Credit
Apr 30	Cash	132	
	Supplies		132
Apr 30	Cash	20	
	Interest revenue		20
Apr 30	Rent Expense	800	
	Cash		800
Apr 30	Accounts Receivable	250	
	Cash		250
Apr 30	Bank Service charges	30	
	Cash		30

AP-10A LO 3

Shine Laundry's bank reconciliation is provided for the month of September 2019. However, due to some errors on the bank reconciliation, the reconciled balance for the ledger and the bank are different from each other.

Shine Laundry Bank Reconciliation September 30, 2019	Ledger	Bank
Opening Balance	$5,100	$3,820
Add: Outstanding deposit—Sep 29	400	
Outstanding deposit—Sep 30	1,220	
Less: Outstanding Cheque #3—Sep 8		(1,000)
Outstanding Cheque #4—Sep 10	(600)	
EFT—Insurance—Sep 15		(400)
EFT—Monthly rent—Sep 18		(600)
NSF Cheque—Sep 19		(250)
Charges for NSF Cheque—Sep 19		(5)
Service charges—Sep 30	(15)	
Interest on bank account—Sep 30	(10)	
Reconciled Balance	$6,095	$1,565

Required

a) Prepare a corrected bank reconciliation. Assume the dollar amounts of the individual items on the bank reconciliation are correct.

Shine laundry Bank reconciliation September 30, 2019					
Cash Balance per ledger		6095	Cash per bank		1565

b)   Prepare all journal entries required by Shine Laundry.

Date	Account Title and Explanation	Debit	Credit

AP-11A LO 3

The bookkeeper for Brose Industrial Supply has prepared a bank reconciliation for the month but, although it balances, it is not correct. Prepare a corrected bank reconciliation for Brose Industrial Supply. Assume that all figures show the correct dollar amounts, and that the opening balances are both correct.

Brose Industrial Supply **Bank Reconciliation** **July 31, 2019**		
	Ledger	**Bank**
Opening Balance	$14,630	$16,070
Add:		
Bank service charges		80
Interest earned	100	
Less:		
Outstanding cheques		(1,600)
Outstanding deposits	(730)	
Unrecorded deposit		(550)
Reconciled Balance	$14,000	$14,000

Analysis

After preparing a bank reconciliation, journal entries must be prepared to record adjustments to cash. Name three items that require an adjusting entry. Why don't all items on the reconciliation require adjusting entries?

_____

_____

_____

_____

AP-12A LO 4

On June 7, 2019, Mary decided to set up a petty cash fund for her small business. A cheque of $125 was issued and cashed. The $125 cash was given to the store supervisor who was to act as petty cash custodian. The petty cash custodian was told to obtain authorized vouchers for all payments. Petty cash was to be replenished when the balance in the cash box reached $23.

Required

a) Record the establishment of the fund on June 7.

Date	Account Title and Explanation	Debit	Credit

b) On June 19, the following summary was prepared.

Delivery Expense	$50.90
Miscellaneous Expense	20.40
Office Expense	24.10
Postage Expense	6.60
Total	$102.00

Prepare the entry to replenish the petty cash.

Date	Account Title and Explanation	Debit	Credit

c) On June 23, it was decided to increase the amount of the petty cash fund from $125 to $175. A cheque of $50 was issued. Record the transaction.

Date	Account Title and Explanation	Debit	Credit

AP-13A LO 4

The petty cash fund was established on August 12, 2019, in the amount of $250. Expenditures from the fund by the custodian as of August 31, 2019, were evidenced by approved receipts for the following.

Postage Expense	$30.00
Supplies Expense	65.00
Maintenance Expense	42.00
Delivery Expense	58.20
Newspaper Advertising	21.95
Miscellaneous Expense	15.75

On August 31, 2019, the petty cash fund was replenished and increased to $300; currency and coin in the fund at that time totalled $15.60.

Prepare the journal entries to record the transactions related to the petty cash fund for the month of August.

Date	Account Title and Explanation	Debit	Credit

AP-14A LO 4

On June 29, 2019, Fire It Up Grill decided to establish a petty cash fund for the office. A cheque for $250 was issued and cashed. The $250 cash was given to the office manager who was to act as the petty cash custodian. He decided that the petty cash fund should be replenished when the balance in the cash box reached $70.

Required

a) Record the establishment of the petty cash fund on June 29.

Date	Account Title and Explanation	Debit	Credit

b) On July 31, the balance in the petty cash account was $70. A summary of the expenses was prepared.

Delivery Expense	$68
Office Supplies Expense	96
Miscellaneous Expense	10
Postage Expense	7
Total	$181

Determine the balance of the petty cash fund after all transactions have occurred for the month of July.

_____

c) Prepare the journal entry to replenish the petty cash fund.

Date	Account Title and Explanation	Debit	Credit

d) Based on your response from part c), determine if the cash amount is over or short.

_____

e) On July 31, with input from the petty cash custodian, management decided to increase the amount of the petty cash fund from $250 to $350. This was based on the fact that more items were approved to be paid by petty cash. A cheque for $100 was issued and cashed. Record the transaction.

Date	Account Title and Explanation	Debit	Credit

AP-15A LO 4

On January 1, 2019, Hit Design set up a petty cash fund for $250. At the end of the first week, the petty cash fund contained the following items.

Cash on hand	$50
Receipt for the purchase of office supplies	40
Receipt for delivery charges	10
Receipt for the purchase of stamps	20
Receipt for travel to a client meeting	50
Receipt for the payment of newspaper advertising	75

Required

a) Calculate any cash overage or shortage.

_____

_____

_____

b) Prepare the journal entries for setting up and replenishing the petty cash fund.

Date	Account Title and Explanation	Debit	Credit

AP-16A LO 4

Eric Dravin Enterprises decided to establish a petty cash fund for the office on January 11, 2019. Management set up the fund and appointed the office administrator as the petty cash custodian. A cheque was issued for the petty cash fund for $175, and was cashed. Management decided that the petty cash fund should be replenished when the balance in the cash box reaches $75.

Required

a) Record the establishment of the petty cash fund on January 11.

Date	Account Title and Explanation	Debit	Credit

b) On January 31, the balance in the petty cash account was $30. The totalled receipts showed the following information.

Delivery Expense	$89
Postage Expense	22
Office Supplies	13
Travel Expense	25
Total	$149

Determine the balance of the petty cash fund based on the receipts provided.

_____

c) Prepare the journal entry to replenish the petty cash fund at the end of the month.

Date	Account Title and Explanation	Debit	Credit

d) Based on your response from part c), determine if the cash amount is over or short.

_____

e) On February 4, 2019, management determined that the petty cash fund's balance ran too low for the month of January. They suggested doubling the petty cash fund balance. A cheque for $175 was issued and cashed. Record the transaction.

Date	Account Title and Explanation	Debit	Credit

AP-17A LO 4

Sky Auctions set up a petty cash fund of $250 on January 1, 2019. The custodian found the following receipts in the cash box for the month.

$35 for food for the office employees
$63 for fuel for the company vehicle
$50 to pay a specialist to update the computer system
$46 to purchase supplies for the office

The custodian counted $81 cash remaining in the cash box. Prepare journal entries to establish the petty cash fund and replenish the petty cash fund on January 31, 2019.

Date	Account Title and Explanation	Debit	Credit

Analysis

What is the purpose of a petty cash system?

_____

_____

_____

Application Questions Group B

AP-1B LO 1

It has been said that all businesses should a good system of internal controls.

Required

a) List 7 general objectives that a good system of internal controls is designed to fulfill.

_____

_____

_____

_____

_____

_____

_____

b) Discuss reasons why, even though a business has set a system of internal controls, such controls do not provide a guarantee against errors, omissions or misuse of company resources.

_____

_____

_____

_____

_____

_____

_____

_____

AP-2B LO 2

The Penny Shack operates a local store that sells a variety of items with nothing costing more than $5.00.

Esther Eaton, the bookkeeper, is unsure of how to record cash transactions when the total is rounded to the nearest nickel. For example the following transactions were recorded.

	Cash received	Total sales
Monday	235.60	235.62
Tuesday	125.95	125.97
Wednesday	343.20	343.22
Thursday	202.75	202.76
Friday	450.30	450.32
Saturday	685.10	685.08
Totals	2,042.90	2,042.97

The bookkeeper has come to you for advice on how to record the above in one entry at the end of the week.

Explain what accounts would be used and show how the journal entry would be recorded.

Date	Account/Description	PR	Debit	Credit

AP-3B LO 3

For the month of September 2019, Jared Anitco noticed that the bank processed a cheque that he was not aware of. He called the bank and determined that the cheque belongs to another account. The following is the general ledger report for cash in the bank and the bank statement for Jared Anitco for the month of September.

GENERAL LEDGER

Account: Cash					GL No: 101	
Date	Description	Debit	Credit	Balance		
Sep 1	Opening Balance			7,000	DR
Sep 6	CandyMan—Cheque #200		500	6,500	DR
Sep 6	Supply Store—Cheque #201		754	5,746	DR
Sep 10	Jordan Lo—Cheque #1000	800		6,546	DR
Sep 25	Book Store—Cheque #202		200	6,346	DR

BANK STATEMENT				
Date	**Description**	**Withdrawal**	**Deposit**	**Balance**
Sep 1	Opening Balance			7,000
Sep 10	CandyMan—Cheque #200	500		6,500
Sep 10	Supply Store—Cheque #201	754		5,746
Sep 14	Jordan Lo—Cheque #1000		800	6,546
Sep 20	Mooris Mo—Cheque #1107	820		5,726
Sep 30	Book Store—Cheque #202	200		5,526

Identify the cheque that does not belong to Jared. Explain why a journal entry is not required to correct the mistake.

_____

_____

_____

AP-4B LO 3

The following financial information is related to a company called World's Computer..

- Cash balance per general ledger is $2,219

- Bank statement balance is $2,478.80

- These cheques were recorded in the ledger but did not appear on the bank statement: Cheque #186 for $100; Cheque #193 for $57; Cheque #199 for $143

- A deposit for $368 dated July 31 was recorded in the ledger but did not appear on the bank statement

- Service charges of $18 are shown on the bank statement

- A cheque for $37.50 has been cashed (correctly) by the bank but was incorrectly recorded in the company's ledger as $375.50. The cheque was issued for the purchase of office supplies.

- The bank automatically deposited interest of $7.80 at the end of the month

Required

a)   Prepare the July 2019 bank reconciliation statement for World's Computer.

b)   Record any journal entries required to bring the company records up to date.

Date	Account Title and Explanation	Debit	Credit

AP-5B LO 3

The bank statement for Fashion Fly had an ending cash balance of $1,500 on December 31, 2019. On this date the cash balance in their general ledger was $2,000. After comparing the bank statement with the company records, the following information was determined.

- The bank returned an NSF cheque in the amount of $320 that Fashion Fly deposited on December 20. The NSF service fee was $5.

- A direct deposit was received from a customer on December 30 in payment of their accounts totalling $3,850. This has not yet been recorded by the company.

- On December 30 the bank deposited $10 for interest earned.

- The bank withdrew $15 for bank service charges.

- Deposits in transit on December 31 totalled $4,020.

Required

a)   Reconcile the ledger and bank statement.

b)   Prepare the required journal entries.

Date	Account Title and Explanation	Debit	Credit

AP-6B LO 3

The bank statement for Flying Fashion had an ending cash balance of $1,640 on March 31, 2019. On this date the cash balance in the general ledger was $1,921. After comparing the bank statement with the company records, the following information was determined.

- The bank returned an NSF cheque in the amount of $264 that Flying Fashion deposited on March 20.
- A direct deposit was received from a customer on March 30 in payment of accounts totalling $3,900. This has not yet been recorded by the company.
- The bank withdrew $41 for all bank service charges.
- On March 30 the bank deposited $14 for interest earned.
- Deposits in transit on March 31 totalled $3,890.

Required

a) Reconcile the ledger and bank statement.

b) Create the required journal entries.

Date	Account Title and Explanation	Debit	Credit

AP-7B LO 3

Lux Transportation Services has just received its bank statement for the month and has compared it to the general ledger cash account.

GENERAL LEDGER

Account: Cash					GL No: 101	
Date	Description	Debit	Credit	Balance	
Oct 1	Opening Balance			13,100	DR
Oct 2	Cheque #401		750	12,350	DR
Oct 5	Cheque #220	900		13,250	DR
Oct 8	Cheque #403		750	12,500	DR
Oct 16	Cheque #404		200	12,300	DR

BANK STATEMENT				
Date	Description	Withdrawal	Deposit	Balance
Oct 1	Opening Balance			13,100
Oct 2	Cheque #401	750		12,350
Oct 6	Cheque #220		900	13,250
Oct 6	EFT Rent Payment	750		12,500
Oct 10	Cheque #403	750		11,750
Oct 16	Cheque #88		445	12,195
Oct 30	Interest		50	12,245
Oct 31	Service Charge	110		12,135

Prepare the bank reconciliation for Lux Transportation as at October 31, 2019.

Lux transportation					
Cash balance per ledger	12300	Cash per Bank			12135
Add:					
Interest on bank	50				
unrecorded cheque 88	443				
	493				
Less: EFT	750	Less:			
Service Charge	110	Cheque 404			200
	860				
Total	11933	Total			11935

Analysis

After some investigation, it is discovered that Cheque #88 is not from a customer and should not have been deposited into the company's bank account by the bank. How does this discovery change the bank reconciliation and any necessary journal entries?

_____

_____

_____

AP-8B LO 3

Shelley Company had completed October's bank reconciliation with an exact reconciled balance on the last day of the month. Consider the bank reconciliation for October.

Shelley Company Bank Reconciliation October 31, 2019		
Description	**Ledger**	**Bank**
Opening Balance	$6,500	$4,725.63
Add: Outstanding deposit 1		700
Error on Cheque #366	189	
Outstanding deposit 2		950
Bank error Cheque #45928		1,000
Interest on bank account	23.63	
Less: Outstanding Cheque #354		(300)
Outstanding Cheque #367		(2,265)
Direct Insurance billing	(1,100)	
EFT—Monthly rent	(1,325)	
NSF Cheque	(875)	
NSF charges	(25)	
Outstanding Cheque #368		(1,463)
Service charges	(40)	
Reconciled Balance	$3,347.63	$3,347.63

The following items were discovered in November.

- An NSF cheque was entered by the bank for $570; it charged the bank account for $25.
- There are three deposits outstanding by the bank for $450, $200, and $1,465 respectively.
- Insurance is a preauthorized payment taken out every month for the same amount month.
- Shelley Company paid its monthly rent via an EFT.
- Cheques #354 and #367 are still outstanding.
- Cheque #378 is outstanding for $675.
- Cheque #379 is outstanding for $1,110.96.
- Interest earned on the bank account is $27.85.
- Total service charges for the bank account are $40.
- The balance of the ledger on November 30 is $6,284.95.
- The bank balance provided from the bank statement dated November 30 is $5,488.76.

Required

a) Complete the bank reconciliation for Shelley Company for the month of November.

b) Prepare the necessary journal entries.

Date	Account Title and Explanation	Debit	Credit

AP-9B LO 3

Consider the following general ledger and bank statement for Saleen Salon.

GENERAL LEDGER

Account: Cash				GL No: 101	
Date	Description	Debit	Credit	Balance	
Dec 1	Opening Balance			8,100	DR
Dec 6	Jonny Supplies—Cheque #120		660	7,440	DR
Dec 10	WalkWalk Supplies—Cheque #121		1,180	6,260	DR
Dec 11	Bethany Balony	230		6,490	DR
Dec 14	Salon Beauty Inc.—Cheque #122		686	5,804	DR
Dec 19	Shona Care Ltd.—Cheque #123		930	4,874	DR
Dec 29	Deposit	2,200		7,074	DR

BANK STATEMENT				
Date	Description	Withdrawal	Deposit	Balance
Dec 1	Opening Balance			8,100
Dec 6	Cheque #120	660		7,440
Dec 10	Cheque #121	1,180		6,260
Dec 10	EFT—Monthly rent	680		5,580
Dec 11	Bethany Balony		230	5,810
Dec 11	NSF Cheque	230		5,580
Dec 11	NSF charge	19		5,561
Dec 14	Cheque #122	866		4,695
Dec 21	Cheque #1470	3,700		995
Dec 31	Service charges	32		963
Dec 31	Interest on bank account		17	980

Additional Information

1. On December 14, Saleen Salon purchased $866 worth of salon supplies from Salon Beauty Inc.
2. The salon's cheque numbers are always three digits in length.

Required

a) Prepare a bank reconciliation for Saleen Salon on December 31, 2019.

b) Prepare the necessary journal entries.

Date	Account Title and Explanation	Debit	Credit

AP-10B LO 3

The owner of Lucy Learning has attempted to prepare the month-end bank reconciliation. However, she has noticed that the ending balances do not match.

Required

a) Prepare a corrected bank reconciliation for Lucy Learning, assuming all figures show the correct dollar amounts.

Lucy Learning		
Bank Reconciliation		
November 30, 2019		
Description	**Ledger**	**Bank**
Opening Balance	$3,400	$200
Add: Outstanding deposits	1,600	
EFT—monthly payment for bank loan		1,500
Interest earned	250	
Less: NSF Cheque	(800)	
NSF charge		(40)
Bank service charge		(60)
Direct customer deposit for balance owed	(550)	
Reconciled Balance	$3,900	$1,600

b) Record any journal entries necessary to update the cash account.

Date	Account Title and Explanation	Debit	Credit

AP-11B LO 3

Tobias has been given the general ledger and bank statement for Eaton Company. Help him prepare the bank reconciliation based on the two documents on September 30, 2019.

GENERAL LEDGER

Account: Cash				GL No: 101	
Date	Description	Debit	Credit	Balance	
Sep 1	Opening Balance			8,400	DR
Sep 7	Cheque #412	500		8,900	DR
Sep 9	Cheque #900—Equipment		4,800	4,100	DR
Sep 16	Cheque #901—Inventory		405	3,695	DR
Sep 19	Cheque #81	2,300		5,995	DR
Sep 27	Cheque #902—Office Supplies		180	5,815	DR

BANK STATEMENT				
Date	Description	Withdawal	Deposit	Balance
Sep 1	Opening Balance			8,400
Sep 7	EFT—Rent payment	1,300		7,100
Sep 9	Cheque #900	4,800		2,300
Sep 16	Cheque #901	450		1,850
Sep 19	Cheque #81		2,300	4,150
Sep 19	NSF—Cheque #81	2,300		1,850
Sep 19	NSF Charge	40		1,810
Sep 30	Interest		80	1,890

Note: In case of any discrepency between dollar amounts, assume the bank statement is correct.

AP-12B LO 1 2 4

Last year, Holtzman Company established a petty cash fund of $100. The custodian complained that she had to reimburse the fund on a weekly basis and suggested that the fund be increased to $400. That way, she would only have to summarize payouts and get a cheque from the cashier once per month.

Management agreed with the custodian, and on April 1, 2019, advised the cashier to increase the fund to $400.

Required

a) Write the journal entry to increase the fund to $400.

Date	Account Title and Explanation	Debit	Credit

b) List five internal controls that should be established around the use of petty cash.

_____

_____

_____

_____

_____

_____

_____

_____

_____

_____

_____

_____

_____

_____

_____

_____

_____

_____

AP-13B LO 4

On April 1, 2019, Clayton Company established a petty cash fund of $200.

During the month the custodian paid out the following amounts.

Apr 6   Purchased stamps for $40

Apr 8   Paid a $20 delivery charge on an outgoing package

Apr 10   Paid $25 for public transit fares for employees on company business

Apr 14   Purchased coffee and doughnuts for $8 for clients during a meeting

Apr 15   Bought a package of paper for $7 for the copy machine

The custodian counted the fund on April 16 and found $105 in the petty cash box.

Required

a) Prepare the journal entry to record the establishment of the fund.

Date	Account Title and Explanation	Debit	Credit

b) Prepare the journal entry to record the reimbursement of the fund on April 16, 2019.

Date	Account Title and Explanation	Debit	Credit

AP-14B LO 4

On March 20, 2019, Skyline Enterprises established a $300 petty cash fund.

Required

a) Prepare the entry to record the establishment of the fund.

b) At the end of the month, the petty cash custodian analyzed all the monthly transactions. She opened the petty cash box and counted $100 cash remaining. There were also two receipts in the petty cash box: receipt #1: $100—Entertainment and receipt #2: $98—Travel. Record the journal entries for this month's expenses and replenish the fund.

c) At the end of the month, Skyline Enterprises wanted to increase the petty cash fund by $100. Prepare the journal entry to record the increase in petty cash fund.

Date	Account Title and Explanation	Debit	Credit

AP-15B LO 4

The following information was taken from the records of the JoJo Store.

Apr 14	Paid $25 for public transit
Apr 16	Paid $20 for food
Apr 17	Purchased stamps for $5
Apr 17	Paid $50 for window washing
Apr 19	Paid $15 for the delivery of packages
Apr 20	Purchased office supplies for $30

JoJo is the owner of the store and he established a petty cash fund of $200 on April 12, 2019. All the transactions listed above were paid using petty cash. Petty cash needs to be replenished when $50 is left in the petty cash box. On April 21, there was $50 left in the petty cash box.

Prepare the journal entries for setting up and replenishing the petty cash fund.

Date	Account Title and Explanation	Debit	Credit

AP-16B LO 1 2 4

On September 24, 2019, Charlie decided to set up a petty cash fund for his small business. Charlie transferred $150 to a cash box and informed his employees that they could use the money for small expenses for the business. He told them to leave a short note with the reason for each withdrawal. Charlie decided to replenish the cash box when its balance reached $30.

The following events took place.

Sep 24   Petty cash fund was established

Oct 10   The following notes and cash were found inside the cash box.

Notes	
Travel	$94
Postage	4
Miscellaneous	17
Office Supplies	9
Total Notes	124
Cash Remaining	15
Total	$139

Nov 3 Charlie decided to increase the amount of the petty cash fund to $200

Record the transactions for the above three events.

Date	Account Title and Explanation	Debit	Credit

Analysis

Charlie has noticed quite a few significant shortages in the cash box since the fund was established. What are two controls that Charlie could implement around the use of petty cash to protect against shortages?

_____

_____

AP-17B LO 4

On March 20, 2019, Michaelangelo's decided to establish a petty cash fund for the restaurant. A cheque of $350 was issued and cashed. The $350 cash was given to the manager, April, who was to act as the petty cashier, and the petty cash box could be locked in her office. At the suggestion of management, it was decided that the petty cash fund should be replenished when the balance in the cash box reached $85.

Required

a) Record the establishment of the petty cash fund on March 20.

Date	Account Title and Explanation	Debit	Credit

b) On March 31, the balance in the petty cash account was $84. A summary of the expenses was prepared.

Advertising Expense	$155
Delivery Expense	76
Miscellaneous Expense	18
Postage Expense	23
Total	$272

Determine the balance of the petty cash fund after all transactions have occurred for the month of April.

_____

c) Prepare the journal entry to replenish the petty cash fund.

Date	Account Title and Explanation	Debit	Credit

d) Based on your response from part c), determine if the cash amount is over or short.

_____

_____

Case Study

CS-1 1 2

M & G Finances (M & G) is an incorporated tax preparation company. Most of its clients pay for the completion of their tax returns with either a debit or a credit card. The rest pay with cash.

M & G employs 20 tax preparers, two supervisors and one manager. The office collects thousands of dollars in cash every day. After a tax return is prepared by one of the 20 tax preparers, a supervisor is responsible for recording information (i.e. customer name, amount charged, payment method) related to the return in a log.

The receipt of cash is recorded immediately when it is received. Receipts are issued immediately, in numerical order. Copies of the receipts are also kept with the logs. The cash is kept in the drawer of the employee who prepared the tax return. At the end of the day, the cash being kept by the various employees is pooled together and then passed on to the supervisor, who keeps it in her drawer. The cash is deposited into the bank at the end of each work week.

Over the past few weeks, the manager has noted that the amount of cash on hand in the office has consistently been less than the amount recorded in the logs. In fact, the difference between the actual cash on hand and the recorded amount is increasing little by little over time.

Required

a) Is M & G exhibiting any positive aspects in its system of cash controls? Explain.

_____

_____

_____

b) What are the negatives in M & G's cash control system? Explain. (You can refer to controls that do not exist, or controls that exist but are ineffective.)

_____

_____

_____

_____

_____

_____

_____

_____

_____

_____

_____

_____

_____

_____

Notes

Chapter 11

PAYROLL

LEARNING OBJECTIVES

LO **1** Describe payroll accounting

LO **2** Calculate gross pay and net pay

LO **3** Describe payroll liabilities, employer's contributions and payroll payments

LO **4** Record payroll liabilities, employer's contributions and payroll payments

LO **5** Prepare payroll registers

LO **6** Describe payroll controls

Appendix

LO **7** Calculate statutory deductions

AMEENGAGE™ *Access **ameengage.com** for integrated resources including tutorials, practice exercises, the digital textbook and more.*

———— Assessment Questions ————

AS-1 LO **1 2**

Define gross pay.

_____

_____

AS-2 LO **1 2**

What is net pay?

_____

_____

AS-3 LO **3 7**

Define statutory deductions, and identify three statutory deductions in Canada.

_____

_____

_____

AS-4 LO **3**

Define voluntary deductions, and provide three examples of voluntary deductions.

_____

_____

_____

_____

AS-5 LO 3

True or False: There is no maximum amount for the Canada Pension Plan (CPP) deductions, so employees will contribute to the CPP no matter how much they earn in a year.

_____

_____

_____

AS-6 LO 3

How much must an employer contribute to CPP on behalf of its employees?

_____

_____

AS-7 LO 3

Is there any limitation to the amount of Employment Insurance (EI) that will be deducted from an employee's pay (i.e. age limit, exemption amounts or maximum deductions)?

_____

_____

_____

AS-8 LO 3

How much must the employer contribute to EI on behalf of its employees?

_____

_____

AS-9 LO 3

True or False: The total cost of paying an employee is equal to the amount of gross pay the employee earns.

_____

_____

_____

AS-10 LO 5

When would a company use a payroll register?

_____

_____

AS-11 LO 6

What type of information is recorded in a payroll record and what is the information used for?

_____

_____

_____

AS-12 `LO 6`

Identify two payroll controls and briefly explain them.

_____

_____

_____

_____

_____

_____

AS-13 `LO 6`

How does an imprest bank account help control payroll?

_____

_____

_____

AS-14 `LO 3 7`

Is there any limitation to the amount of income tax that will be deducted from an employee's pay (i.e. age limit, exemption amounts or maximum amounts)?

_____

_____

_____

AS-15 `LO 7`

How much is the annual CPP exemption amount, and what does it mean for employees?

_____

_____

_____

Application Questions Group A

AP-1A LO 1

Payroll accounting is important to any business that has employees. Discuss the objectives and/or requirements and obligations of employees, government and the employer where payroll is concerned.

_____

_____

_____

_____

_____

_____

AP-2A LO 2

The records of Dipsum Soft Drinks show the following figures. Calculate the missing amounts.

Employee Earnings	
Salaries for the month	
Overtime Pay	2,200
Total Gross Pay	
Deductions and Net Pay	
Withheld Statutory Deductions	3,000
Charitable Contributions	
Medical Insurance	150
Total Deductions	3,250
Net Pay	5,650

AP-3A LO 2

Phineas Company has two employees who are paid on an hourly basis every week. Payroll information for the week ending June 28, 2019, is listed below. Overtime is paid on hours over 48 hours per week.

Employee	Hours	Hourly Rate	Income Tax	CPP	EI
H. Farnsworth	37	$16.25	$120.25	$27.23	$9.74
P. Fry	42	19.00	155.80	37.27	12.93

Calculate the gross pay and net pay for each employee.

Employee	Gross Pay	Net Pay
H. Farnsworth		
P. Fry		

AP-4A LO 3

Identify the following payroll deductions and expenses as statutory or voluntary, based on legislation.

Description	Statutory	Voluntary
Income taxes		
Dental benefits		
Union dues		
Savings bond purchase		
Uniform allowance		
Tuition		
Canada Pension Plan		
Prescription coverage		
Retirement deduction		
Employment Insurance		
Long-term disability		
Professional dues		
Charitable donations		
Tools and safety apparel		

AP-5A LO 2 3 4

An employer has calculated the following amounts for an employee during the last week of March 2019.

Gross wages	$1,500
Income taxes	331
Canada Pension Plan	73.07
Employment Insurance	24.30

Required

a) Calculate the employee's net pay.

_____

_____

b) Assuming the employer's contribution is 100% for Canada Pension Plan and 140% for Employment Insurance, what is the employer's total expense?

_____

_____

_____

c)   Prepare the journal entries to record payroll for the employee and record the employer's contribution.

JOURNAL			
Date	Account Title and Explanation	Debit	Credit

AP-6A LO 2 3 4

An employee has the following information for her pay for the week ending September 27, 2019. Her employer contributes 100% toward CPP and 140% toward EI. Vacation pay is accrued at 4% of gross pay. Workers' Compensation is 1% of gross pay.

Hours	38
Hourly Rate	$16.50
Income Tax	$100.32
Canada Pension Plan	$28.54
Employment Insurance	$10.16
Union Dues	$20.00
Charitable Donations	$5.00

Required

a)   Prepare the journal entry to record the payroll entry for the employee. The employee will be paid immediately.

JOURNAL			
Date	Account Title and Explanation	Debit	Credit

b) Prepare the journal entry to record accrued vacation pay.

JOURNAL			
Date	Account Title and Explanation	Debit	Credit

c) Prepare the journal entry to record the employer's payroll expense.

JOURNAL			
Date	Account Title and Explanation	Debit	Credit

d) Prepare the journal entry on October 10, 2019, to record the cash payment for statutory amounts owed to the CRA.

JOURNAL			
Date	Account Title and Explanation	Debit	Credit

e) Prepare the journal entry on October 20, 2019, to record the cash payment to Workers' Compensation.

JOURNAL			
Date	Account Title and Explanation	Debit	Credit

AP-7A LO 2 3 4

Sampson Company has three employees who are paid on an hourly basis, plus time and a half for hours in excess of 44 hours per week. Payroll information for the week ending August 16, 2019, is listed below.

Employee	Hours	Hourly Rate	Income Tax	CPP	EI	Union Dues
A. Knopf	41	$14.25	$116.85	$26.36	$9.46	$10
B. Penguin	48	16.00	160.00	37.37	12.96	10
D. House	38	15.75	119.70	27.09	9.70	10

Required

a) Calculate the gross pay for each employee and the amount the employer will have to pay for CPP and EI.

Employee	Gross Pay	Employer CPP	Employer EI
A. Knopf			
B. Penguin			
D. House			
Total			

b) Prepare the journal entries for the August 14 payroll and the employer's portion of payroll. Employees will not be paid until the next week.

JOURNAL			
Date	Account Title and Explanation	Debit	Credit

c) Record the payment of the statutory deductions to the CRA on August 31, 2019.

JOURNAL			
Date	Account Title and Explanation	Debit	Credit

AP-8A LO 3 4

Bertrand Company has calculated the gross pay of one of its employees to be $2,500 semi-monthly. The company must pay 4% of the gross pay as vacation pay and 0.5% for Workers' Compensation. The pay date is August 15, 2019.

Required

a) Calculate and prepare the journal entry for accrued vacation pay.

JOURNAL			
Date	**Account Title and Explanation**	**Debit**	**Credit**

b) Calculate and prepare the journal entry for Workers' Compensation.

JOURNAL			
Date	**Account Title and Explanation**	**Debit**	**Credit**

AP-9A LO 2 3·4 5

The payroll records of Russon Corporation's district office provided the following information for the weekly pay period ended December 27, 2019.

Employee	Hours	Hourly Rate	Income Tax	CPP	EI	Union Dues
Clay York	43	$12	$61	$24	$9	$10
Karen Cooper	46	15	101	34	12	10
Stephen James	48	17	134	42	14	10
Jessie Moore	40	14	66	25	9	10

Note
All employees are paid 1.5 times their hourly wage for hours worked in excess of 40 hours per week.
The company contributes 100% for its share of CPP and 140% of EI.

Required

a) Calculate gross and net pay for each employee. Round all answers to the nearest whole number.

Employee	Gross Pay	Income Tax	CPP	EI	Union Dues	Net Pay	Employer's Cost: CPP	Employer's Cost: EI
Clay York								
Karen Cooper								
Stephen James								
Jessie Moore								
Total								

b) Prepare the payroll journal entries for December 27, 2019.

JOURNAL			
Date	Account Title and Explanation	Debit	Credit

c) Prepare a journal entry to record cash payment of the payroll liabilities due to the CRA on January 15, 2020.

JOURNAL			
Date	Account Title and Explanation	Debit	Credit

AP-10A LO 6

Payroll is an area of a business that requires adequate internal controls to ensure that employees are paid properly on a timely basis and that abuse of business resources has not occurred in the process. Discuss five internal controls specifically related to payroll.

AP-11A LO 2 7

Beverly earns a salary of $48,000 per year and is paid semi-monthly. Assuming her income tax rate is 21%, calculate her net pay for each semi-monthly pay period in 2019.

AP-12A LO 2 3 4 5 7

Tremolo Manufacturing has three employees who work on an hourly basis and are paid bi-weekly. The current CPP rate is 5.1%, the current EI rate is 1.62%, and the appropriate income tax rate is 18%. Each employee contributes a portion of their pay to the United Way. The employer pays the entire amount of the health care premium for the employees. Assume the employer contributes 100% toward CPP and 140% toward EI. Payroll information for the week ending August 23, 2019, is listed below.

Employee	Total Hours	Hourly Rate	United Way	Health Care
Sing Ing	80	$12.50	$5.00	$14.00
Roc N. Role	78	14.00	7.00	20.00
Hip Hopp	75	13.50	4.00	17.00

Required

a) Calculate gross and net pay for each employee.

		Deductions					
Employee	**Gross**	**Income Tax**	**CPP***	**EI**	**United Way**	**Total Deductions**	**Net Pay**
Sing Ing							
Roc N. Role							
Hip Hopp							
Total							

Payroll Register

*Remember to properly account for the $3,500 exemption

b) Calculate the employer contributions.

Employer Contributions	
CPP	
EI	
Health Care	

c) Prepare the payroll journal entries for August 23, 2019, to record the salaries payable to the employees and accrue the employer contributions.

JOURNAL			
Date	**Account Title and Explanation**	**Debit**	**Credit**

d)   Prepare the entry to pay the employees on August 30, 2019.

JOURNAL			
Date	Account Title and Explanation	Debit	Credit

e)   Prepare the entries to pay the liabilities to the United Way and the health insurance company on August 31, 2019.

JOURNAL			
Date	Account Title and Explanation	Debit	Credit

f)   Prepare the entry to pay the liabilities to the government on September 15, 2019.

JOURNAL			
Date	Account Title and Explanation	Debit	Credit

Application Questions Group B

AP-1B `LO` **1**

Payroll accounting involves the calculation of gross and net pay. Explain how each is calculated.

_____

_____

_____

_____

AP-2B `LO` **2**

Hurley Johnson works as a janitor in a hospital and earns $11.00 per hour. Johnson's payroll deductions include withheld income tax of 7% of total earnings, CPP of $79, EI amounting to $30, and a monthly deduction of $40 for a charitable contribution.

Calculate Hurley Johnson's gross pay and net pay assuming he worked 168 hours during the month of June 2019. Round to the nearest whole dollar.

_____

_____

_____

_____

_____

_____

_____

_____

_____

_____

AP-3B `LO` **2**

Sigma Five Consulting has two employees who are paid on an hourly basis every week. Payroll information for the week ending July 26, 2019, is listed below. Overtime is paid on hours over 48 hours per week.

Employee	Hours	Hourly Rate	Income Tax	CPP	EI
K. Bill	39	$22.50	$175.50	$41.32	$14.22
Q. Tarantino	43	24.00	204.00	49.20	16.72

Calculate the gross pay and net pay for each employee.

Employee	Gross Pay	Net Pay
K. Bill		
Q. Tarantino		

AP-4B LO 2 3

ABC Company showed the following information relating to employees' salaries for the month of October 2019.

Gross wages	$4,300
Income taxes	739
Canada Pension Plan contributions	204
Employment Insurance contributions	70

Note: The company matches 100% of employees' CPP and 140% of employees' EI.

Required

a) Calculate the company's total expense.

_____

_____

_____

_____

_____

b) Calculate the employee's net pay.

_____

_____

_____

_____

_____

AP-5B LO 2 3 4

An employer has calculated the following amounts for an employee during the last week of March 2019.

Gross wages	$1,800
Income taxes	445
Canada Pension Plan	88
Employment Insurance	29
Workers' Compensation	20

Required

a) Calculate the employee's net pay.

_____

_____

b) Assuming the employer's contribution is 100% for CPP and 140% for EI, what is the employer's total expense?

_____

_____

_____

c) Prepare the journal entries to record payroll for the employee and record the employer's contribution.

JOURNAL			
Date	**Account Title and Explanation**	**Debit**	**Credit**

AP-6B LO 2 3 4

An employee has the following information for his pay for the week ending April 26, 2019. His employer contributes 100% toward CPP and 140% toward EI. Vacation pay is accrued at 4% of gross pay. Workers' Compensation is 0.8% of gross pay. Any hours worked over 40 per week are paid overtime at 1.5 times the hourly rate.

Hours	44
Hourly Rate	$18.00
Income Tax	$126.72
Canada Pension Plan	$38.80
Employment Insurance	$13.41

Required

a) Prepare the journal entry to record the payroll entry for the employee. The employee will be paid immediately.

JOURNAL			
Date	**Account Title and Explanation**	**Debit**	**Credit**

b) Prepare the journal entry to record accrued vacation pay.

JOURNAL			
Date	Account Title and Explanation	Debit	Credit

c) Prepare the journal entry to record the employer's payroll expense.

JOURNAL			
Date	Account Title and Explanation	Debit	Credit

d) Prepare the journal entry on May 9, 2019, to record the cash payment for statutory amounts owed to the CRA.

JOURNAL			
Date	Account Title and Explanation	Debit	Credit

e) Prepare the journal entry on May 15, 2019, to record the cash payment to Workers' Compensation.

JOURNAL			
Date	Account Title and Explanation	Debit	Credit

AP-7B LO 2 3 4

Ridell Company has two employees who are paid on an hourly basis, plus time and a half for hours in excess of 44 hours per week. Payroll information for the week ending May 31, 2019, is listed below.

Employee	Hours	Hourly Rate	Income Tax	CPP	EI
D. Troi	38	$15.25	$115.90	$26.12	$9.39
W. Crusher	50	18.00	190.80	45.22	15.45

Required

a) Calculate the gross pay for each employee and the amount the employer will have to pay for CPP and EI.

Employee	Gross Pay	Employer CPP	Employer EI
D. Troi			
W. Crusher			
Total			

b) Prepare the journal entries for the May 31 payroll and the employer's portion of payroll. Employees will not be paid until the next week.

JOURNAL			
Date	Account Title and Explanation	Debit	Credit

c) Record the payment of the statutory deductions to the CRA on June 15, 2019.

JOURNAL			
Date	Account Title and Explanation	Debit	Credit

AP-8B LO 3 4

Sigmund Accounting has calculated the gross pay of all its employees for the month of August 2019 to be $43,000. The company must pay 4% of the gross pay as vacation pay and 1.5% for Workers' Compensation. The pay date is August 31, 2019.

Required

a) Calculate and prepare the journal entry for accrued vacation pay.

JOURNAL			
Date	Account Title and Explanation	Debit	Credit

b) Calculate and prepare the journal entry for Workers' Compensation.

JOURNAL			
Date	Account Title and Explanation	Debit	Credit

AP-9B LO 2 3 4 5

Learn Company has four employees who are paid on an hourly basis, plus time and a half for hours in excess of 40 hours per week. Payroll information for the week ending June 14, 2019, is listed below.

Employee	Total Hours	Hourly Rate	Income Tax	CPP	EI	Union Dues
A. Bee	40	$9.50	$26.00	$15.95	$6.16	$25.00
E. Fields	47	11.00	64.85	24.90	9.00	0.00
L. Parsons	42	11.75	55.15	22.34	8.19	15.00
I. Jay	44	10.50	51.45	21.20	7.82	15.00

Required

a) Assume the employer contributes 100% toward CPP and 140% toward EI. Calculate gross and net pay for each employee.

Payroll Register							
		Deductions					
Employee	Gross*	Income Tax	CPP	EI	Union Dues	Total Deductions	Net Pay
A. Bee	380	26	15.95	6 16	25	73.11	306.89
E. Fields	555.5	64.05	24.90	9	0	98.75	456.75
L. Parsons	505.25	55.15	22.34	8.19	15	100.68	404.57
I. Jay	485	51 45	21.20	7.82	15	95.47	387.53
Total	1925.75	197.43	84.39	31.17	55.00	368.01	1555.74

*Remember to calculate time and a half for overtime hours.

b) Prepare the payroll journal entries for June 14 to pay the employees and accrue the employer contributions.

JOURNAL			
Date	Account Title and Explanation	Debit	Credit
Jun 14 2019	Salaries expense		
	Income Tax		
	Canada Pension Plan		
	EI payable		
	Union Dues payable		
	Cash		

c) Prepare the journal entry to record the cash payment on June 30 for the employer's liability to the government.

JOURNAL			
Date	Account Title and Explanation	Debit	Credit

AP-10B LO 6

Determine which internal controls have been violated in the following independent scenarios.

a) Simon's Shoes is a local footwear retailer that employs five people. The owner, Preeti Simon, hired Janel Carew as the store's manager. Janel is responsible for hiring all other staff. Each employee is required to fill out and submit forms containing their personal information, such as social insurance number and contact information. Janel is also responsible for collecting the weekly time cards, which she uses to prepare the weekly paycheques.

_____

_____

_____

b) Ravi's Appliance Repair Depot employs 25 people, of which 20 are full-time and 5 part-time. Employees are paid weekly by manual cheque. The owner, Ravi Rajinder, believes that his employees are honest and trusts that they will submit their hours worked by Thursday morning each week, so his bookkeeper can then prepare the payroll entry in time for employees to be given their paycheque by 3 p.m. each Friday.

_____

_____

_____

_____

_____

c) County Cleaners employs 50 full-time people, who are paid on the 15th and last day of the month by cheque from the main bank account of the business. Often, employees have not cashed their cheques as of end-of-business-day on the last day of the month. Therefore, since the bank statement is prepared on that same day, the majority of these cheques are usually listed, along with other non-payroll related cheques, as outstanding. Management has noticed that it seems to take longer each month to prepare the bank reconciliation due to the large number of outstanding cheques.

_____

_____

_____

_____

_____

AP-11B LO 2 7

Katrina earns a salary of $43,000 per year and is paid bi-weekly. Assuming her income tax rate is 19%, calculate her net pay for each bi-weekly pay period in 2019.

_____

_____

_____

_____

AP-12B LO 2 3 4 5 7

Rippling Waters rents canoes and other watercraft to campers and hikers. On May 15, 2019, Rippling Waters prepared its semi-monthly payroll for employees. The current CPP rate is 5.1%, the current EI rate is 1.62%, and the appropriate income tax rate is 20%. The employer pays half of the health care premium, and the employees pay the other half. Assume the employer contributes 100% toward CPP and 140% toward EI. Payroll information for May 15, 2019, is listed below.

Employee	Total Hours	Hourly Rate	Health Care
M. Swift	87.5	$14.50	$18.00
S. Current	85.5	15.00	20.00
B. Wavey	73.5	13.50	14.00

Required

a) Calculate gross and net pay for each employee.

Payroll Register							
		Deductions					
Employee	Gross	Income Tax	CPP*	EI	Health Care	Total Deductions	Net Pay
M. Swift							
S. Current							
B. Wavey							
Total							

*Remember to properly account for the $3,500 exemption

b) Calculate the employer contributions.

Employer Contributions	
CPP	
EI	
Health Care	

c) Prepare the payroll journal entries for May 15, 2019, to record the salaries payable to the employees and accrue the employer contributions.

JOURNAL			
Date	Account Title and Explanation	Debit	Credit

d) Prepare the entry to pay the employees on May 17, 2019.

JOURNAL			
Date	Account Title and Explanation	Debit	Credit

e) Prepare the entry to pay the liability to the health insurance company on May 31, 2019.

JOURNAL			
Date	Account Title and Explanation	Debit	Credit

f) Prepare the entry to pay the liabilities to the government on June 15, 2019.

JOURNAL			
Date	Account Title and Explanation	Debit	Credit

Case Study

CS-1 **6**

Tarantula Publishing prints advertising flyers, booklets and magazines for customers. The company has 12 employees who work the small printing presses and binding machines. Susan is the bookkeeper and deals with all items relating to the financial recordkeeping of the business. Among her many duties, she prepares all the paperwork for new hires, collects the punch cards from the employees at the end of each pay period and completes and signs the paycheques.

When a new employee is hired, the general manager sends the individual to Susan to complete the appropriate paperwork for payroll. Susan is responsible for properly completing the paperwork regarding the employee's SIN, gross pay and other details.

Susan sometimes has to track down employees to get their time cards so she can pay them. Employees manually fill out the time cards and sometimes take them home in their uniforms.

The general manager does not review the paycheques that Susan writes. He is often too busy dealing with customers and planning the production runs to have time to do much of the paperwork that Susan presents to him. Since Susan is allowed to sign cheques, she prepares the cheques and hands them out to the employees.

Susan prepares the paycheques manually and is currently using the 2018 payroll tables to calculate income tax, CPP and EI deductions. The 2019 year has just started, and Susan is unaware that the rates for income tax, CPP and EI change each year. She is still using the 2018 payroll tables for 2019 paycheques.

Required

a) What are the consequences of using older payroll tables to calculate payroll deductions?

_____

_____

_____

_____

_____

_____

_____

b) Discuss the control issues with this company and what can be done to implement better controls.

_____

_____

_____

_____

_____

_____

_____

_____

_____

_____

_____

Notes

Chapter 12

ANALYZING ACCOUNTING INFORMATION

LEARNING OBJECTIVES

LO 1 Explain the shareholders' equity section of a corporation's balance sheet

LO 2 Explain the key items in a corporation's income statement

LO 3 Prepare a horizontal and vertical analysis of financial statements

LO 4 Assess a company's liquidity, profitability, operations management and leverage using financial ratios

LO 5 Analyze the statement of cash flows by interpreting the three sources and uses of cash

AMEENGAGE™ Access **ameengage.com** *for integrated resources including tutorials, practice exercises, the digital textbook and more.*

Assessment Questions

AS-1 LO 1

For the equity section of a balance sheet, describe the differences between how a corporation and a sole proprietorship would present the information.

_____

_____

_____

_____

AS-2 LO 1

Describe the three primary differences between common shares and preferred shares.

_____

_____

_____

_____

AS-3 LO 2

On an income statement, what is a gain and how does a gain occur?

_____

_____

AS-4 LO 3

Describe horizontal analysis.

_____

_____

AS-5 LO 3

Describe vertical analysis.

_____

_____

_____

AS-6 LO 4

What is the formula for gross profit margin?

_____

_____

AS-7 LO 4

What does gross profit margin tell us?

_____

_____

_____

_____

AS-8 LO 4

What is the formula for net profit margin?

_____

_____

AS-9 LO 4

What is the formula for return on equity?

_____

_____

AS-10 LO 4

For a particular company, if net income increases significantly from one year to the next, does this guarantee that the return on equity will also increase? Explain.

_____

_____

_____

AS-11 LO 4

What is the formula for working capital?

_____

_____

AS-12 LO 4

What does working capital indicate?

_____

_____

_____

AS-13 LO 4

If current assets decrease from one period to the next, but current liabilities remain constant, what will happen to working capital?

_____

_____

AS-14 LO 4

What is the formula for the current ratio?

_____

_____

AS-15 LO 4

What does the current ratio indicate?

_____

_____

_____

AS-16 LO 4

If current assets stay constant from one period to the next, but current liabilities increases, what will happen to the current ratio?

_____

_____

AS-17 LO 4

What is the formula for the quick ratio?

_____

_____

AS-18 LO 4

How do you calculate the debt-to-equity ratio?

_____

_____

AS-19 LO 4

If liabilities increase from one period to the next, but equity remains constant, what will happen to the debt-to-equity ratio?

_____

_____

AS-20 LO 4

Consider the following changes that occurred from one accounting period to the next. Current liabilities decreased, while cash, short term investments and accounts receivable all increased. What will happen to the quick ratio?

_____

_____

AS-21 LO 4

What does the inventory turnover ratio tell you?

_____

_____

_____

AS-22 LO 4

How is days' sales in inventory calculated?

_____

_____

AS-23 LO 4

What is the formula for the inventory turnover ratio?

_____

_____

AS-24 LO 4

If the inventory turnover ratio increases, what will happen to the days' sales in inventory ratio?

_____

_____

AS-25 LO 5

Is the statement of cash flows an optional statement? Explain.

_____

_____

AS-26 `LO 5`

Identify the three ways a business can generate and use cash.

AS-27 `LO 5`

What does cash flow from operating activities represent?

AS-28 `LO 5`

What does cash flow from investing activities represent?

AS-29 `LO 5`

What does cash flow from financing activities represent?

AS-30 `LO 5`

What does the statement of cash flows show?

Application Questions Group A

AP-1A LO 5

Indicate the section of the statement of cash flows where each item would be located (operating activities, investing activities or financing activities).

Item	Section
Net Income	
Increase in Accounts Payable	
Decrease in Accounts Receivable	
Purchase of Equipment	
Payment of Bank Loan	
Increase in Inventory	
Pay Dividends	
Increase in Prepaid Insurance	

AP-2A LO 5

Bonus Company had the following amounts in its statement of cash flows for the year ended December 31, 2019.

Net decrease in cash from operating activities	$100,000
Net decrease in cash from investing activities	400,000
Net increase in cash from financing activities	350,000
Cash balance, January 1, 2019	600,000

Calculate the cash balance at December 31, 2019.

AP-3A LO 5

Mark Mortton Company had the following totals in its statement of cash flows for the year ended October 31, 2019.

Net increase from investing activities	$250,000
Net decrease from operating activities	120,000
Net increase from financing activities	330,000
Cash balance, November 1, 2018	65,000

Calculate the net increase (decrease) in the cash balance at October 31, 2019.

AP-4A LO 4

A company reports current assets of $6,572 and current liabilities of $2,786. Calculate the current ratio. Round your answer to two decimal places.

AP-5A LO 4

Selected financial data from Crew Company is provided below.

	As at December 31, 2019
Cash	$75,000
Accounts Receivable	225,000
Merchandise Inventory	270,000
Short-Term Investments	40,000
Land and Building	500,000
Current Portion of Long-Term Debt	30,000
Accounts Payable	120,000

Required

a) Calculate the quick ratio. Round your answer to two decimal places.

b) What does Crew Company's quick ratio suggest about the company's performance?

AP-6A LO 4

A company had a debt-to-equity ratio last year of 1.46. This year's liabilities totalled $452,000, while shareholders' equity amounted to $226,000 for the year.

Required

a) Calculate the debt-to-equity ratio.

b) Comparing year over year, is the company managing its debt-to-equity ratio better or worse? Explain your answer.

AP-7A LO 4

A company reported the following

- Sales: $1 million
- Cost of Goods Sold: $0.7 million
- Operating Expenses: $0.2 million

Calculate the gross profit margin. Differentiate between gross profit margin and gross profit.

_____

_____

_____

_____

_____

_____

_____

AP-8A LO 4

The income statement of Raphael Inc. for 2019 and 2018 shows the following information.

	2019	2018
Service Revenue	$856,000	$813,000
Cost of Goods Sold	545,000	529,000
Operating Expenses	208,000	203,000

Required

a) Calculate the gross profit and the net income for both years.

	2019	2018
Sales Revenue	$856,000	$813,000
Cost of Goods Sold	545,000	529,000
Operating Expenses	208,000	203,000

b) Calculate the net profit margin for both years. Round your answer to the nearest whole percent.

_____

_____

c) In which year does Raphael Inc. have a better net profit margin? Explain.

_____

_____

AP-9A LO 4

The following data pertains to Frost Company for the year ended December 31, 2019.

Net Sales	$60,000
Net Income	15,000
Total Assets (January 1, 2019)	200,000
Total Assets (December 31, 2019)	300,000

Calculate Frost Company's return on assets for 2019. Explain what the ratio means.

_____

_____

_____

_____

_____

_____

_____

_____

_____

AP-10A LO 4

The following financial data is given for two companies, TIX and SUBA. They are both in the business of selling fresh produce to large supermarkets across North America. Both companies have a year end of December 31.

TIX Company	December 31, 2019	December 31, 2018
Net Sales	$2,500,000	$2,250,000
Total Assets	$4,700,000	$4,200,000
Net Income	$310,000	$300,000
Gross Profit	$1,000,000	$900,000

SUBA Company	December 31, 2019	December 31, 2018
Net Sales	$1,900,000	$2,200,000
Total Assets	$1,500,000	$1,800,000
Net Income	$400,000	$421,000
Gross Profit	$855,000	$990,000

Required

Based on the information provided, answer the following questions. Round your answers to two decimal places.

a)   Calculate the asset turnover of each company for 2019.

_____
_____
_____
_____
_____
_____
_____
_____
_____
_____
_____
_____
_____
_____

b)   In 2019, which company performed better when it comes to managing assets? Explain.

_____
_____
_____
_____

AP-11A LO 4

At the beginning of 2019, Acatela Corp. had inventory of $350,000. They ended the year with inventory of $70,000 after purchasing $220,000 worth of inventory. The cost of goods sold totalled $500,000.

Required

a)   Calculate the inventory turnover ratio.

_____
_____
_____

b)   Calculate the days' sales in inventory ratio.

_____
_____
_____

c)   What does Acatela Corp.'s inventory turnover ratio mean?

_____
_____

d)   What does Acatela Corp.'s days' sales in inventory ratio mean?

_____

_____

AP-12A LO 4

Wechsler Company has a net accounts receivable opening balance of $250,000 and an ending balance of $300,000. The total sales amount for the year is $1,700,000, of which 80% is on credit. Normal credit terms are 30 days. Calculate the days' sales outstanding and the accounts receivable turnover. Comment on the calculated ratios.

_____

_____

_____

_____

_____

_____

_____

_____

_____

_____

_____

_____

_____

AP-13A LO 4

The following information relevant to accounts receivable is presented for Dommar Company (in thousands of dollars).

	2019	2018	2017
Accounts Receivable	$300	$404	$481
Net Credit Sales	4,377	3,598	2,937

Required

a)   Calculate the accounts receivable turnover ratio for the years 2018 and 2019.

_____

_____

_____

b)   Calculate the days' sales outstanding for the years 2018 and 2019.

_____

_____

_____

AP-14A LO 3

Perform a horizontal analysis for Groff Inc. Use 2017 as the base year and comment on the results. A table has been provided to conduct the analysis.

Groff Inc. Income Statement (in Thousands) For Years Ended December 31, 2017–2019			
	2019	**2018**	**2017**
Revenue	500	400	300
Expenses	334	242	156
Net Income	166	158	144

Groff Inc. Income Statement (in Thousands) For Years Ended December 31, 2017–2019									
	2019			**2018**			**2017**		
	Value	**% of 2017**	**% Ch**	**Value**	**% of 2017**	**% Ch**	**Value**	**% of 2017**	**% Ch**
Revenue	500			400			300		
Expenses	334			242			156		
Net Income	166			158			144		

AP-15A LO 3

Perform a vertical analysis for Hiltonia Inc., using sales as the base figure for both years. The comparative income statement has already been done for you. Calculate the percentages to two decimal places. Comment on the results of significant changes.

Hiltonia Inc. Income Statement (in Millions) For Years Ended June 30, 2019 and 2018		
	2019	**2018**
Sales	$210	$250
COGS	150	200
Gross Profit	60	50
Expenses		
Advertising Expense	12	8
Insurance Expense	2	1.8
Rent Expense	4	3
Salaries Expense	20	19
Selling Expenses	3	2
Total Expenses	41	33.8
Net Income	$19	$16.2

Use the modified income statement below to perform a vertical analysis.

Hiltonia Inc. Income Statement (in Millions) and Vertical Analysis For Years Ended June 30, 2019 and 2018				
	2019	**% of Base Figure**	**2018**	**% of Base Figure**
Sales	$210		$250	
COGS	150		200	
Gross Profit	60		50	
Expenses				
Advertising Expense	12		8	
Insurance Expense	2		1.8	
Rent Expense	4		3	
Salaries Expense	20		19	
Selling Expenses	3		2	
Total Expenses	41		33.8	
Net Income	$19		$16.2	

_____

_____

_____

_____

_____

AP-16A LO 3

The following financial statements are taken from the records of Abaya Inc.

Abaya Inc. Balance Sheet As at December 31, 2019 and 2018		
	2019	**2018**
Assets		
Current Assets		
Cash	$315,000	$325,000
Accounts Receivable	140,000	198,000
Inventory	411,000	397,000
Short-Term Investments	115,000	100,000
Total Current Assets	981,000	1,020,000
Other Assets	356,000	250,000
Total Assets	**$1,337,000**	**$1,270,000**
Liabilities and Equity		
Current Liabilities	$214,000	$265,000
Long-Term Debt	22,000	150,000
Total Liabilities	236,000	415,000
Shareholders' Equity	1,101,000	855,000
Total Liabilities and Equity	**$1,337,000**	**$1,270,000**

Abaya Inc. Income Statement For the Years Ended December 31, 2019 and 2018		
	2019	**2018**
Sales	$701,000	$689,000
COGS	379,000	396,000
Gross Profit	322,000	293,000
Operating Expenses		
Advertising Expense	4,200	3,100
Bank Charges Expense	2,400	1,600
Communication Expense	5,600	3,700
Depreciation Expense	2,500	2,500
Professional Fees Expense	11,800	5,400
Rent Expense	5,000	5,000
Repairs and Maintenance Expense	3,000	3,000
Salaries and Wages Expense	41,000	11,500
Transportation Expense	8,950	6,400
Utilities Expense	8,600	7,580
Total Operating Expenses	93,050	49,780
Net Income	**$228,950**	**$243,220**

Required

a) Use horizontal analysis tools to compare the changes between 2018 and 2019 line items for the balance sheet. The comparative balance sheet has already been done for you. For all percentages, calculate to two decimal places. Comment on the results of significant changes.

Abaya Inc. Balance Sheet and Horizontal Analysis As at December 31, 2019 and 2018				
	2019	**2018**	**% of 2018**	**% Change**
Assets				
Current Assets				
Cash	$315,000	$325,000		
Accounts Receivable	140,000	198,000		
Inventory	411,000	397,000		
Short-Term Investments	115,000	100,000		
Total Current Assets	981,000	1,020,000		
Other Assets	356,000	250,000		
Total Assets	**$1,337,000**	**$1,270,000**		
Liabilities and Equity				
Current Liabilities	214,000	265,000		
Long-Term Debt	22,000	150,000		
Total Liabilities	236,000	415,000		
Shareholders' Equity	1,101,000	855,000		
Total Liabilities and Equity	**$1,337,000**	**$1,270,000**		

b) Use horizontal analysis tools to compare the changes between 2018 and 2019 line items for the income statement. The comparative income statement has already been done for you. For all percentages, calculate to two decimal places. Comment on the results of significant changes.

Abaya Inc. Income Statement and Horizontal Analysis For the Years Ended December 31, 2019 and 2018				
	2019	**2018**	**% of 2018**	**% Change**
Sales	$701,000	$689,000		
COGS	379,000	396,000		
Gross Profit	322,000	293,000		
Operating Expenses				
Advertising Expense	4,200	3,100		
Bank Charges Expense	2,400	1,600		
Communication Expense	5,600	3,700		
Depreciation Expense	2,500	2,500		
Professional Fees Expense	11,800	5,400		
Rent Expense	5,000	5,000		
Repairs and Maintenance Expense	3,000	3,000		
Salaries and Wages Expense	41,000	11,500		
Transportation Expense	8,950	6,400		
Utilities Expense	8,600	7,580		
Total Operating Expenses	93,050	49,780		
Net Income	$228,950	$243,220		

c) Use vertical analysis tools to compare line items to the total assets base figure. For all percentages, calculate to two decimal places. Comment on the results.

	Abaya Inc. **Balance Sheet and Vertical Analysis** **As at December 31, 2019 and 2018**			
	2019		**2018**	**Vertical**
Assets				
Current Assets				
Cash	$315,000		$325,000	
Accounts Receivable	140,000		198,000	
Inventory	411,000		397,000	
Short-Term Investments	115,000		100,000	
Total Current Assets	981,000		1,020,000	
Other Assets	356,000		250,000	
Total Assets	**$1,337,000**		**$1,270,000**	
Liabilities and Equity				
Current Liabilities	214,000		265,000	
Long-Term Debt	22,000		150,000	
Total Liabilities	**236,000**		**415,000**	
Shareholders' Equity	1,101,000		855,000	
Total Liabilities and Equity	**$1,337,000**		**$1,270,000**	

_____

_____

_____

_____

_____

_____

_____

d) Use vertical analysis tools to compare line items to the sales base figure. For all percentages, calculate to two decimal places. Comment on the results.

	2019	Vertical	2018	Vertical
Abaya Inc. Income Statement and Vertical Analysis For the Years Ended December 31, 2019 and 2018				
Sales	$701,000		$689,000	
COGS	379,000		396,000	
Gross Profit	322,000		293,000	
Operating Expenses				
Advertising Expense	4,200		3,100	
Bank Charges Expense	2,400		1,600	
Communication Expense	5,600		3,700	
Depreciation Expense	2,500		2,500	
Professional Fees Expense	11,800		5,400	
Rent Expense	5,000		5,000	
Repairs and Maintenance Expense	3,000		3,000	
Salaries and Wages Expense	41,000		11,500	
Transportation Expense	8,950		6,400	
Utilities Expense	8,600		7,580	
Total Operating Expenses	93,050		49,780	
Net Income	$228,950		$243,220	

_____

_____

_____

_____

AP-17A LO 4

The income statements and balance sheets for Hathaway Inc. are shown below for the last three fiscal years. All sales are on credit.

	2019	2018	2017
Hathaway Inc. Income Statement For the Years Ended December 31, 2017–2019			
Sales	$800,000	$720,000	$760,000
Cost of Goods Sold	260,000	288,000	266,000
Gross Profit	540,000	432,000	494,000
Expenses			
Operating expense	320,000	216,000	342,000
Depreciation expense	64,000	72,000	76,000
Advertising expense	80,000	72,000	114,000
Interest expense	10,000	10,000	10,000
Total expenses	474,000	370,000	542,000
Net income (loss) before taxes	66,000	62,000	(48,000)
Income tax expense (return)	29,700	27,900	(21,600)
Net income (loss) after taxes	$36,300	$34,100	($26,400)

Hathaway Inc. Balance Sheet As at the Years Ended December 31, 2017–2019			
	2019	**2018**	**2017**
Cash	$234,400	$149,600	$80,000
Accounts Receivable	84,000	70,000	56,000
Inventory	136,000	102,000	61,200
Equipment	110,000	174,000	246,000
Total Assets	**$564,400**	**$495,600**	**$443,200**
Accounts Payable	$54,600	$45,500	$36,400
Unearned Revenue	21,000	23,100	18,900
Long-Term Debt	50,000	50,000	50,000
Common Shares	85,500	60,000	55,000
Retained Earnings	353,300	317,000	282,900
Total Liabilities and Shareholders' Equity	**$564,400**	**$495,600**	**$443,200**

Required

a) Calculate the following ratios for Hathaway Inc. for 2018 and 2019, and state whether the ratios improved or weakened in 2019.

	2019	**2018**	**Improved or Weakened**
Gross Profit Margin			
Net Profit Margin			
Return on Equity (ROE)			
Current Ratio			
Quick Ratio			
Debt-to-Equity Ratio			
Inventory Turnover			
Days' Sales in Inventory			

b) The owner of Hathaway Inc. is pleased to see that the company has started generating profits again and assumes that profitability must be improving. Perform a ratio analysis to determine if the owner's assumption is correct or not. Explain.

_____

_____

_____

_____

_____

c) What does the company's inventory turnover ratio indicate?

_____

_____

_____

Application Questions Group B

AP-1B LO 5

Indicate the section of the statement of cash flows where each item would be located (operating activities, investing activities or financing activities).

Item	Section
Change in Accounts Payable	
Change in Inventory	
Change in Equipment	
Change in Long-Term portion of Bank Loan	
Change in Current portion of Bank Loan	
Change in Prepaid Rent	
Change in Accounts Receivable	
Change in Common Shares	

AP-2B LO 5

The Grading Company's cash account decreased by $14,000 and its short-term investment account increased by $18,000. Cash increase from operations was $21,000. Net cash decrease from investments was $22,000.

Based on the above information, calculate the cash increase (or decrease) from financing.

AP-3B LO 5

Brothers Christoph and Wilson Adler are the owners of Adler Bros Company. They had the following totals in their statement of cash flows for the year ended February 28, 2019.

Net increase from financing activities	$560,000
Net increase from operating activities	112,000
Net decrease from investing activities	400,000
Cash balance, March 1, 2018	88,000

Calculate the net increase (decrease) in the cash balance at February 28, 2019.

AP-4B LO 4

Total current liabilities for a company are $2,786. If cash is $2,000, short-term investments are $3,000, long-term investments are $1,000 and accounts receivable is $1,200, calculate the quick ratio. Round your answer to two decimal places.

AP-5B LO 4

Information from Silky Company's year-end financial statements is as follows.

	2019	2018
Current Assets	$200,000	$210,000
Current Liabilities	100,000	90,000
Shareholders' Equity	250,000	270,000
Net Sales	830,000	880,000
Cost of Goods Sold	620,000	640,000
Income from Operations	50,000	55,000

Required

a) Calculate the current ratio for both years.

b) In which year does Silky Company have a better current ratio? Explain.

AP-6B LO 4

Gross profit increased from $0.3 million in 2018 to $0.4 million in 2019. Gross profit margin decreased from 30% in 2018 to 28% in 2019. Comment on whether or not the company's profitability improved or deteriorated.

AP-7B LO 4

The income statement of Ellen Corporation for the years 2019 and 2018 showed the following gross profit calculation.

	2019	2018
Sales Revenue	$97,200	$80,000
Cost of Goods Sold	72,000	50,000
Gross Profit	$25,200	$30,000

Required

a) Calculate the gross profit margin for both years.

_____

_____

_____

_____

_____

b) In which year does Ellen Corporation have a better gross profit margin? Explain.

_____

_____

_____

_____

AP-8B LO 4

Selected information for the Universal Company is as follows.

	December 31		
	2019	**2018**	**2017**
Common Shares	$840,000	$648,000	$550,000
Retained Earnings	370,000	248,000	150,000
Net income for the year	240,000	122,000	98,000

Required

a) Calculate the return on equity ratio for 2019 and 2018.

_____

_____

_____

_____

_____

b) Has the Universal Company's performance improved in 2019? Explain using the return on equity ratio.

_____

_____

AP-9B LO 4

Joe Corporation's selected financial data is given below.

Net Sales for 2019	$180,000
Cost of Goods Sold for 2019	99,000
Average Total Assets for 2019	120,000

Calculate the company's asset turnover. Explain what the ratio means.

_____

_____

_____

_____

_____

_____

_____

_____

AP-10B LO 4

The following financial data is given for two companies, LIN and WOK. They both manufacture and sell office furniture across the US and Canada. Both companies have a year end of June 30.

LIN Company	June 30, 2019	June 30, 2018
Net Sales	$3,500,000	$3,000,000
Total Assets	$2,200,000	$1,150,000
Net Income	$590,000	$500,000
Gross Profit	$1,575,000	$1,350,000

WOK Company	June 30, 2019	June 30, 2018
Net Sales	$4,500,000	$4,120,000
Total Assets	$5,500,000	$4,800,000
Net Income	$840,000	$620,000
Gross Profit	$1,575,000	$1,442,000

Required

Based on the information provided, answer the following questions. Round your final answers to the nearest whole percentage.

a) Calculate the return on assets for each company in 2019.

_____

_____

_____

_____

_____

_____

_____

_____

_____

_____

b) In 2019, which company performed better when it comes to managing assets? Explain.

_____

_____

_____

_____

AP-11B LO 4

The balance sheet of Leonardo Corporation for 2019 and 2018 shows the following information.

	2019	2018
Current Assets	$7,000	$13,000
Current Liabilities	$10,000	$9,000

Required

a) Calculate the working capital for both years.

_____

_____

b) In which year does Leonardo Corporation have a better working capital? Explain.

_____

_____

_____

c) What are some implications regarding the working capital for 2019?

_____

_____

AP-12B LO 4

A company's relevant accounts receivable information for the years 2018 and 2019 is provided below. Round your answers to one decimal place, where appropriate.

	2019	2018
Average Net Accounts Receivable	$1,486,739	$1,769,032
Net Credit Sales	23,075,635	22,107,539

Required.

a) Calculate the accounts receivable turnover ratio for 2018 and 2019.

_____

_____

_____

b) Calculate the days' sales outstanding for 2018 and 2019.

_____

_____

_____

c) Compare and discuss the results from parts a) and b).

_____

_____

_____

AP-13B LO 4

The following information is taken from the records of Hanlan Corporation. Normal credit terms are 30 days.

	2019	2018	2017
Net Credit Sales	$250,000	$200,000	$190,000
Account Receivable	16,450	23,040	31,008

Required

a) Calculate the accounts receivable turnover ratio for 2018 and 2019. Round your answers to two decimal places.

_____

_____

_____

b) Calculate the days' sales outstanding for the years 2018 and 2019. Round your answers to the nearest whole number.

_____

_____

_____

c) Comment on the accounts receivable ratios calculated from 2018 and 2019.

_____

_____

_____

_____

AP-14B LO 3

Perform a horizontal analysis for Gob Blooth Inc. Use 2017 as the base year and comment on the results.

Gob Blooth Inc. Income Statement (in Thousands) For Years Ended October 31, 2017–2019			
	2019	2018	2017
Revenue	1,234	1,100	988
Expenses	907	1,009	678
Net Income	327	91	310

A table has been provided to conduct the analysis.

	2019			2018			2017		
Gob Blooth Inc. **Horizontal Analysis** **For Years Ended October 31, 2017–2019**	Value	% of 2017	% Change	Value	% of 2017	% Change	Value	% of 2017	% Change
Revenue	1,234			1,100			988		
Expenses	907			1,009			678		
Net Income	327			91			310		

_____

_____

_____

_____

AP-15B LO 3

Perform a vertical analysis for G Michael Inc., using sales as the base figure for both years. The comparative income statement has already been done for you. For all percentages, calculate to two decimal places. Comment on the results of significant changes.

G Michael Inc. Income Statement (in Millions) For Years Ended August 31, 2019 and 2018	2019	2018
Sales	$456	$386
COGS	222	201
Gross Profit	234	185
Expenses		
Advertising Expense	15	12
Insurance Expense	3	2
Rent Expense	21	19
Salaries Expense	55	50
Selling Expenses	34	31
Total Expenses	128	114
Net Income	$106	$71

Use the modified income statement below to perform your vertical analysis.

G Michael Inc. Income Statement (in Millions) and Vertical Analysis For Years Ended August 31, 2019 and 2018				
	2019	% of Base Figure	2018	% of Base Figure
Sales	$456		$386	
COGS	222		201	
Gross Profit	234		185	
Expenses				
Advertising Expense	15		12	
Insurance Expense	3		2	
Rent Expense	21		19	
Salaries Expense	55		50	
Selling Expenses	34		31	
Total Expenses	128		114	
Net Income	$106		$71	

AP-16B LO 3

The following financial statements are taken from the records of Pop-Pop Products Inc.

Pop-Pop Products Inc. Balance Sheet (in Thousands) As at April 30, 2019 and 2018		
	2019	2018
Assets		
Current Assets		
Cash	$35	$12
Accounts Receivable	147	188
Inventory	249	267
Short-Term Investments	98	34
Total Current Assets	529	501
Other Assets	521	487
Total Assets	$1,050	$988
Liabilities and Equity		
Current Liabilities	$298	$379
Long-Term Debt	101	321
Total Liabilities	399	700
Shareholders' Equity	651	288
Total Liabilities and Equity	$1,050	$988

Pop-Pop Products Inc. Income Statement (in Thousands) For the Years Ended April 30, 2019 and 2018		
	2019	**2018**
Sales	**$2,139**	**$2,395**
COGS	1,098	1,230
Gross Profit	**1,041**	**1,165**
Operating Expenses		
Advertising Expense	10	14
Bank Charges Expense	5	6
Communication Expense	13	11
Depreciation Expense	112	98
Professional Fees Expense	0	30
Rent Expense	103	307
Repairs and Maintenance Expense	62	86
Salaries and Wages Expense	212	178
Transportation Expense	52	50
Utilities Expense	24	22
Total Operating Expenses	**593**	**802**
Net Income	**$448**	**$363**

Required

a) Use horizontal analysis tools to compare the changes between 2018 and 2019 line items for the balance sheet. The comparative balance sheet has already been done for you. For all percentages, calculate to two decimal places. Comment on the results of significant changes.

Pop-Pop Products Inc. Balance Sheet (in Thousands) and Horizontal Analysis As at April 30, 2019 and 2018				
	2019	**2018**	**% of 2018**	**% Change**
Assets				
Current Assets				
Cash	$35	$12		
Accounts Receivable	147	188		
Inventory	249	267		
Short-Term Investments	98	34		
Total Current Assets	**529**	**501**		
Other Assets	521	487		
Total Assets	**$1,050**	**$988**		
Liabilities and Equity				
Current Liabilities	$298	$379		
Long-Term Debt	101	321		
Total Liabilities	**399**	**700**		
Shareholders' Equity	651	288		
Total Liabilities and Equity	**$1,050**	**$988**		

_____

_____

_____

_____

_____

_____

_____

b) Use horizontal analysis tools to compare the changes between 2018 and 2019 line items for the income statement. The comparative income statement has already been done for you. For all percentages, calculate to two decimal places. Comment on the results of significant changes.

Pop-Pop Products Inc. Income Statement (in Thousands) and Horizontal Analysis For the Years Ended April 30, 2019 and 2018				
	2019	2018	% of 2018	% Change
Sales	$2,139	$2,395		
COGS	1,098	1,230		
Gross Profit	1,041	1,165		
Operating Expenses				
Advertising Expense	10	14		
Bank Charges Expense	5	6		
Communication Expense	13	11		
Depreciation Expense	112	98		
Professional Fees Expense	0	30		
Rent Expense	103	307		
Repairs and Maintenance Expense	62	86		
Salaries and Wages Expense	212	178		
Transportation Expense	52	50		
Utilities Expense	24	22		
Total Operating Expenses	593	802		
Net Income	$448	$363		

_____

_____

_____

_____

c) Use vertical analysis tools to compare line items to the total assets base figure. For all percentages, calculate to two decimal places. Comment on the results.

Pop-Pop Products Inc. Balance Sheet (in Thousands) and Vertical Analysis As at April 30, 2019 and 2018				
	2019	**Vertical**	**2018**	**Vertical**
Assets				
Current Assets				
Cash	$35		$12	
Accounts Receivable	147		188	
Inventory	249		267	
Short-Term Investments	98		34	
Total Current Assets	529		501	
Other Assets	521		487	
Total Assets	**$1,050**		**$988**	
Liabilities and Equity				
Current Liabilities	298		379	
Long-Term Debt	101		321	
Total Liabilities	399		700	
Shareholders' Equity	651		288	
Total Liabilities and Equity	**$1,050**		**$988**	

_____

_____

_____

_____

_____

_____

d) Use vertical analysis tools to compare line items to the sales base figure. For all percentages, calculate to two decimal places. Comment on the results.

Pop-Pop Products Inc. Income Statement (in Thousands) and Vertical Analysis For the Years Ended April 30, 2019 and 2018				
	2019	Vertical	2018	Vertical
Sales	**$2,139**		**$2,395**	
COGS	1,098		1,230	
Gross Profit	**1,041**		**1,165**	
Operating Expenses				
Advertising Expense	10		14	
Bank Charges Expense	5		6	
Communication Expense	13		11	
Depreciation Expense	112		98	
Professional Fees Expense	0		30	
Rent Expense	103		307	
Repairs and Maintenance Expense	62		86	
Salaries and Wages Expense	212		178	
Transportation Expense	52		50	
Utilities Expense	24		22	
Total Operating Expenses	**593**		**802**	
Net Income	**$448**		**$363**	

_____

_____

_____

_____

AP-17B LO 4

Chicken Inc. and Egg Inc. are both in the toy retail business. All sales are on credit. Below is select financial information for the current year.

	Chicken Inc.	Egg Inc.
Income Statement:		
Sales	$150,000	$135,000
Cost of Goods Sold	48,750	41,850
Gross Profit	101,250	93,150
Expenses:		
Salaries Expense	22,500	27,000
Depreciation Expense	15,000	13,500
Advertising Expense	7,500	6,750
Interest Expense	6,750	5,130
Total Expenses	51,750	52,380
Net Income Before Taxes	49,500	40,770
Income Tax Expense	26,250	24,300
Net Income After Taxes	**$23,250**	**$16,470**
Balance Sheet:		
Cash	$40,850	$24,510
Accounts Receivable	15,000	9,000
Inventory	34,500	20,125
Equipment	85,800	51,480
Total Assets	**$176,150**	**$105,115**
Accounts Payable	21,000	32,000
Unearned Revenue	27,800	18,670
Long-Term Debt	39,350	15,635
Shareholders' Equity	88,000	38,810
Total Liabilities and Shareholders' Equity	**$176,150**	**$105,115**

a) Calculate each ratio listed below for each company and indicate which company is stronger for each one. If averages are required in any of your ratios, use the current period.

	Chicken Inc.	Egg Inc.	Which company is stronger?
Gross Profit Margin			
Net Profit Margin			
Return on Equity (ROE)			
Current Ratio			
Quick Ratio			
Debt-to-Equity Ratio			
Inventory Turnover			
Days' Sales in Inventory			

b)   Examining all of the ratios, explain which company has a stronger financial position with respect to the following.

i.   Profitability

_____

_____

_____

_____

ii.   Liquidity

_____

_____

_____

_____

iii. Operations mangement

_____

_____

Case Study

CS-1 LO 1 2 3 4 5

After learning that you are taking an accounting course, Kim, your close friend, has come to ask you for investment advice. She went skiing at Rocky Alpine Retreat last winter and was so impressed by the resort that she has been thinking about investing in it. Because she doesn't know how to read financial statements, she asked you to analyze Rocky Alpine Retreat's financial statements and comment on the company's liquidity, profitability and leverage. The statements are presented below.

Rocky Alpine Retreat Consolidated Balance Sheet (in thousands) As at September 30, 2019 and 2018		
	2019	**2018**
Assets		
Cash	$ 8,410	$ 41,353
Short-term investments	145	311
Accounts receivable	4,496	3,323
Inventory	18,633	15,856
Prepaid expenses	3,985	2,727
Total Current Assets	**35,669**	**63,570**
Notes receivable	777	2,636
Property, buildings and equipment	319,897	322,316
Property held for development	9,244	9,244
Intangible assets	300,778	311,428
Goodwill	137,354	137,259
Total Assets	**$803,719**	**$846,453**
Liabilities		
Accounts payable and accrued liabilities	25,715	24,927
Income taxes payable	2,403	1,645
Provisions	2,139	2,858
Deferred revenue	27,610	22,347
Total Current Liabilities	**57,867**	**51,777**
Long-term debt	229,855	258,042
Deferred income tax liability	21,974	20,690
Limited partner's interest	72,796	72,796
Total Liabilities	**382,492**	**403,305**
Shareholders' Equity		
Common shares	495,176	497,929
Retained earnings (deficit)	(73,949)	(54,781)
Total Shareholders' Equity	**421,227**	**443,148**
Total Liabilities and Shareholders' Equity	**$ 803,719**	**$ 846,453**

Rocky Alpine Retreat Consolidated Income Statement (in thousands) For the Years Ended September 30, 2019 and 2018		
	2019	2018
Resort revenue	$ 254,517	$ 240,780
Operating expenses	134,081	126,673
Depreciation and amortization expenses	41,254	40,249
Selling, general and administrative expenses	27,761	27,673
Total Expenses	203,096	194,595
Income from Operations before Tax	**51,421**	**46,185**
Other income	3,068	0
Other expense	(30,712)	(25,607)
Income Before Income Tax	23,777	20,578
Income tax expense	5,737	7,248
Net Income	**$ 18,040**	**$ 13,330**

Rocky Alpine Retreat Summary of the Statement of Cash Flows (in thousands) For the Years Ended September 30, 2019 and 2018		
	2019	2018
Net cash provided by operating activities	$ 67,848	$ 64,725
Net cash used by investing activities	(28,398)	(24,345)
Net cash used by financing activities	(72,393)	(42,661)
Net increase (decrease) in cash	$ (32,943)	$ (2,281)

For the calculation that requires average shareholders' equity, the Rocky Alpine Retreat's shareholders' equity balance at the end of 2017 is $544,479.

Required

a) Explain to Kim what a retained earnings deficit in Rocky Alpine Retreat's balance sheet means.

b) Perform horizontal and vertical analyses on Rocky Alpine Retreat's balance sheet and income statement. Interpret the figures for Kim.

	Horizontal Analysis			Vertical Analysis	
	2019	2018	% Change	2019	2018

Rocky Alpine Retreat
Horizontal and Vertical Analysis on the Balance Sheet
As at September 30, 2019 and 2018

	Horizontal Analysis			Vertical Analysis	
	2019	2018	% Change	2019	2018

Rocky Alpine Retreat
Horizontal and Vertical Analysis on the Income Statement
For the Years Ended September 30, 2019 and 2018

c) Assess Rocky Alpine Retreat's liquidity using relevant ratios and provide an explanation.

_____
_____
_____
_____
_____
_____
_____
_____
_____
_____
_____
_____
_____
_____
_____
_____
_____
_____
_____

d) Assess Rocky Alpine Retreat's profitability using relevant ratios and provide an explanation.

_____
_____
_____
_____
_____
_____
_____
_____
_____
_____
_____
_____
_____
_____
_____
_____

e)   Assess Rocky Alpine Retreat's leverage using the relevant ratio and provide an explanation.

_____

_____

_____

_____

_____

_____

_____

_____

_____

_____

_____

f)   Based on all of the above analyses, would you advise Kim to invest in Rocky Alpine Retreat?

_____

_____

_____

_____

_____

_____

_____

_____

_____

_____

_____

_____

_____